CARTOONS from MAINE

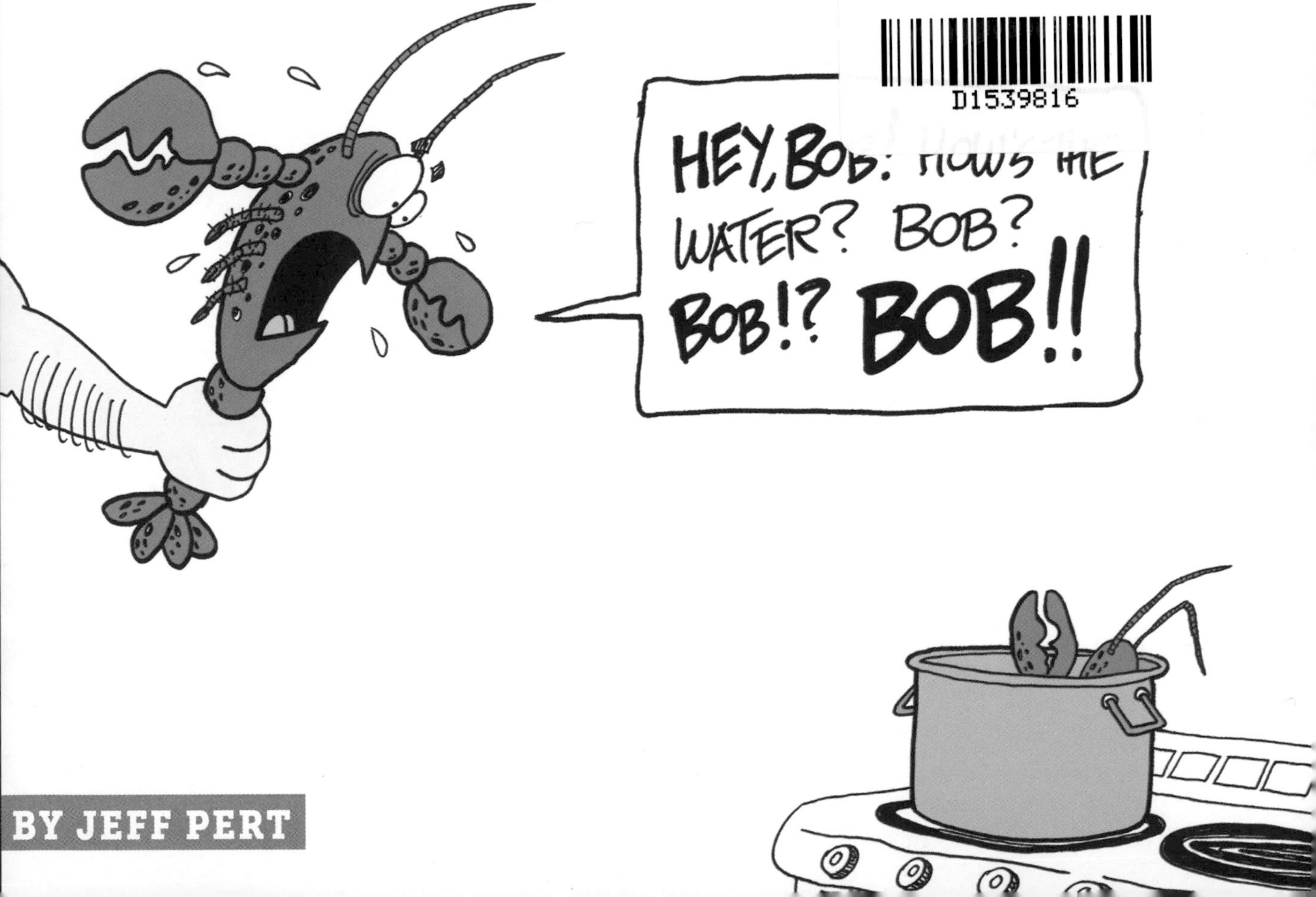
HEY, BOB! HOW'S THE WATER? BOB? BOB!? BOB!!

BY JEFF PERT

ISBN 978-1-60893-042-5

Down East Books
www.nbnbooks.com
Distributed by
National Book Network
800-462-6420

Printed in Yuanzhou, China October 2016

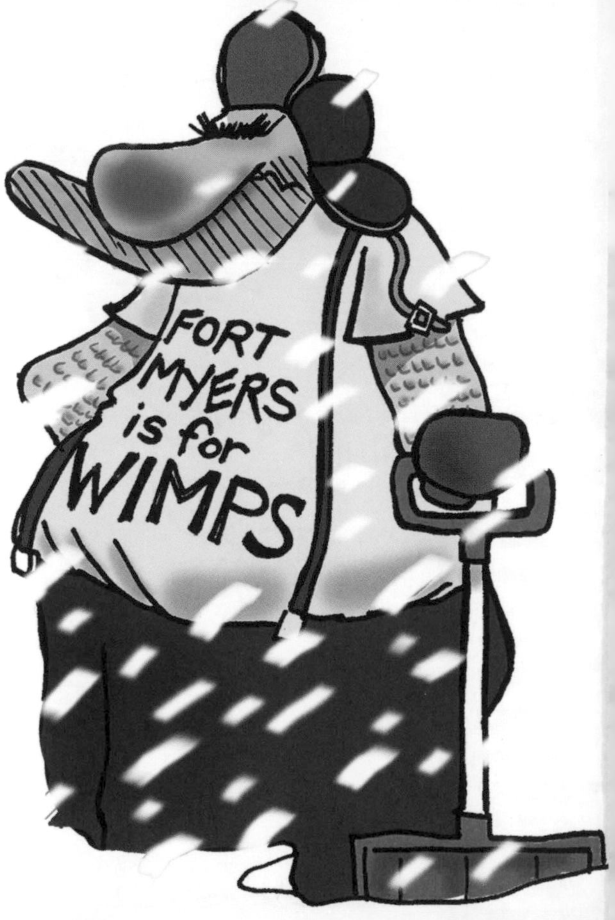
FORT MYERS is for WIMPS

To Dad

Introduction

These toons are wicked funny! I've been a fan for years. This is a great book for next to the toilet, on the coffee table, side table, dinin' room table, ping-pong table, next to the bed, on the bed, in the bed. Turn these pages and laugh yourself silly, bubba! Jeff is a wicked stitch!
He's a good Mainer as well. Enjoy, ya dinks!!

—Bob Marley, Maine's favorite comedian

JEFF PERT

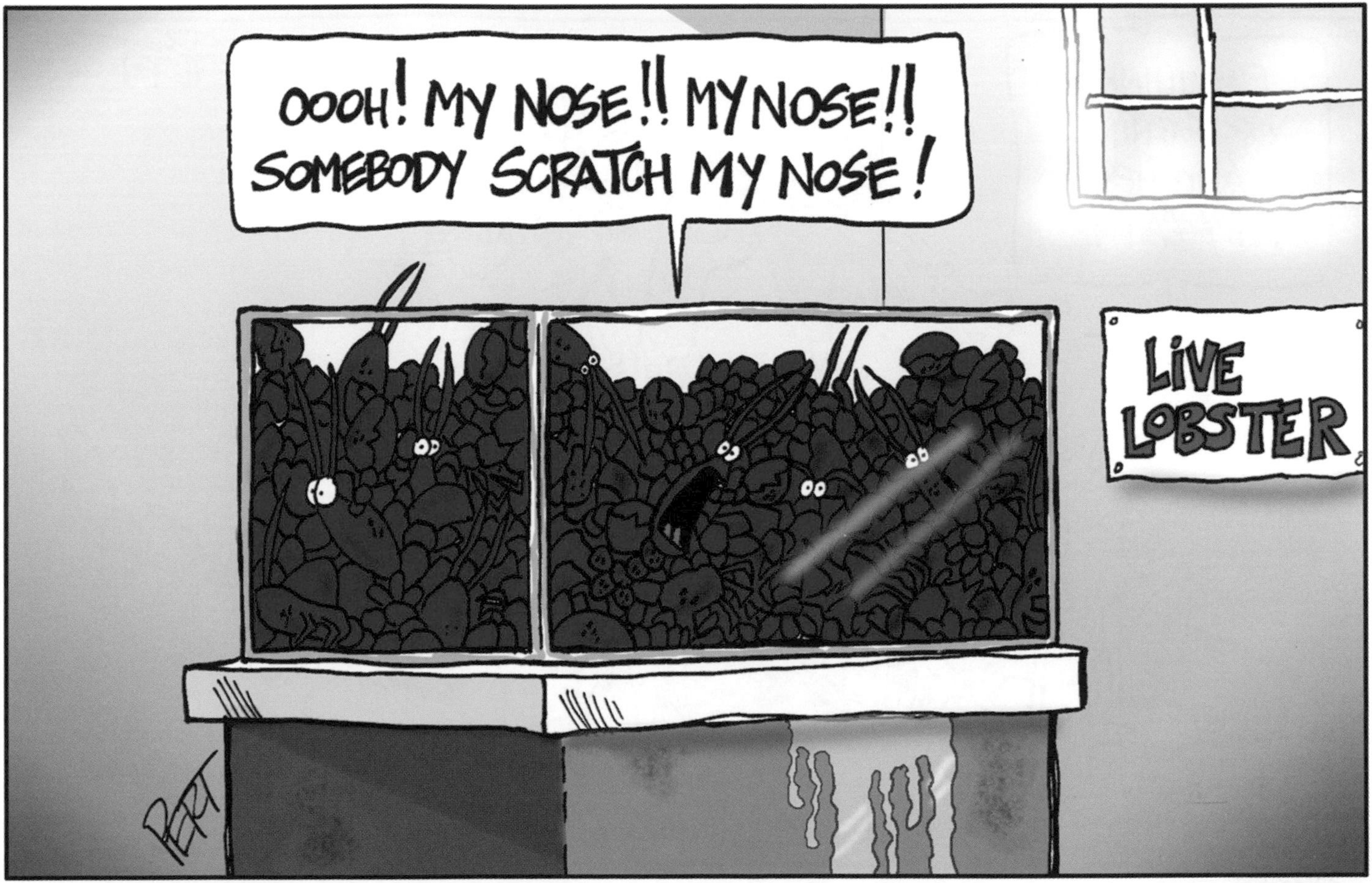
OOOH! MY NOSE!! MY NOSE!! SOMEBODY SCRATCH MY NOSE!
LIVE LOBSTER
REPRT

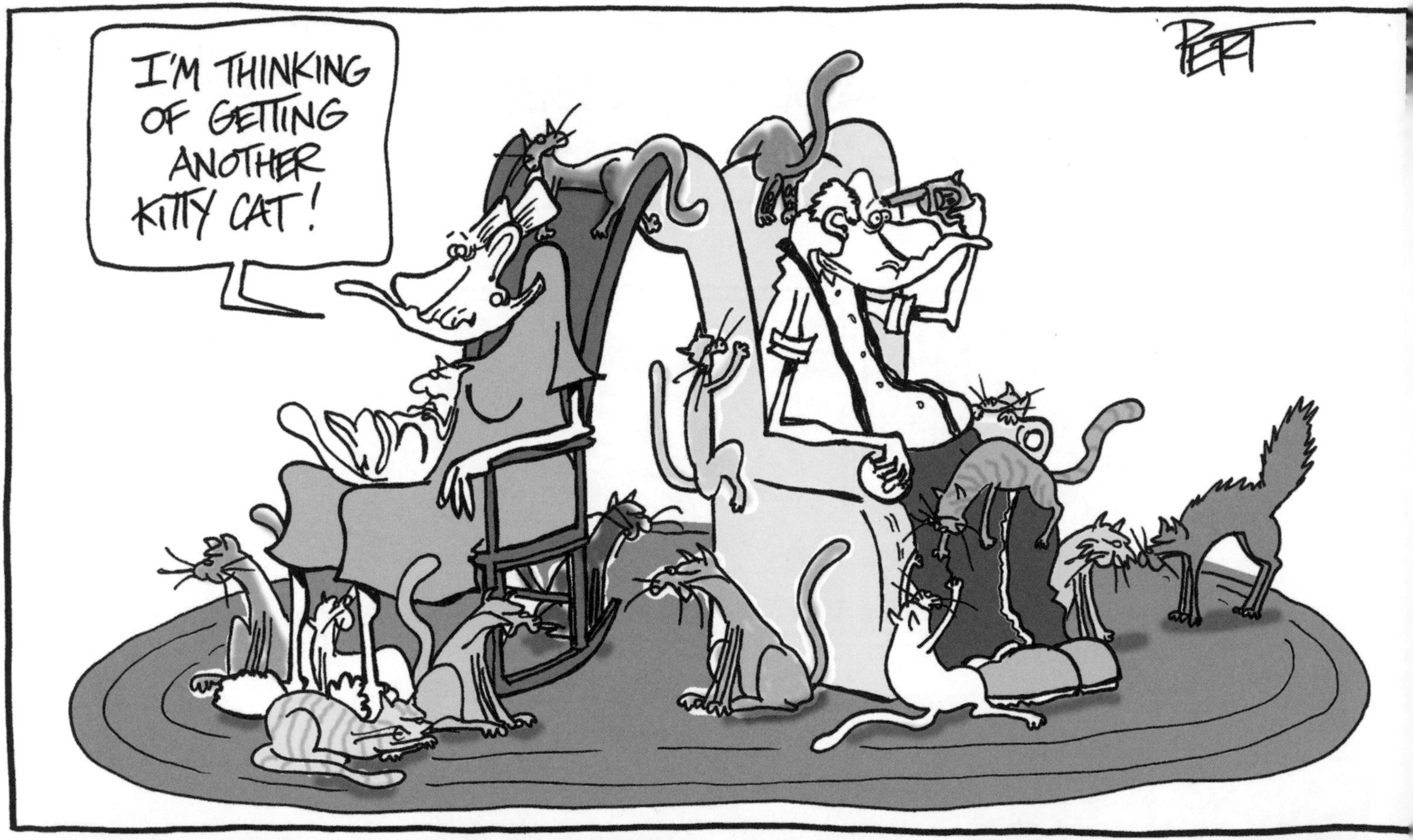
I'M THINKING OF GETTING ANOTHER KITTY CAT!
PERT

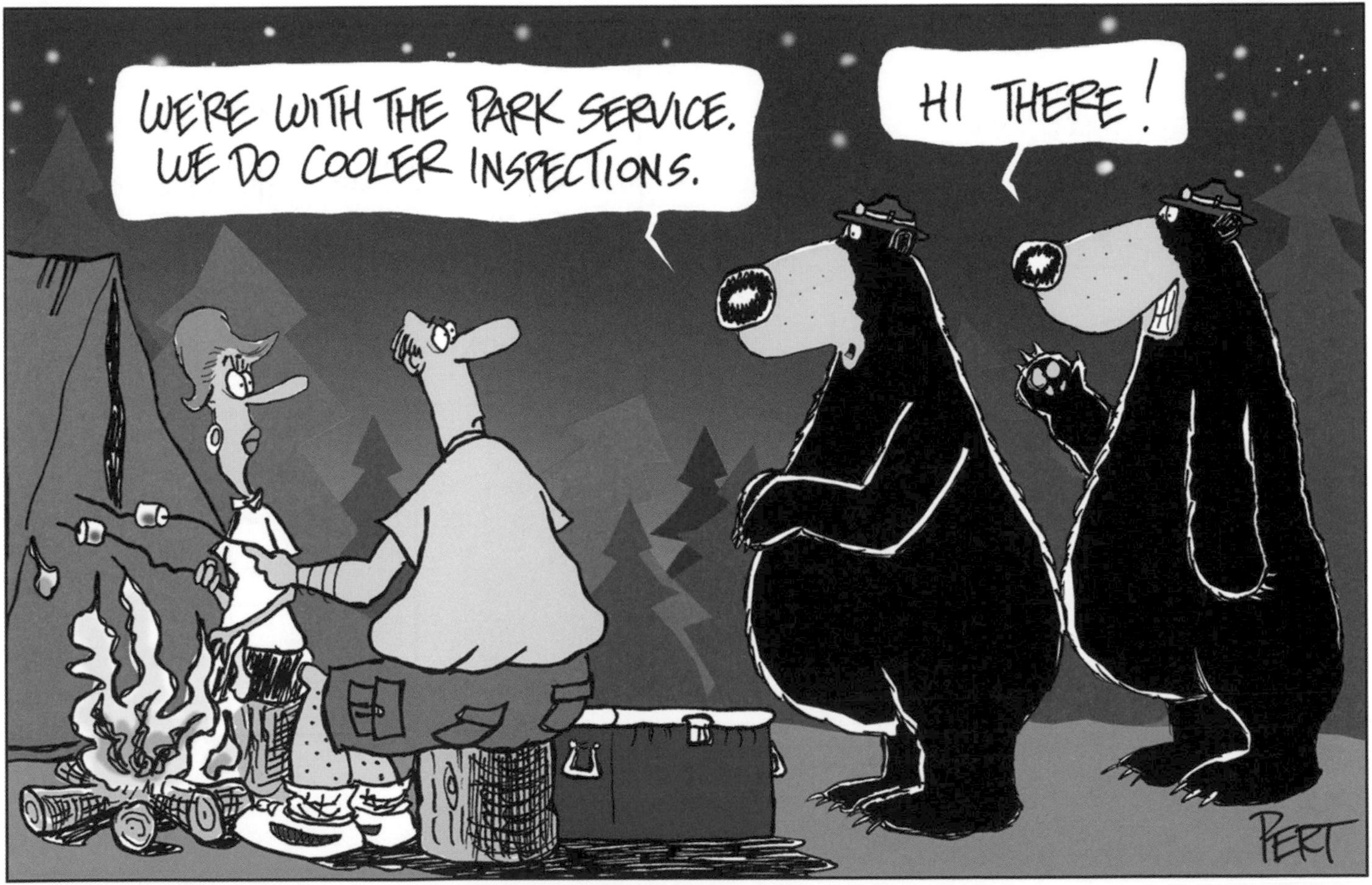
WE'RE WITH THE PARK SERVICE. WE DO COOLER INSPECTIONS.
HI THERE!
PERT

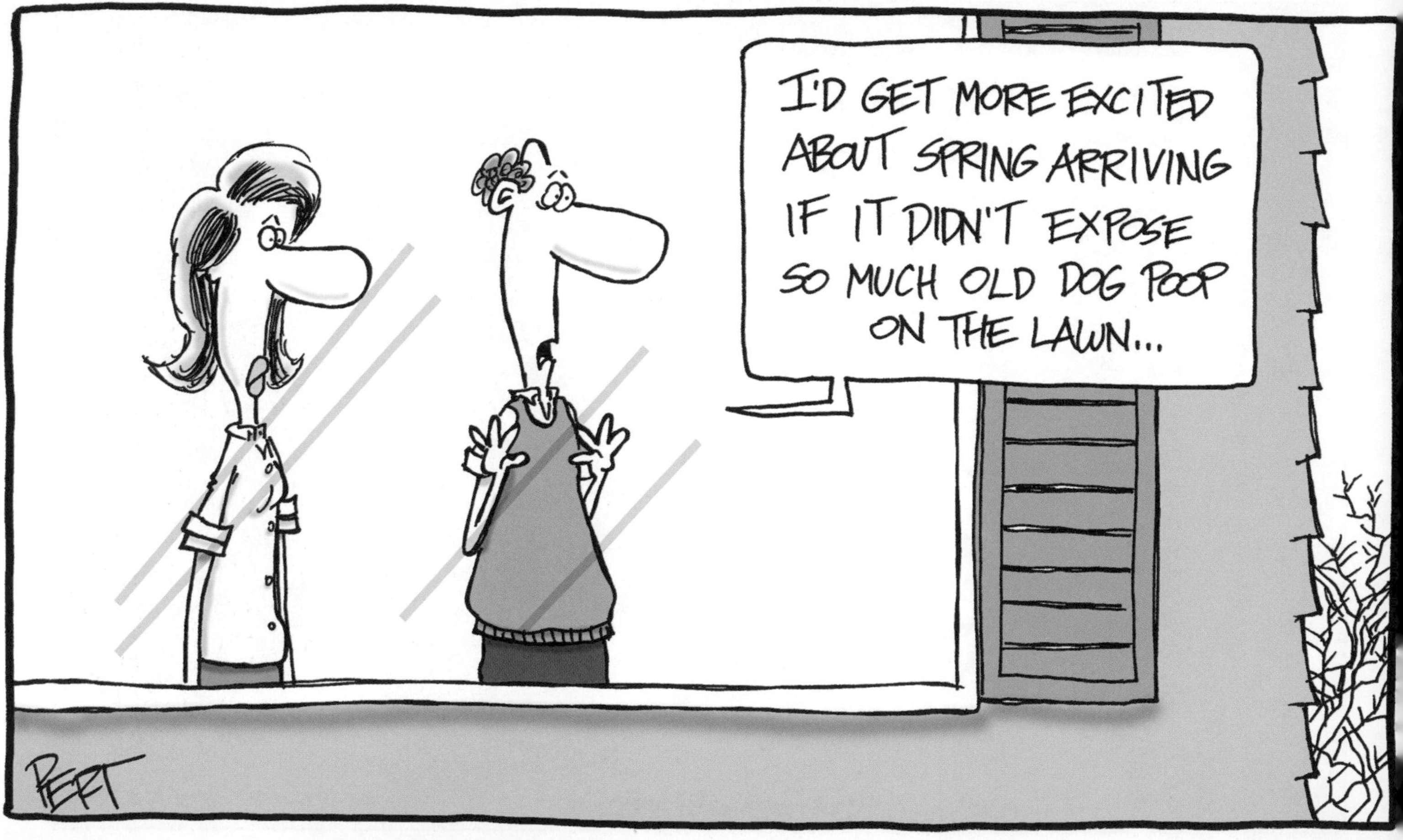
I'D GET MORE EXCITED ABOUT SPRING ARRIVING IF IT DIDN'T EXPOSE SO MUCH OLD DOG POOP ON THE LAWN...
PEPT

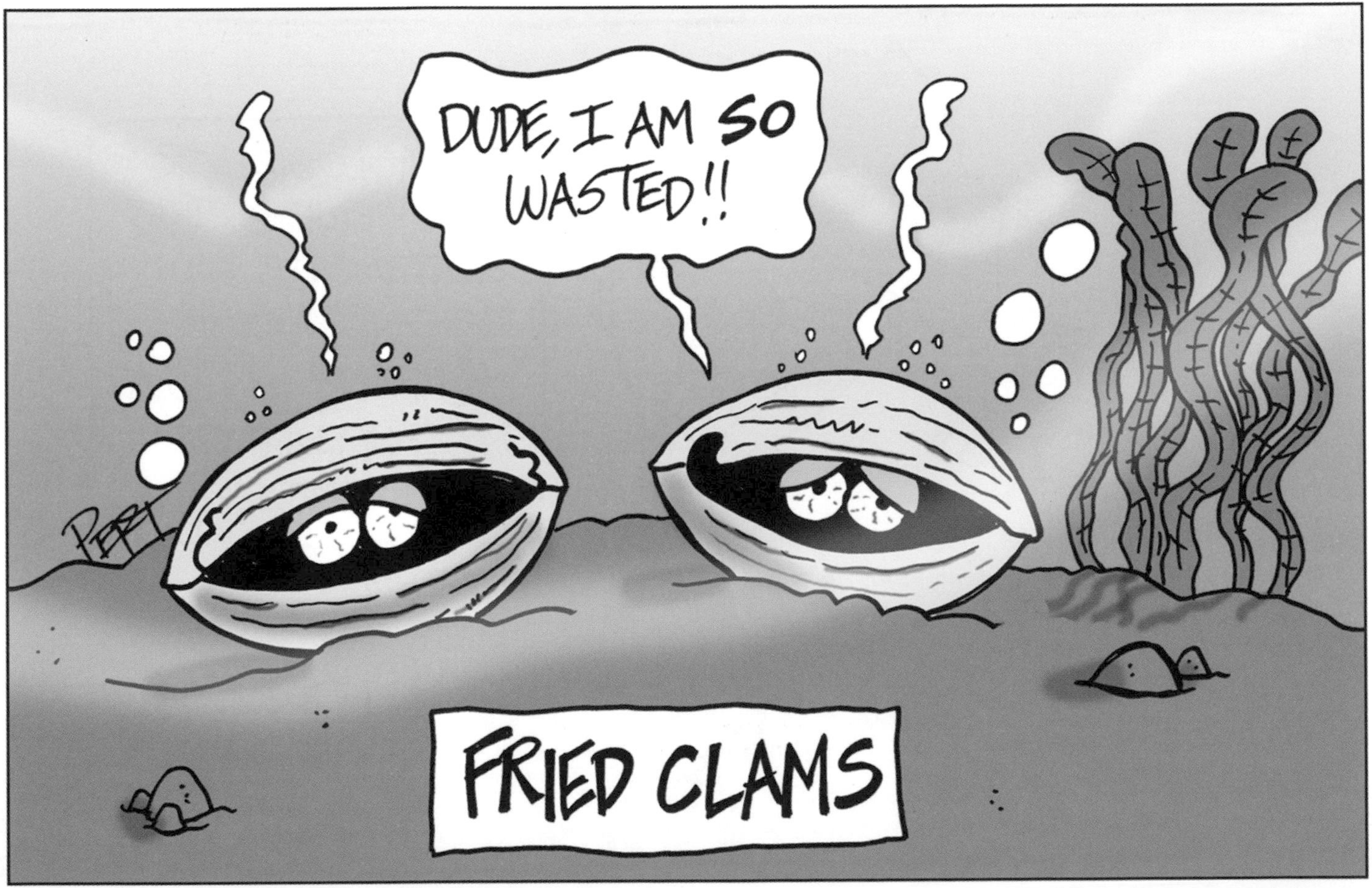
DUDE, I AM SO WASTED!!
PEPI
FRIED CLAMS

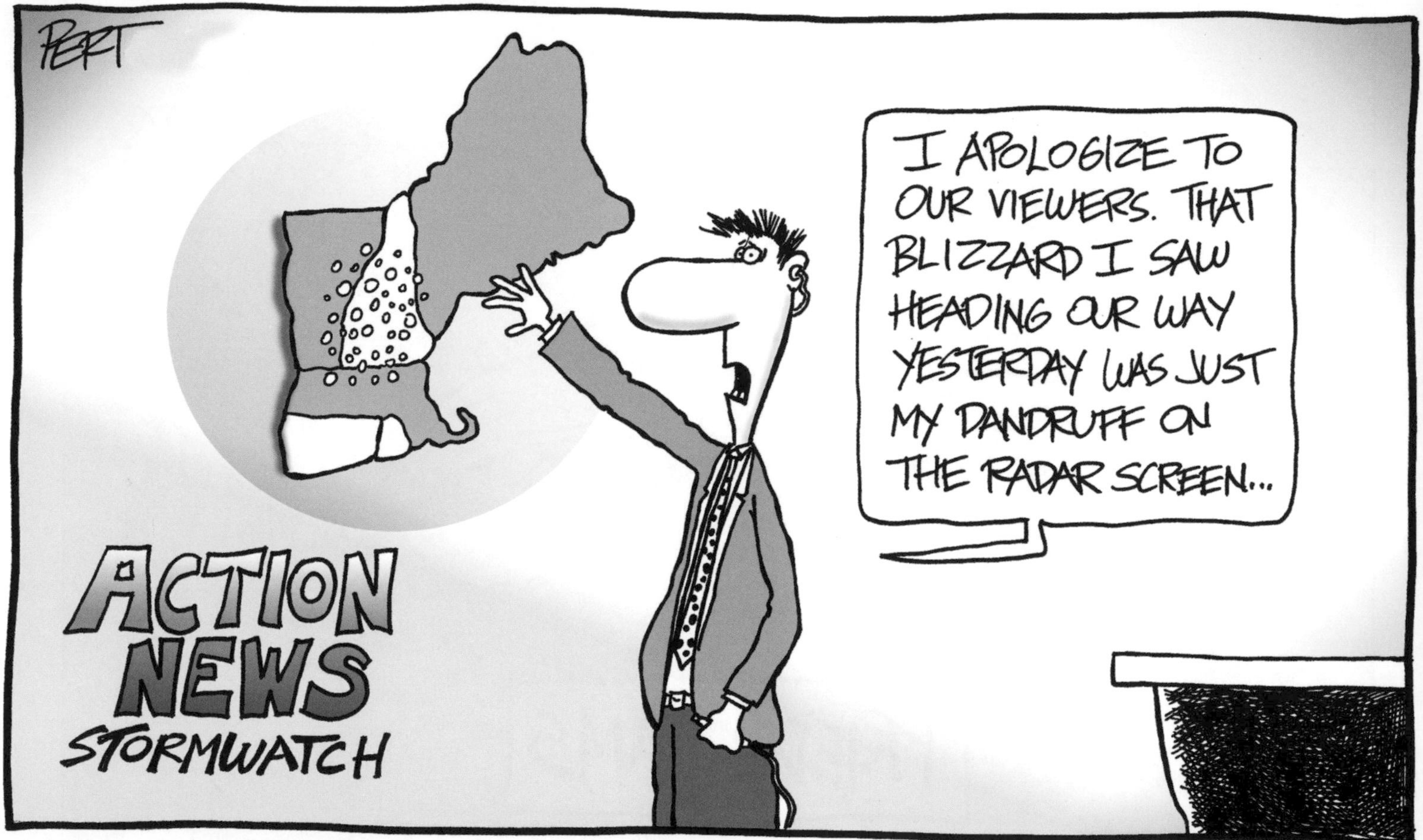
PERT
I APOLOGIZE TO OUR VIEWERS. THAT BLIZZARD I SAW HEADING OUR WAY YESTERDAY WAS JUST MY DANDRUFF ON THE RADAR SCREEN...
ACTION NEWS
STORMWATCH

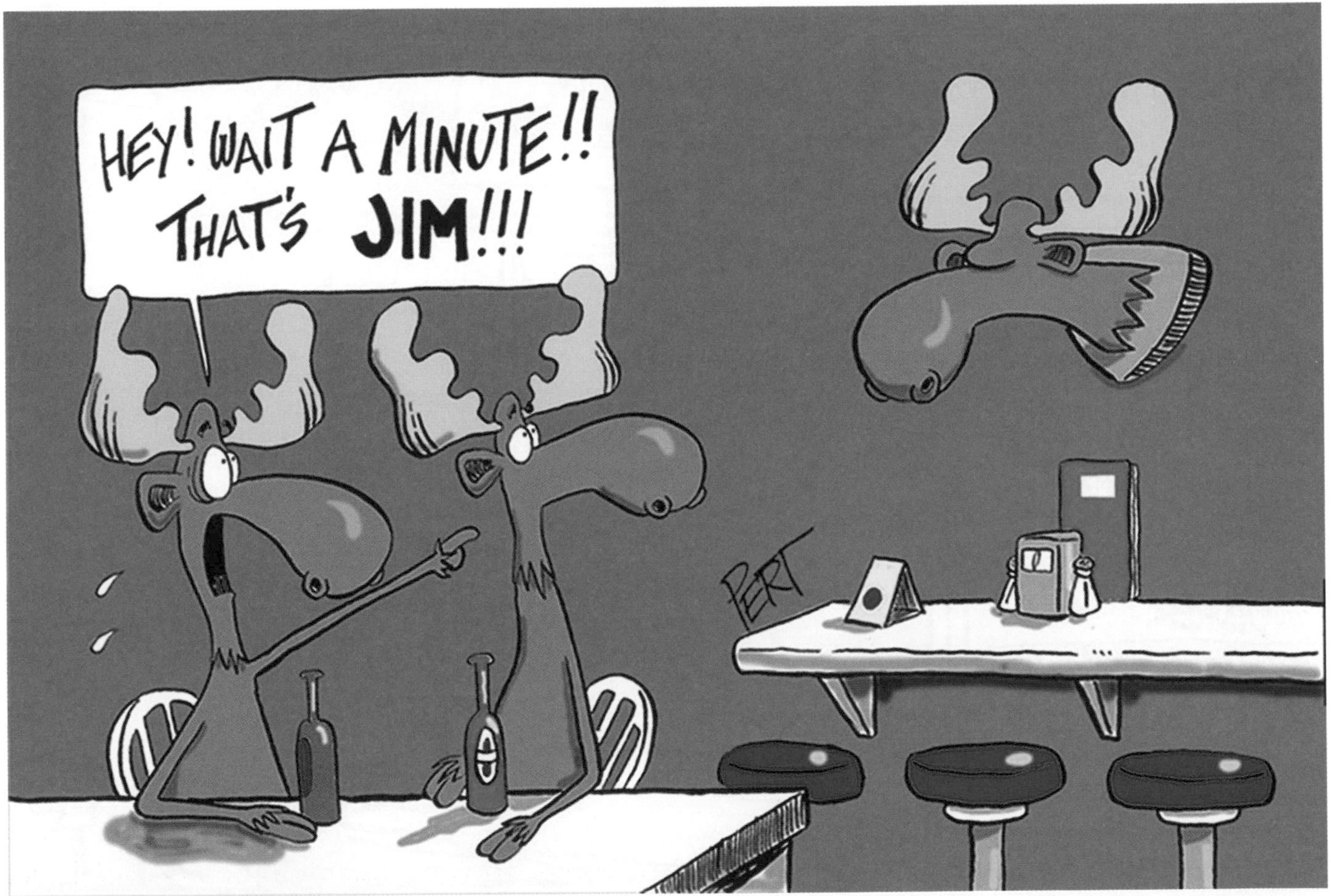
HEY! WAIT A MINUTE!!
THAT'S JIM!!!
PERT

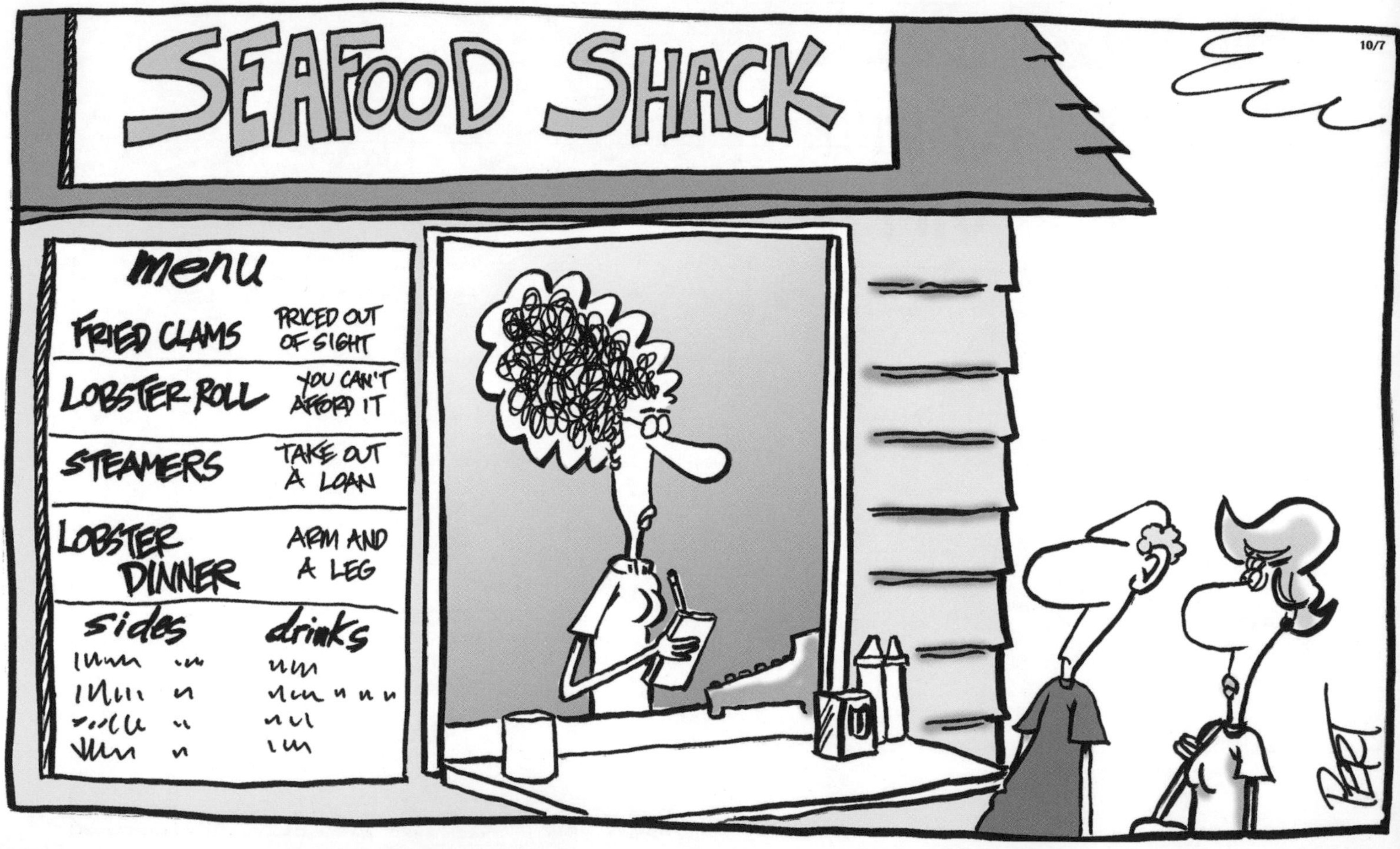
SEAFOOD SHACK
10/7
menu
FRIED CLAMS
PRICED OUT OF SIGHT
LOBSTER ROLL
YOU CAN'T AFFORD IT
STEAMERS
TAKE OUT A LOAN
LOBSTER DINNER
ARM AND A LEG
sides
drinks

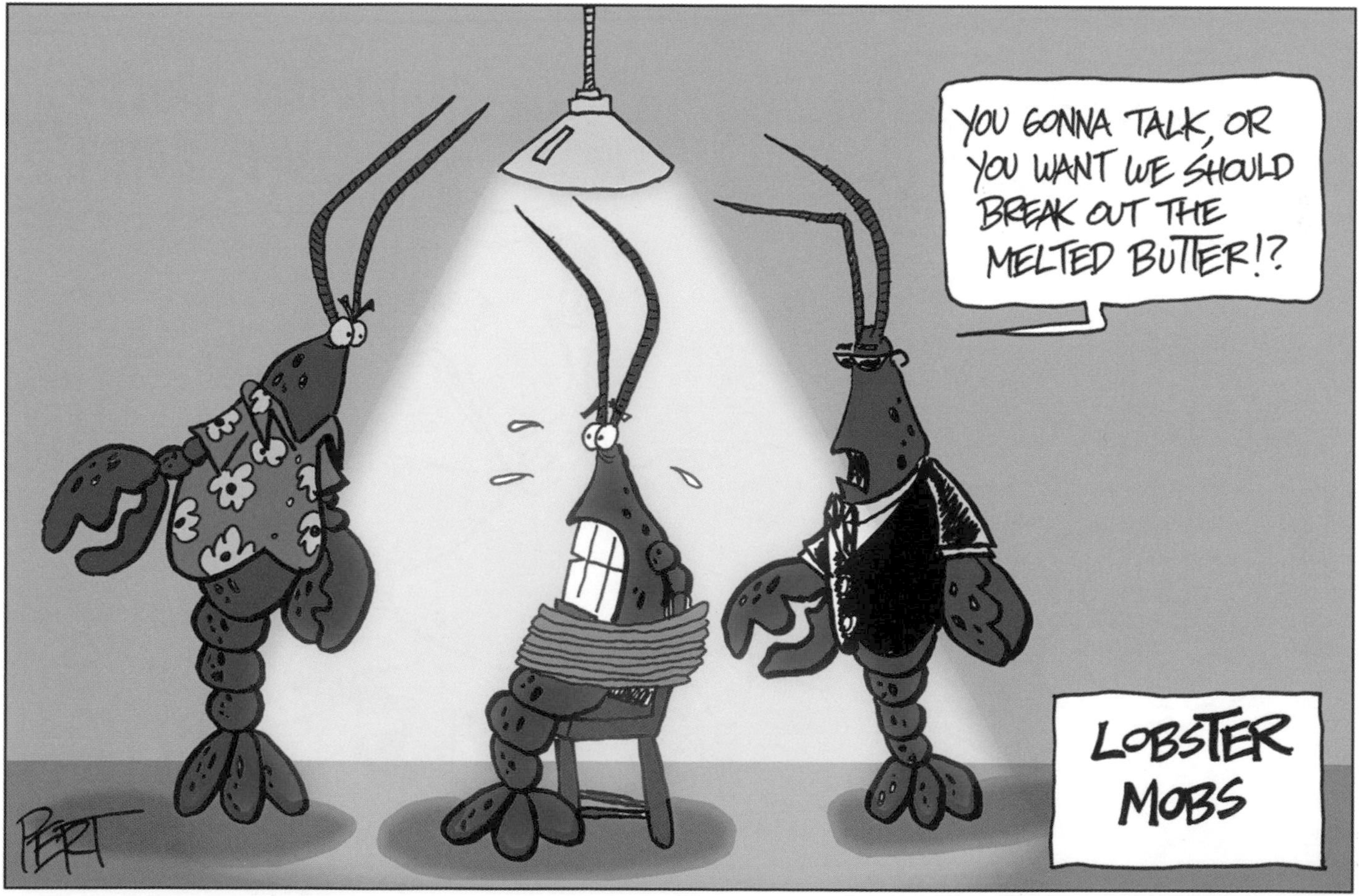
YOU GONNA TALK, OR YOU WANT WE SHOULD BREAK OUT THE MELTED BUTTER!?
LOBSTER MOBS
PEIRT

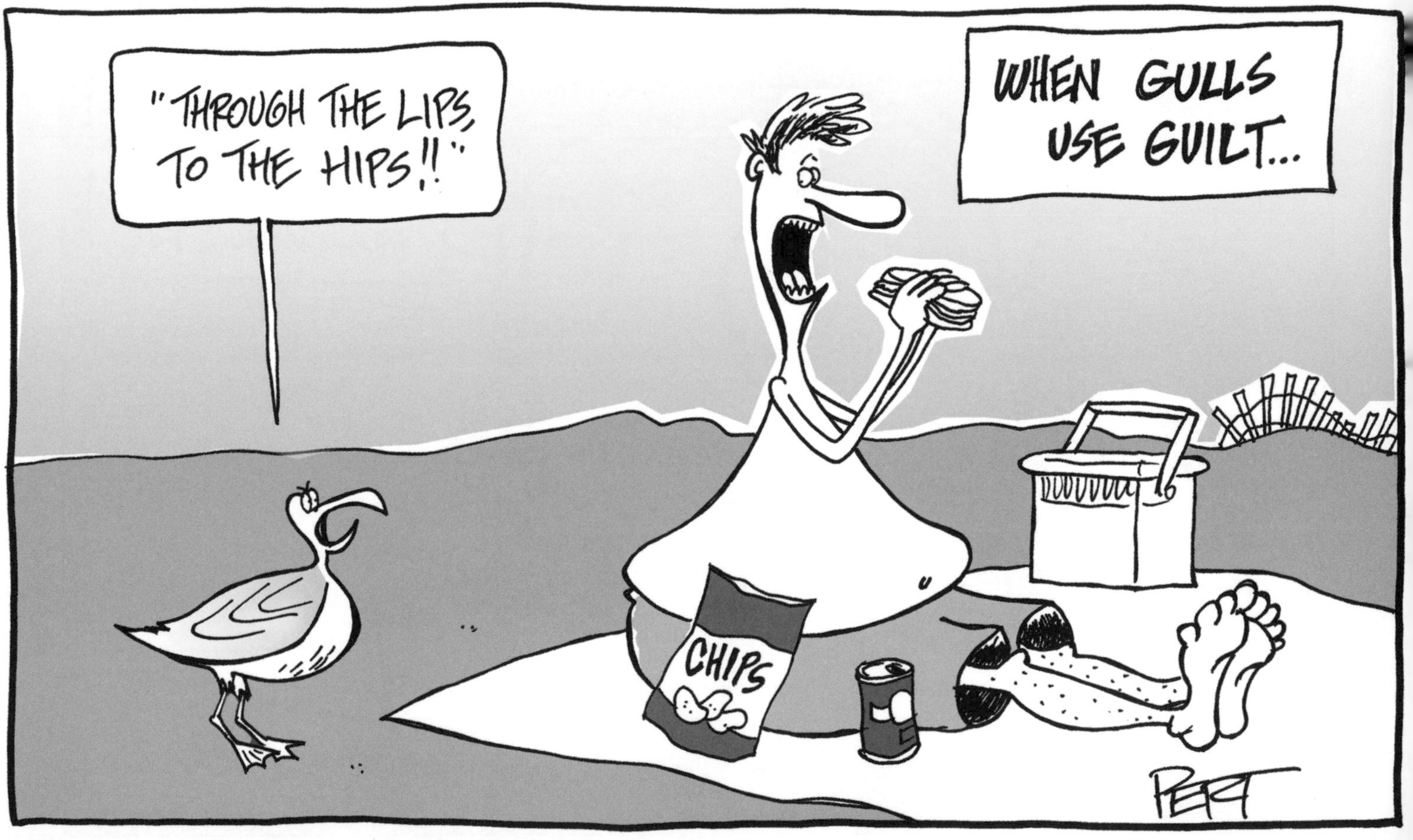
"THROUGH THE LIPS, TO THE HIPS!!"
WHEN GULLS USE GUILT...
CHIPS
PETT

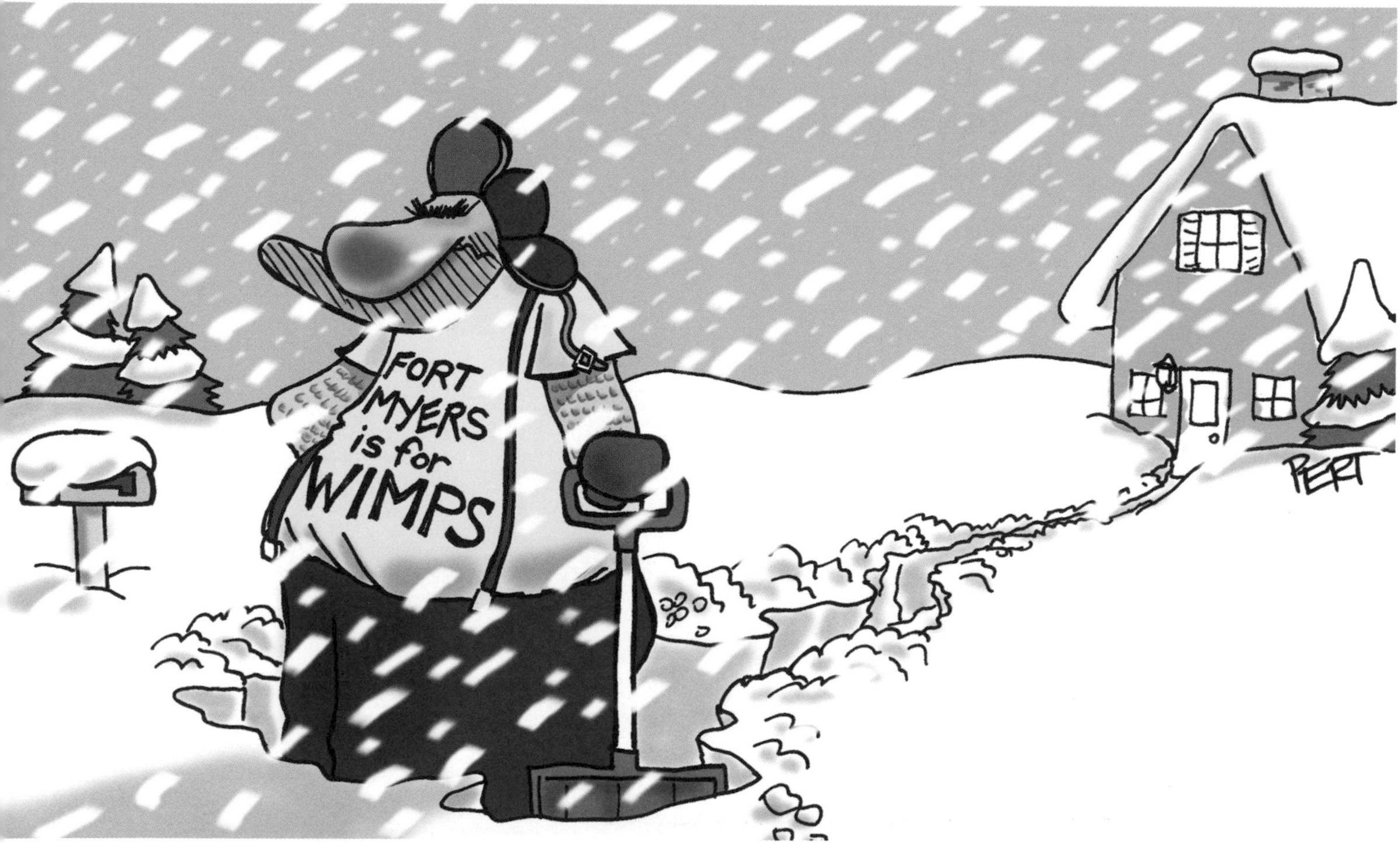
FORT MYERS is for WIMPS
PERT

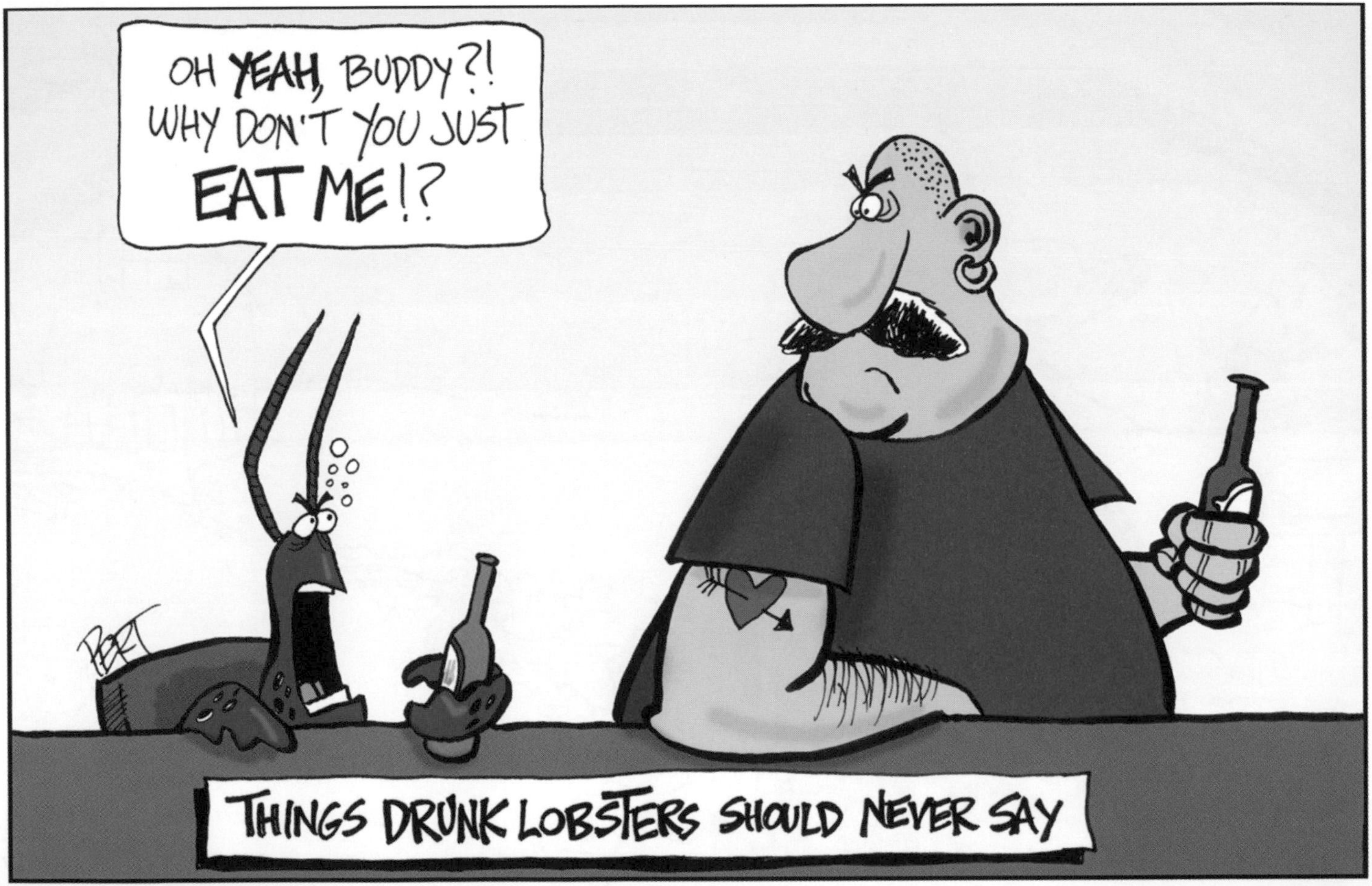
OH YEAH, BUDDY?!
WHY DON'T YOU JUST
EAT ME!?
PERT
THINGS DRUNK LOBSTERS SHOULD NEVER SAY

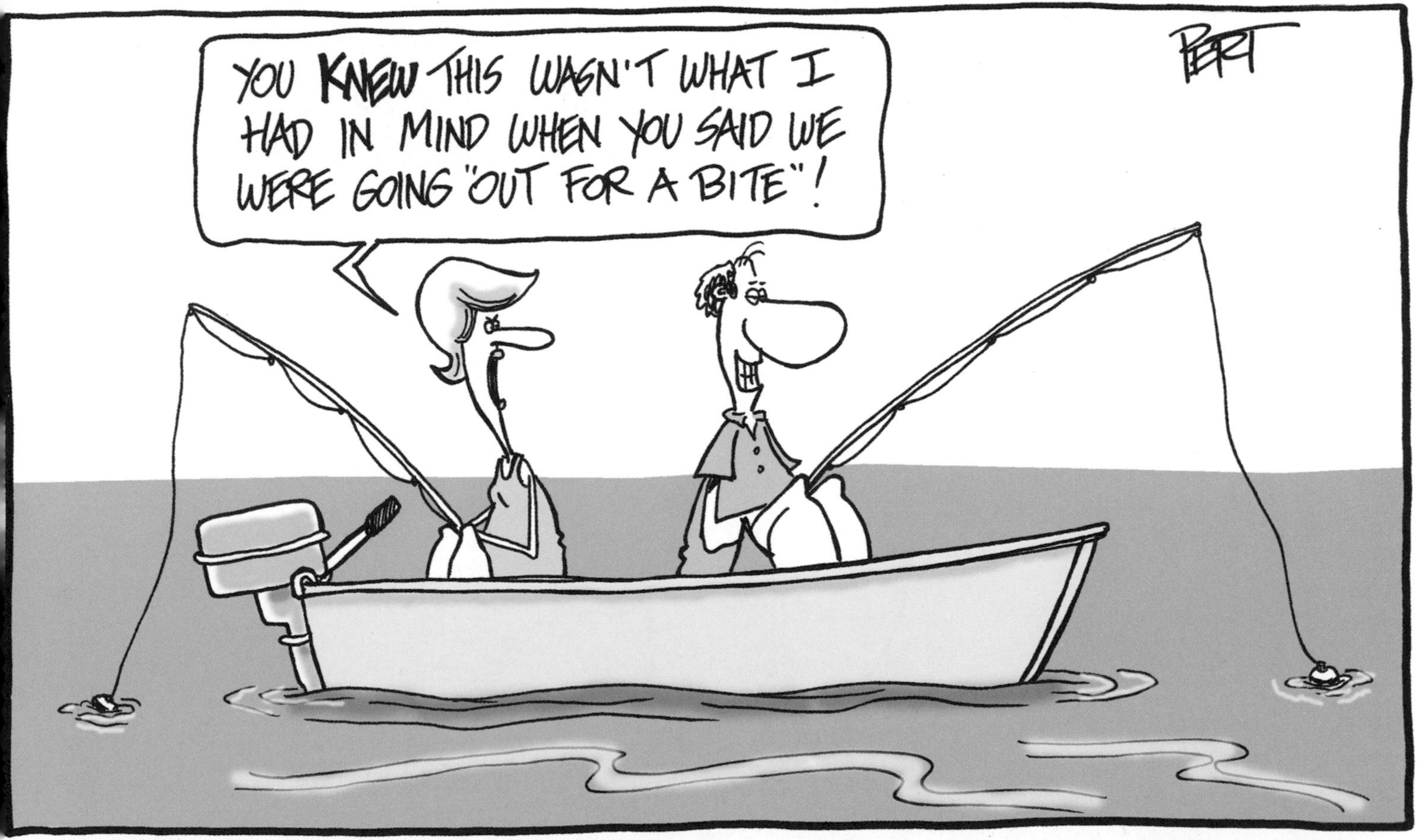
YOU KNEW THIS WASN'T WHAT I HAD IN MIND WHEN YOU SAID WE WERE GOING "OUT FOR A BITE"!
PERT

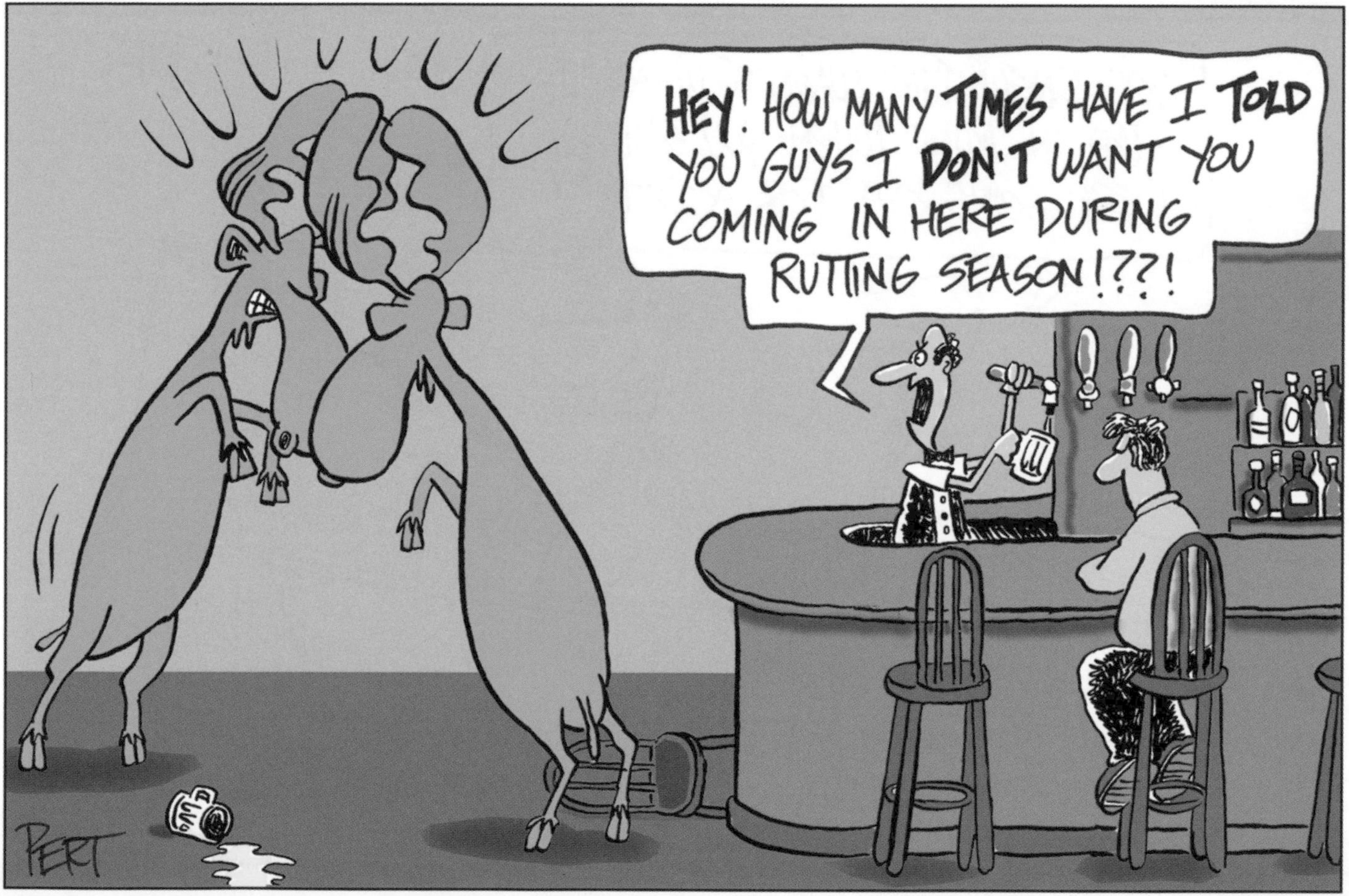
HEY! HOW MANY TIMES HAVE I TOLD YOU GUYS I DON'T WANT YOU COMING IN HERE DURING RUTTING SEASON!??!
PERT

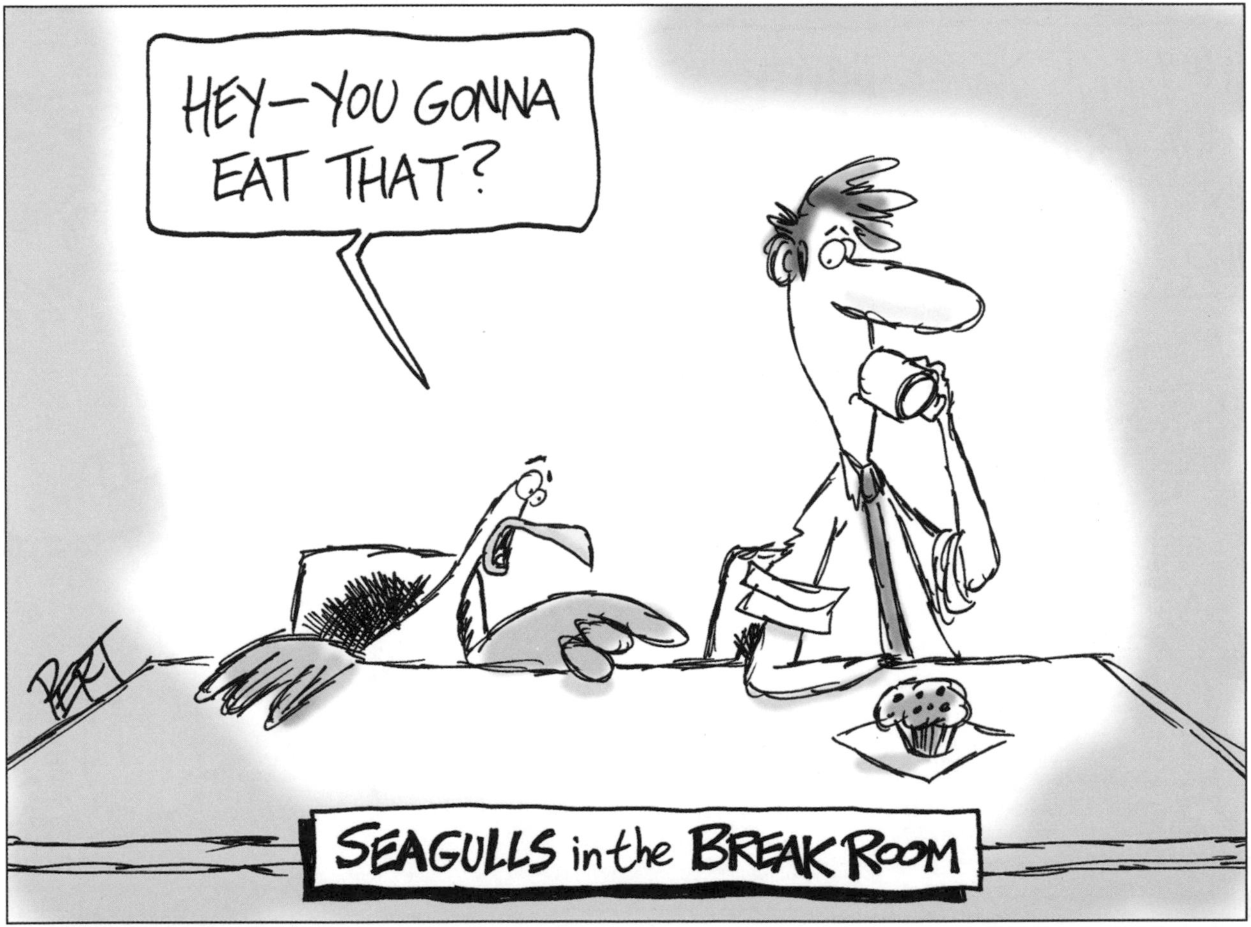
HEY—YOU GONNA EAT THAT?
SEAGULLS in the BREAK ROOM

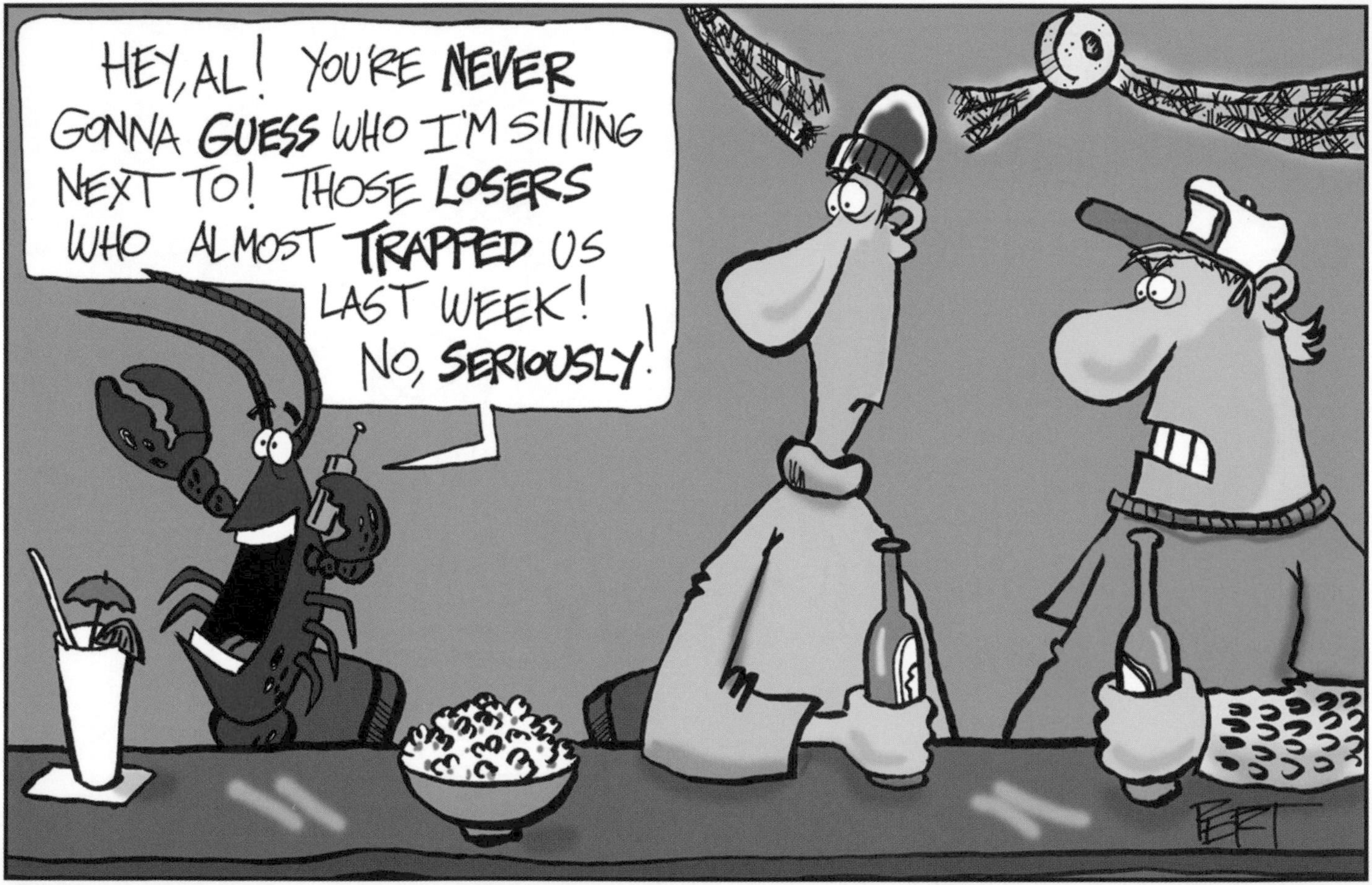
HEY, AL! YOU'RE NEVER GONNA GUESS WHO I'M SITTING NEXT TO! THOSE LOSERS WHO ALMOST TRAPPED US LAST WEEK! NO, SERIOUSLY!
BERT

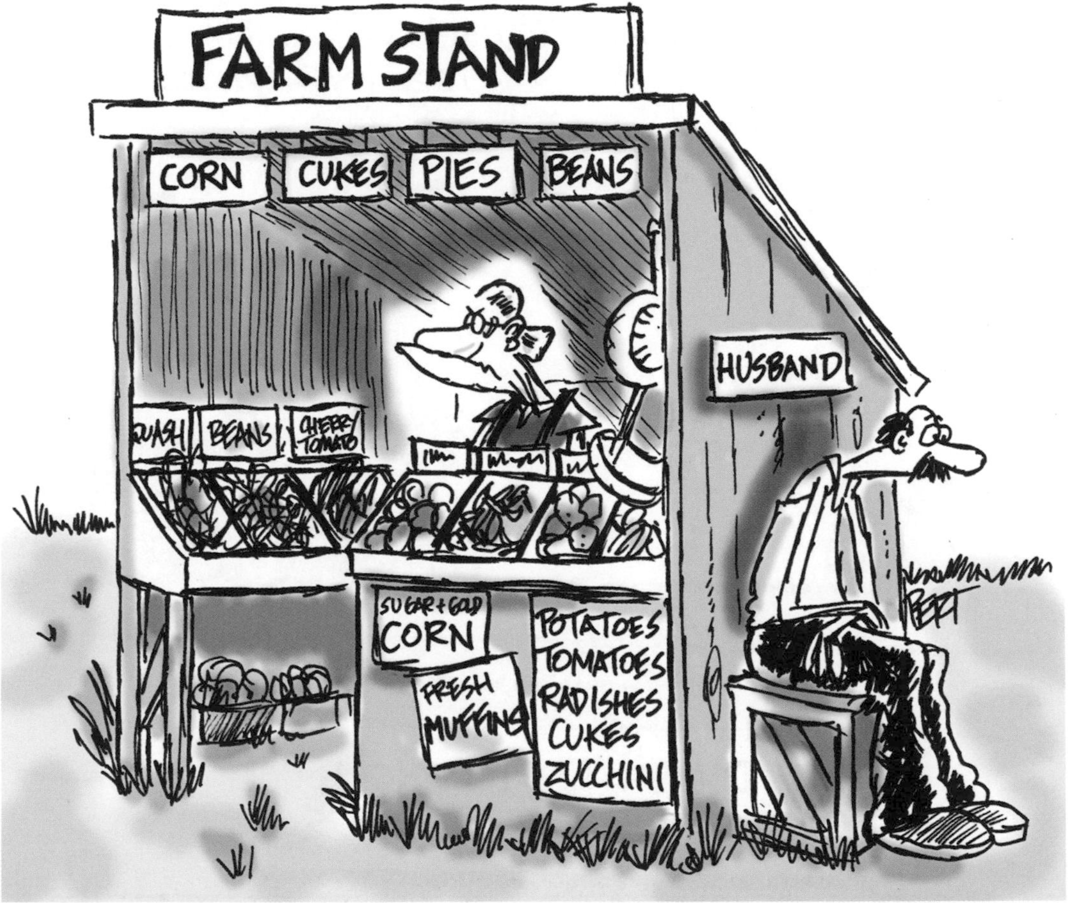
FARM STAND
CORN
CUKES
PIES
BEANS
HUSBAND
BEANS
CHERRY TOMATO
SUGAR + GOLD CORN
FRESH MUFFINS
POTATOES
TOMATOES
RADISHES
CUKES
ZUCCHINI
BERT

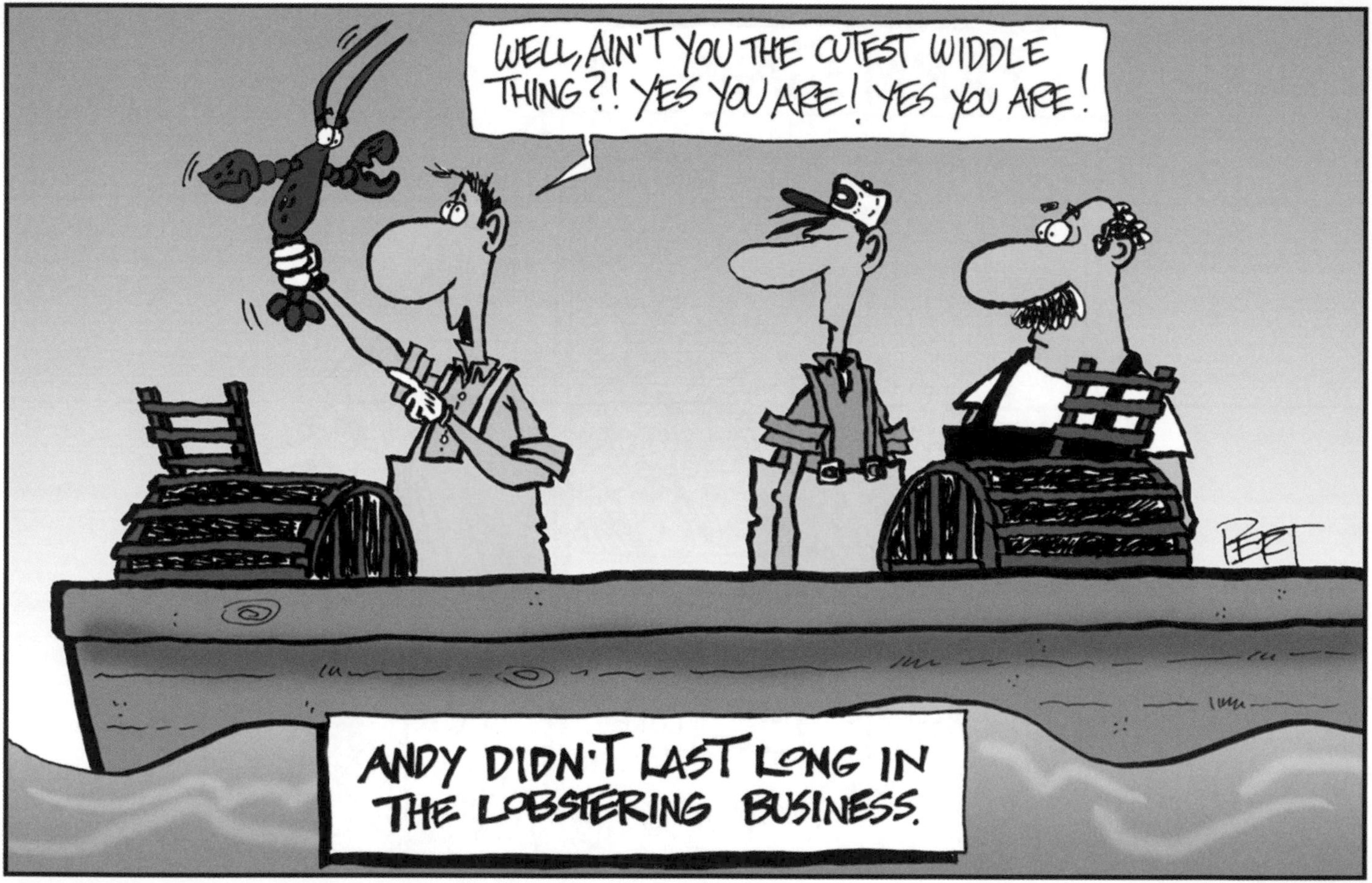
WELL, AIN'T YOU THE CUTEST WIDDLE THING?! YES YOU ARE! YES YOU ARE!
BERT
ANDY DIDN'T LAST LONG IN THE LOBSTERING BUSINESS.

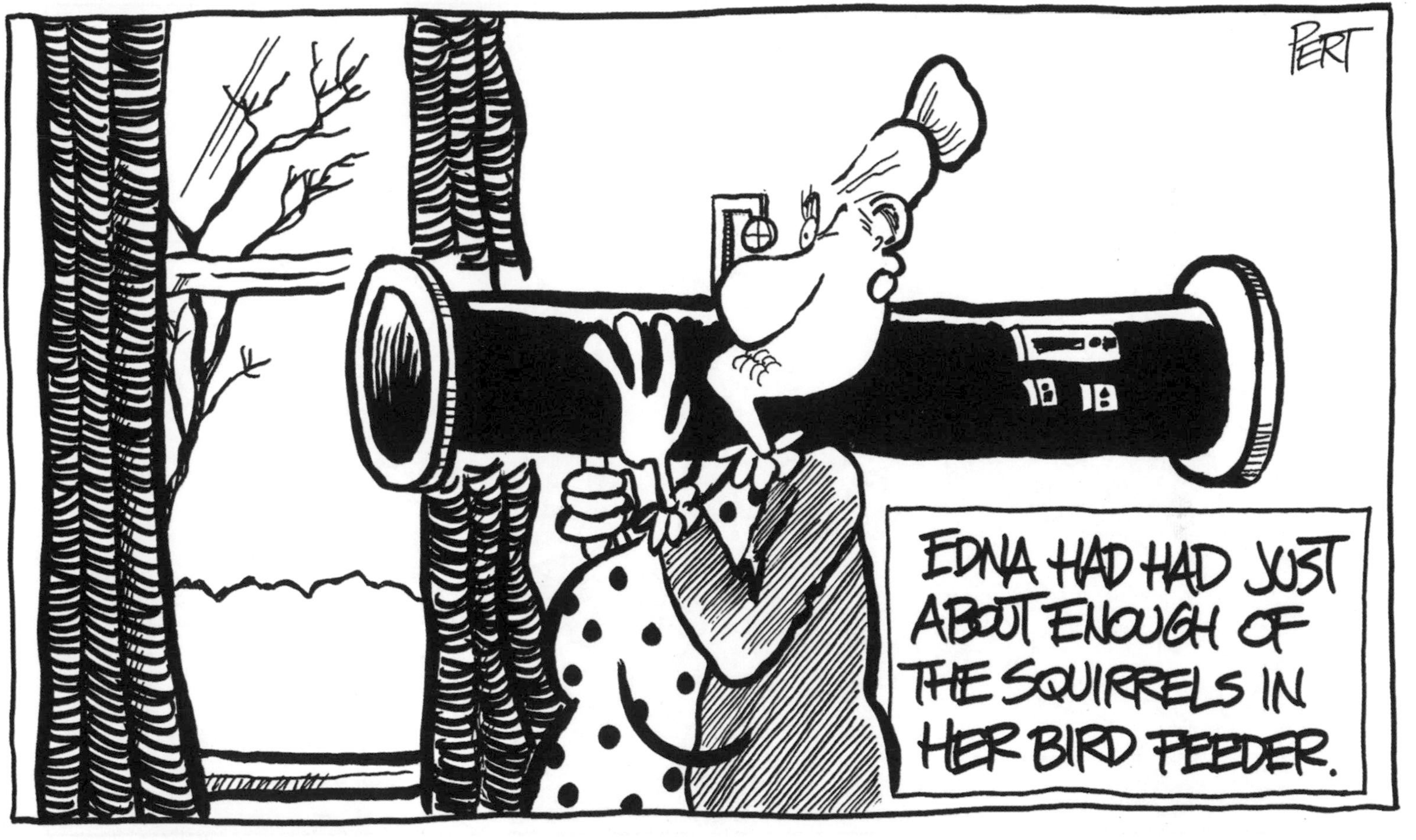
PERT
EDNA HAD HAD JUST ABOUT ENOUGH OF THE SQUIRRELS IN HER BIRD FEEDER.

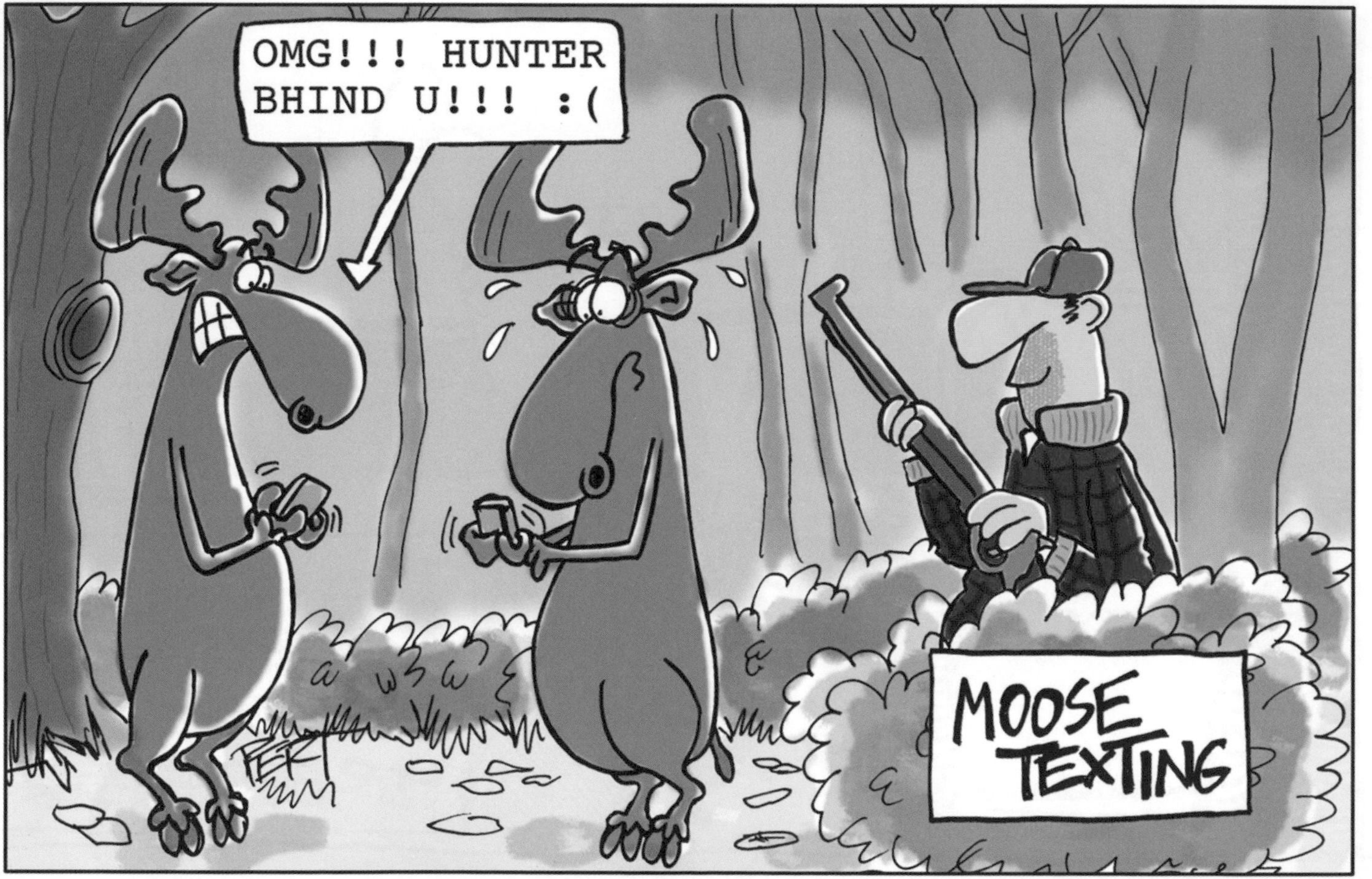
OMG!!! HUNTER BHIND U!!! :(
MOOSE TEXTING

ALDEN DIDN'T LIVE ANYWHERE NEAR THE OCEAN, BUT HE MADE DO...

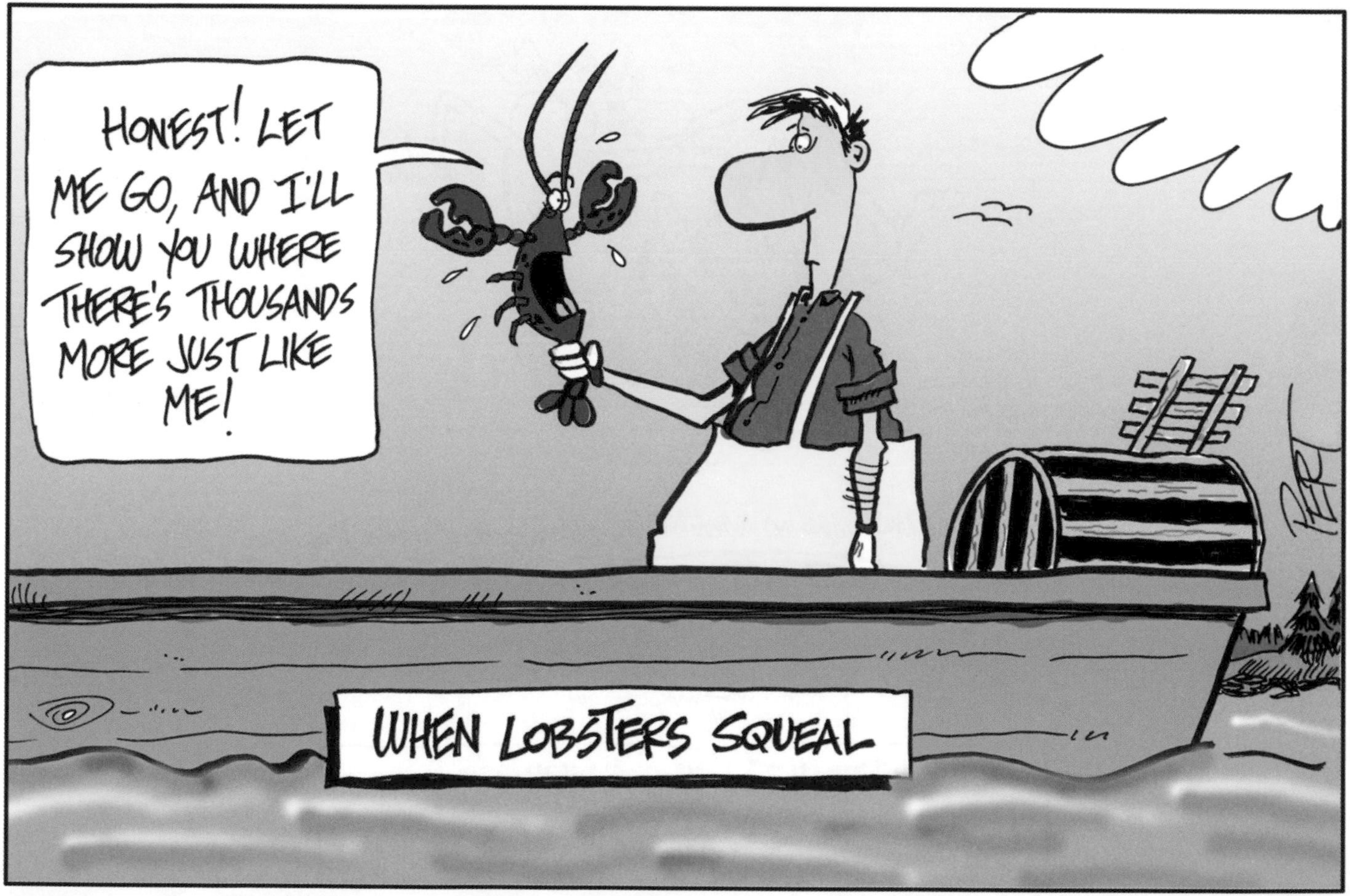
HONEST! LET ME GO, AND I'LL SHOW YOU WHERE THERE'S THOUSANDS MORE JUST LIKE ME!
WHEN LOBSTERS SQUEAL

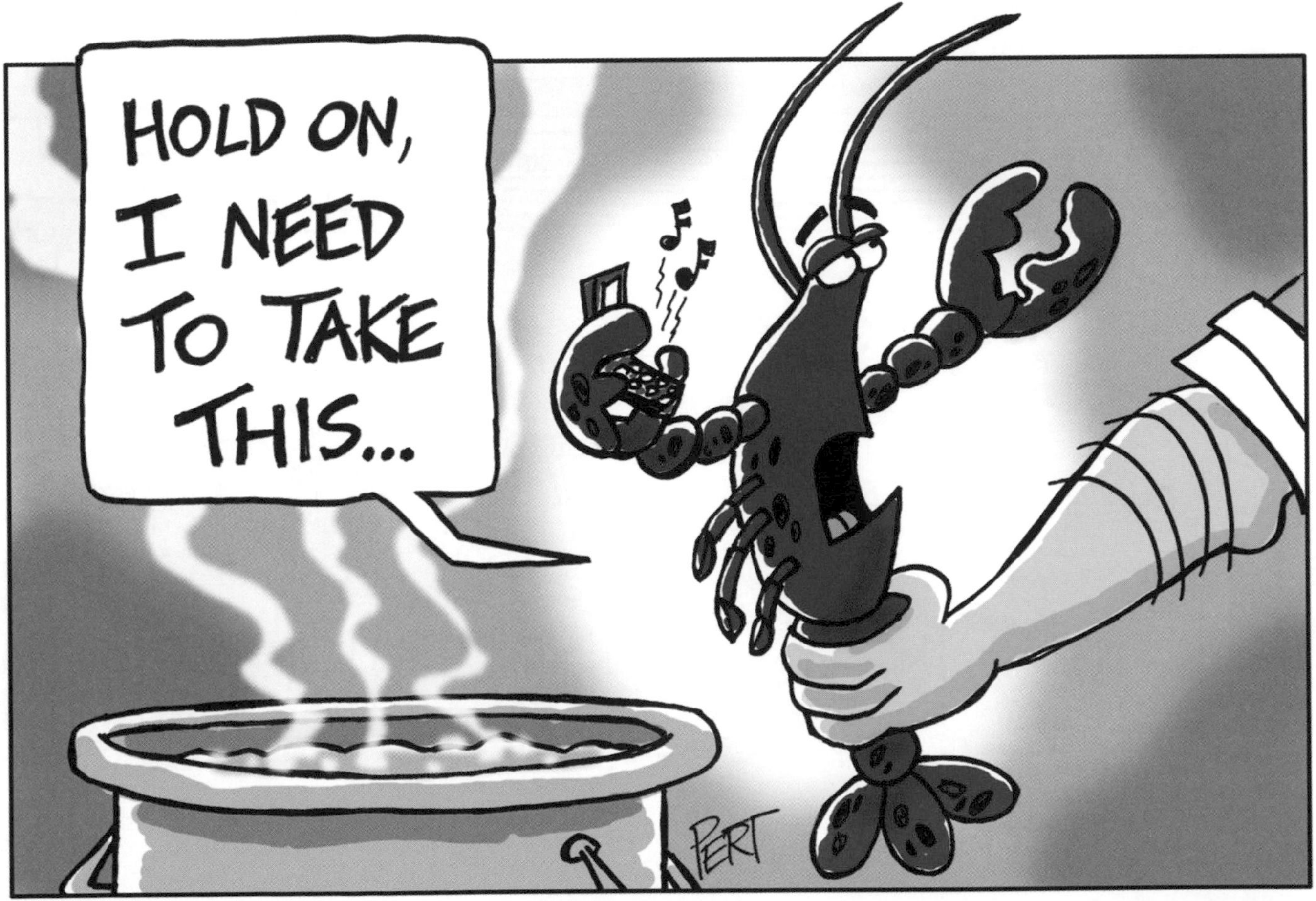
HOLD ON, I NEED TO TAKE THIS...
PERT

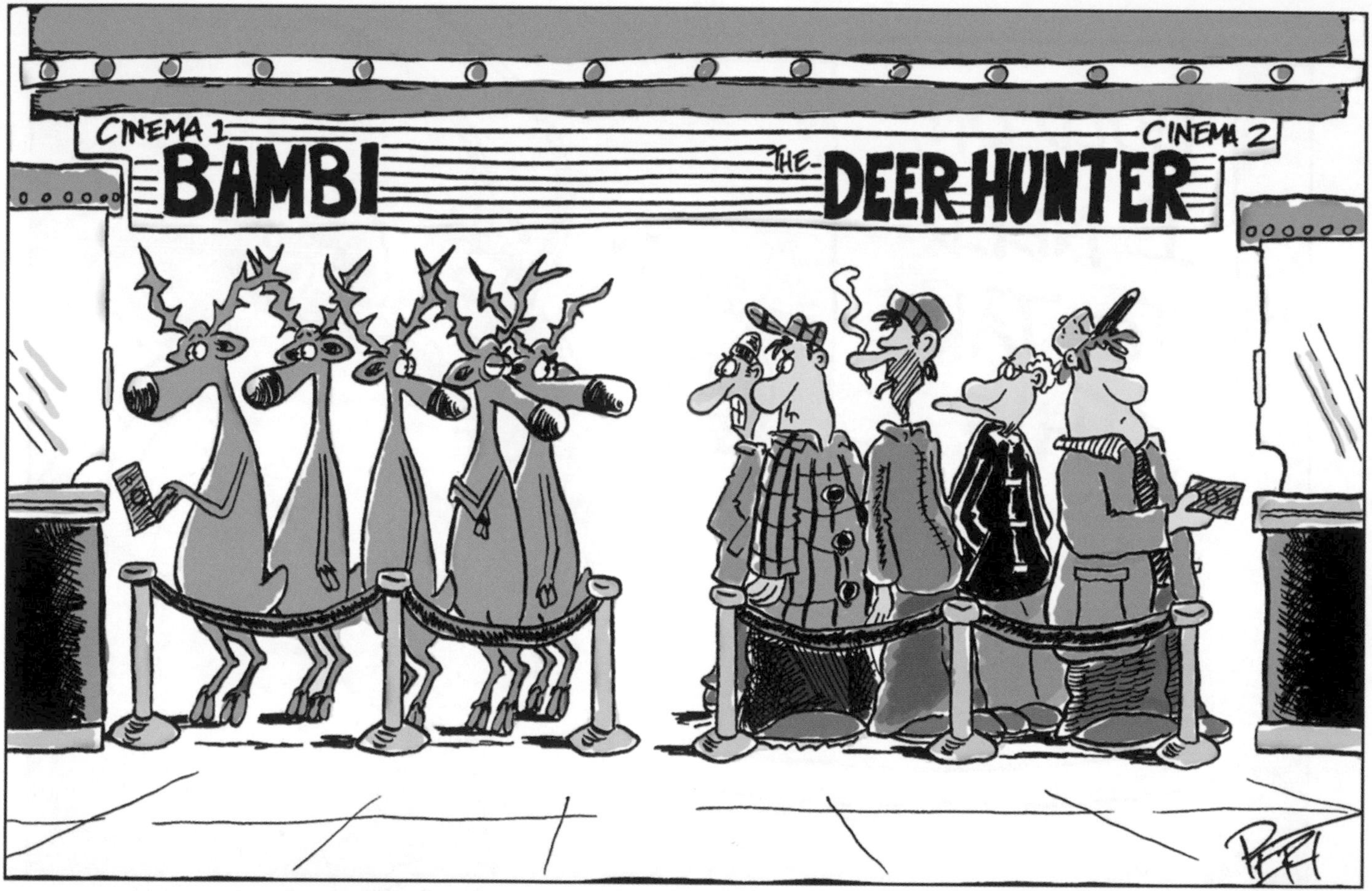
CINEMA 1
BAMBI
CINEMA 2
THE DEER HUNTER

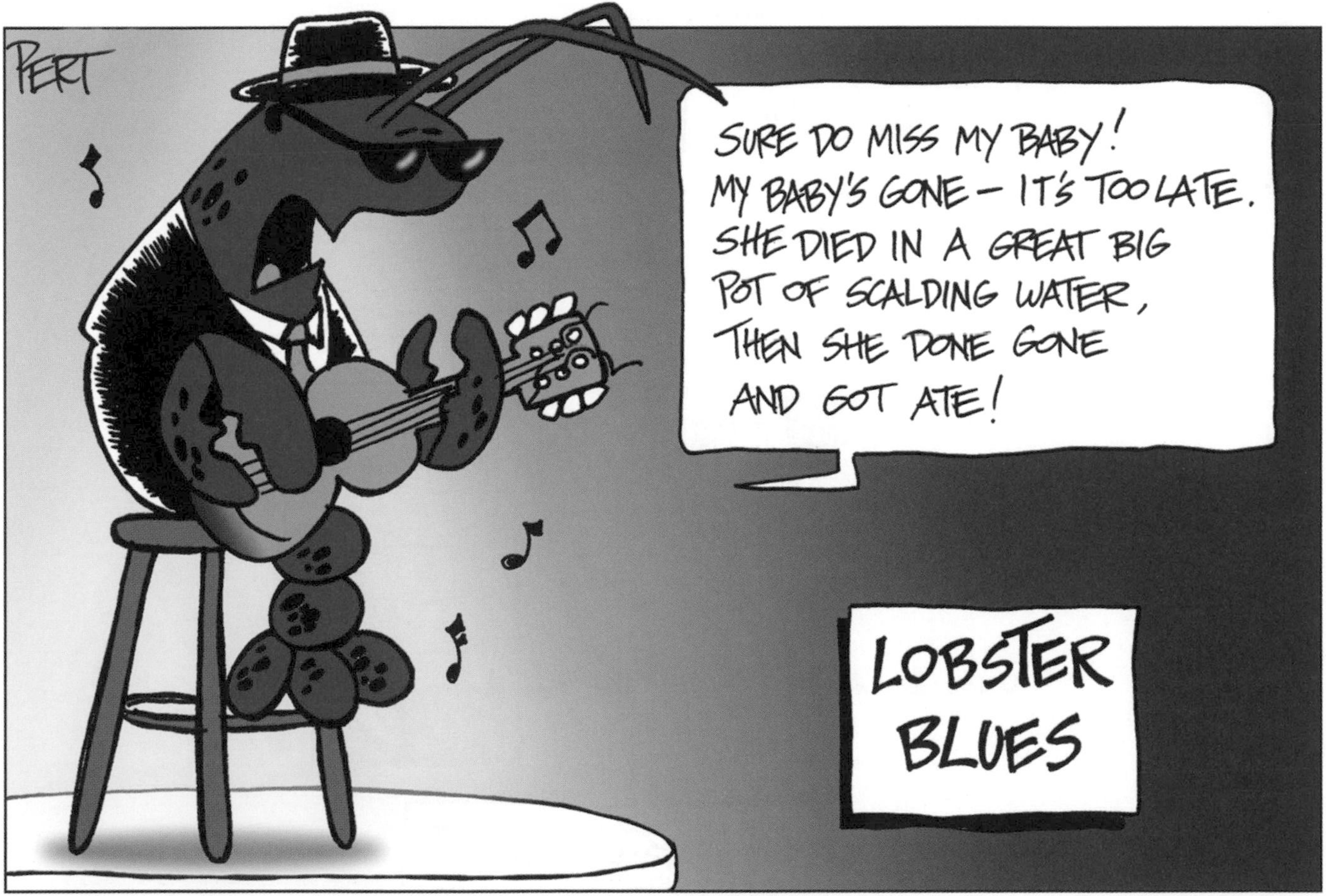
PERT
SURE DO MISS MY BABY! MY BABY'S GONE – IT'S TOO LATE. SHE DIED IN A GREAT BIG POT OF SCALDING WATER, THEN SHE DONE GONE AND GOT ATE!
LOBSTER BLUES

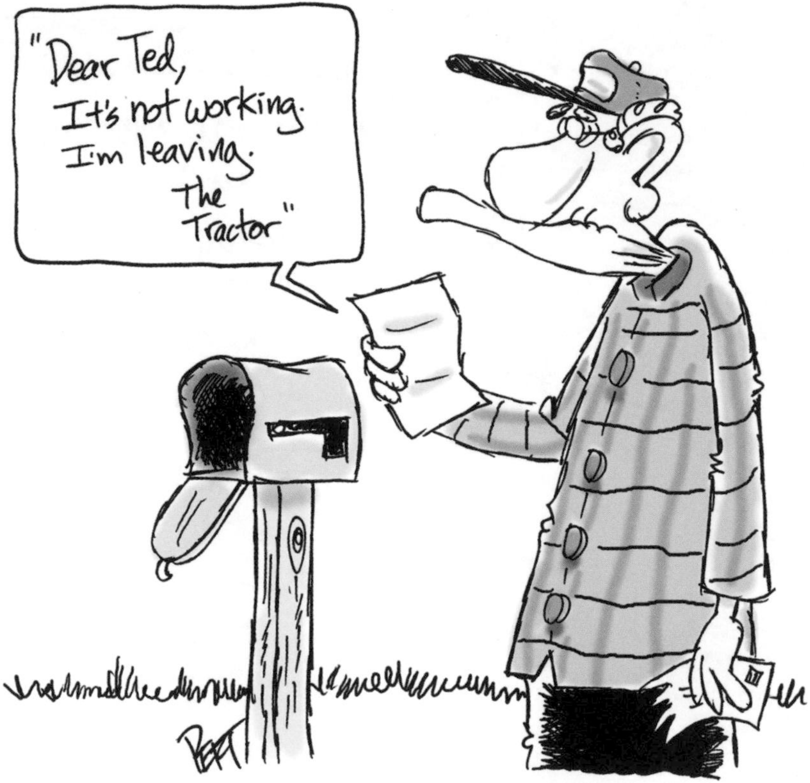
"Dear Ted, It's not working. I'm leaving. The Tractor"

"JOHN DEERE" LETTER

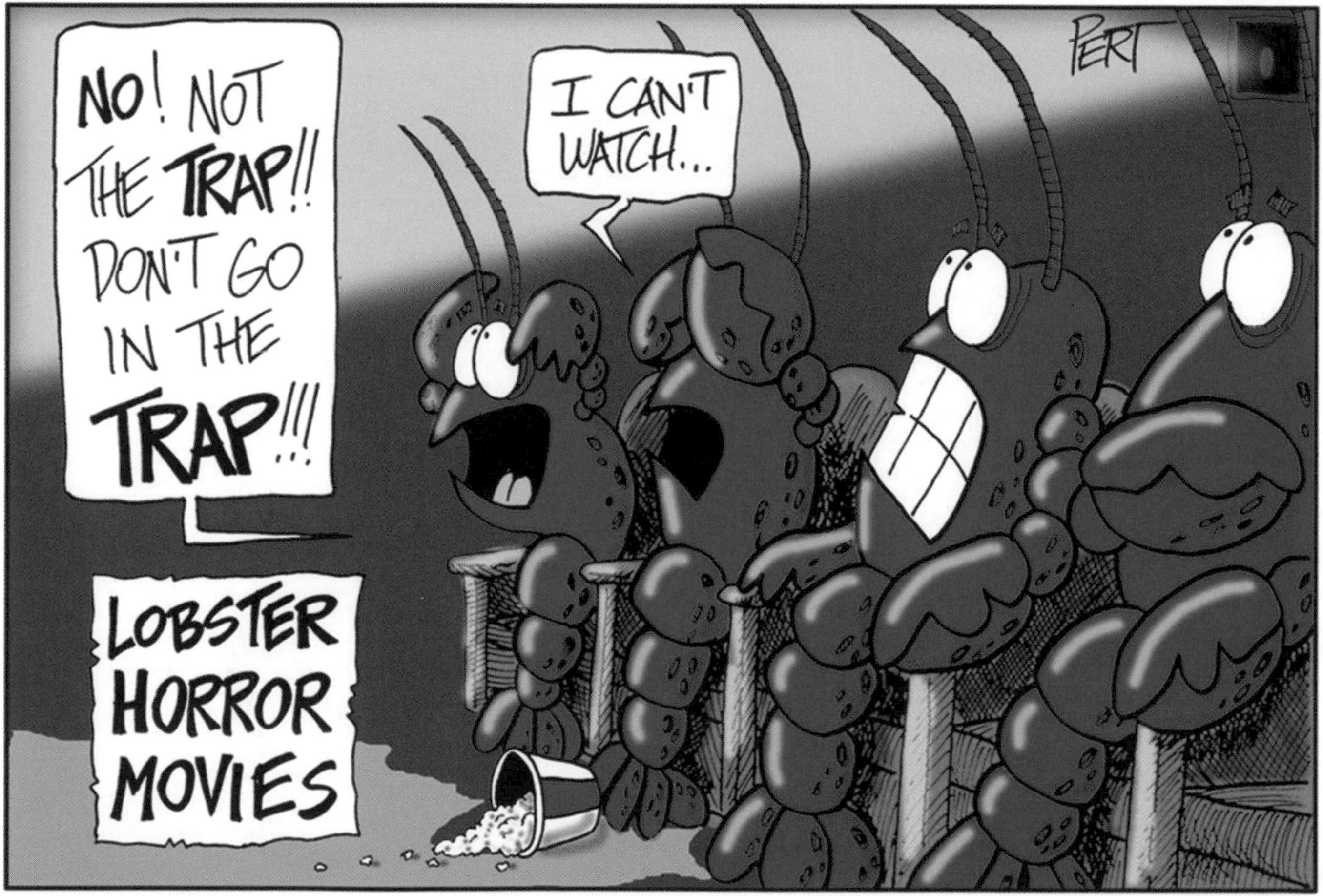
PERT
NO! NOT THE TRAP!! DON'T GO IN THE TRAP!!!
I CAN'T WATCH...
LOBSTER HORROR MOVIES

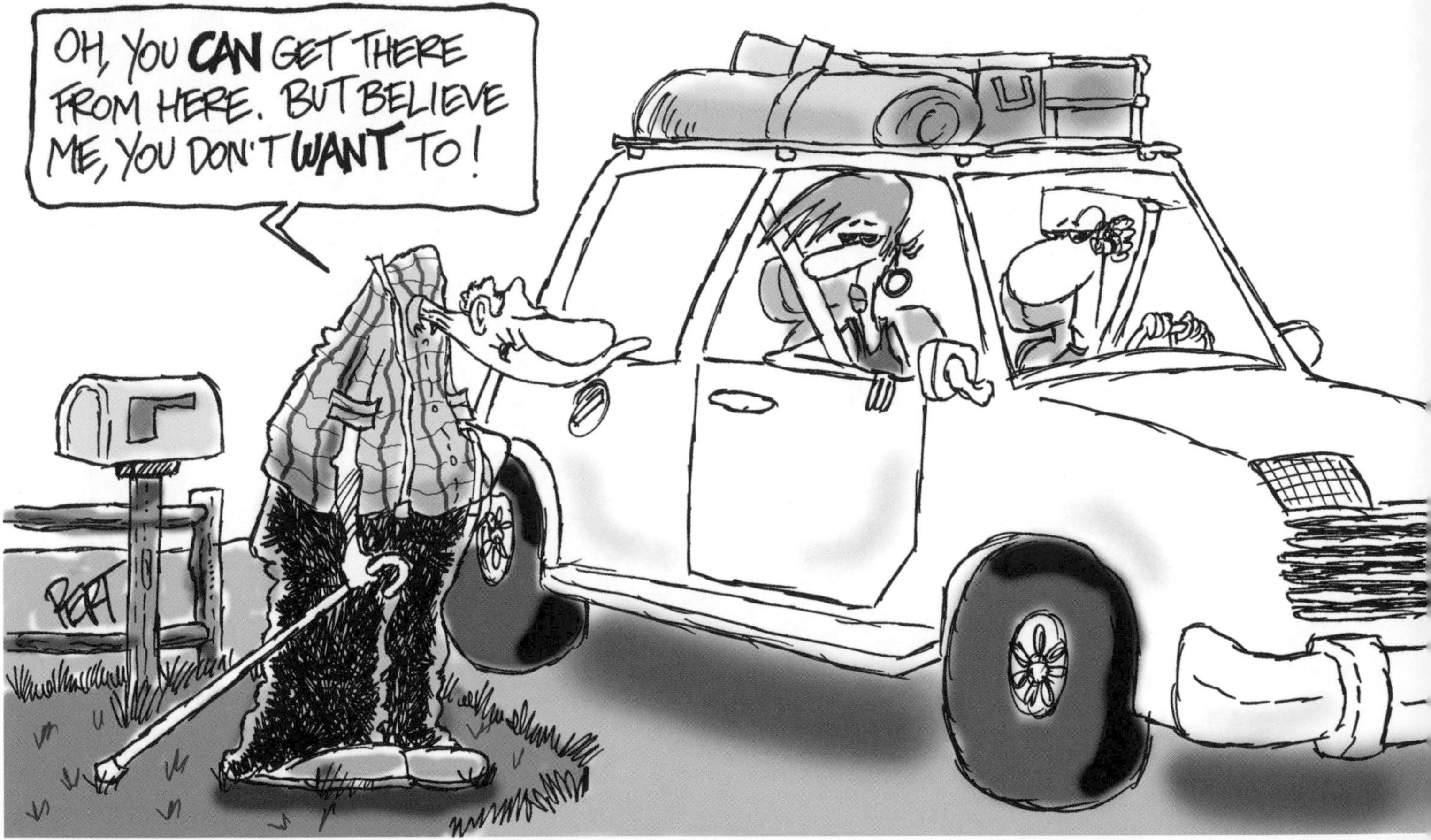

OH, YOU CAN GET THERE FROM HERE. BUT BELIEVE ME, YOU DON'T WANT TO!
PERT

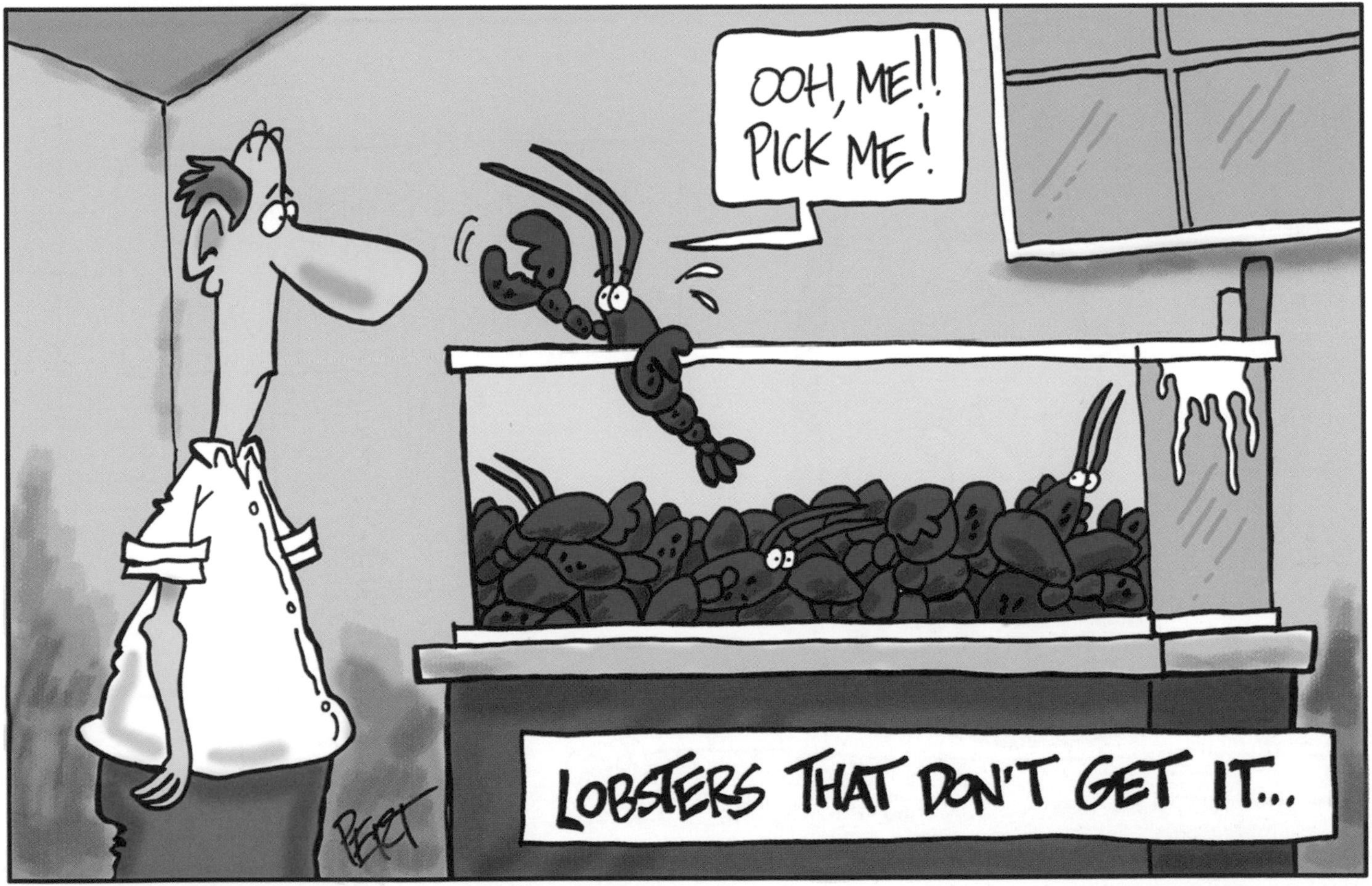
OOH, ME!! PICK ME!
LOBSTERS THAT DON'T GET IT...
PEARCE

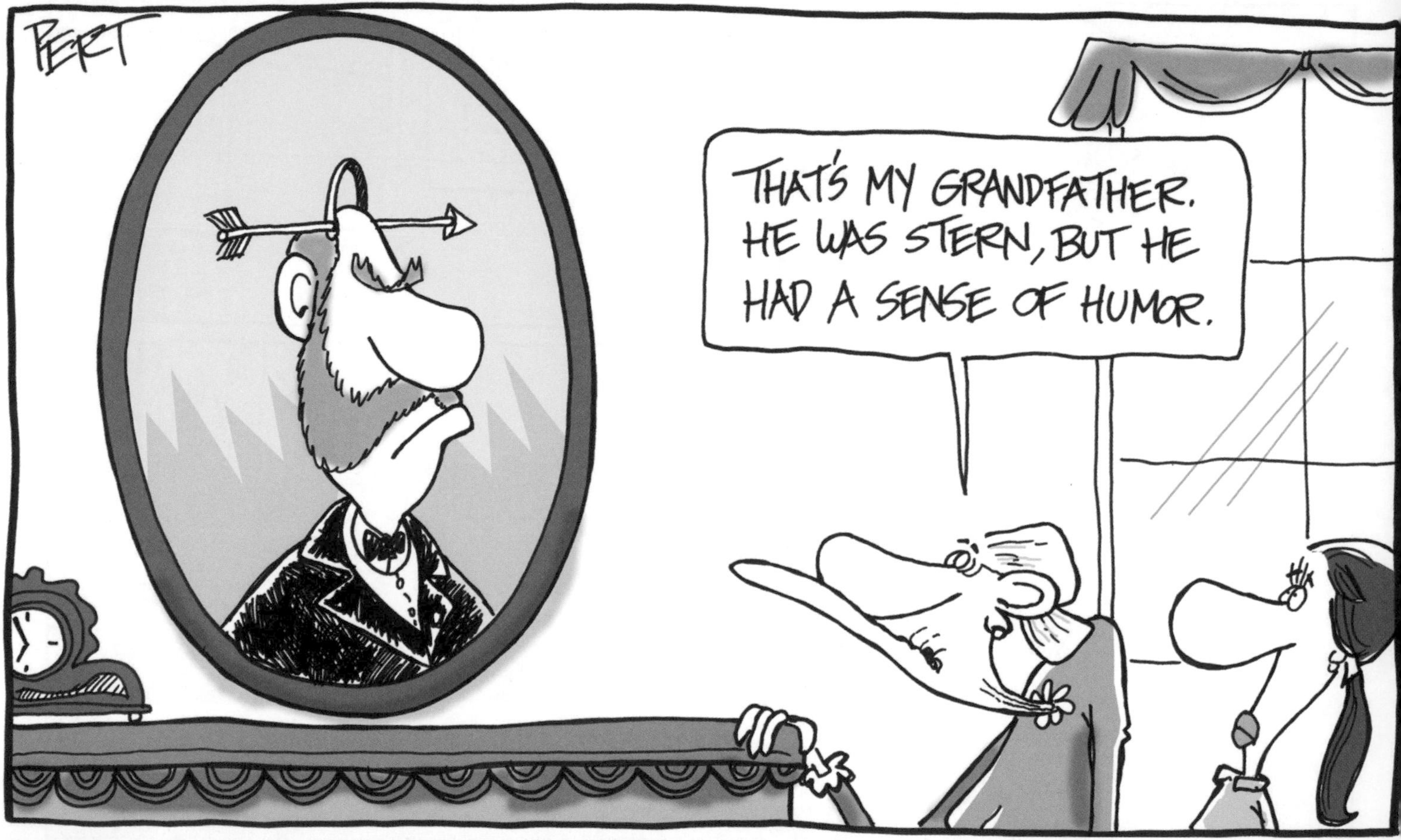
PEERT
THAT'S MY GRANDFATHER. HE WAS STERN, BUT HE HAD A SENSE OF HUMOR.

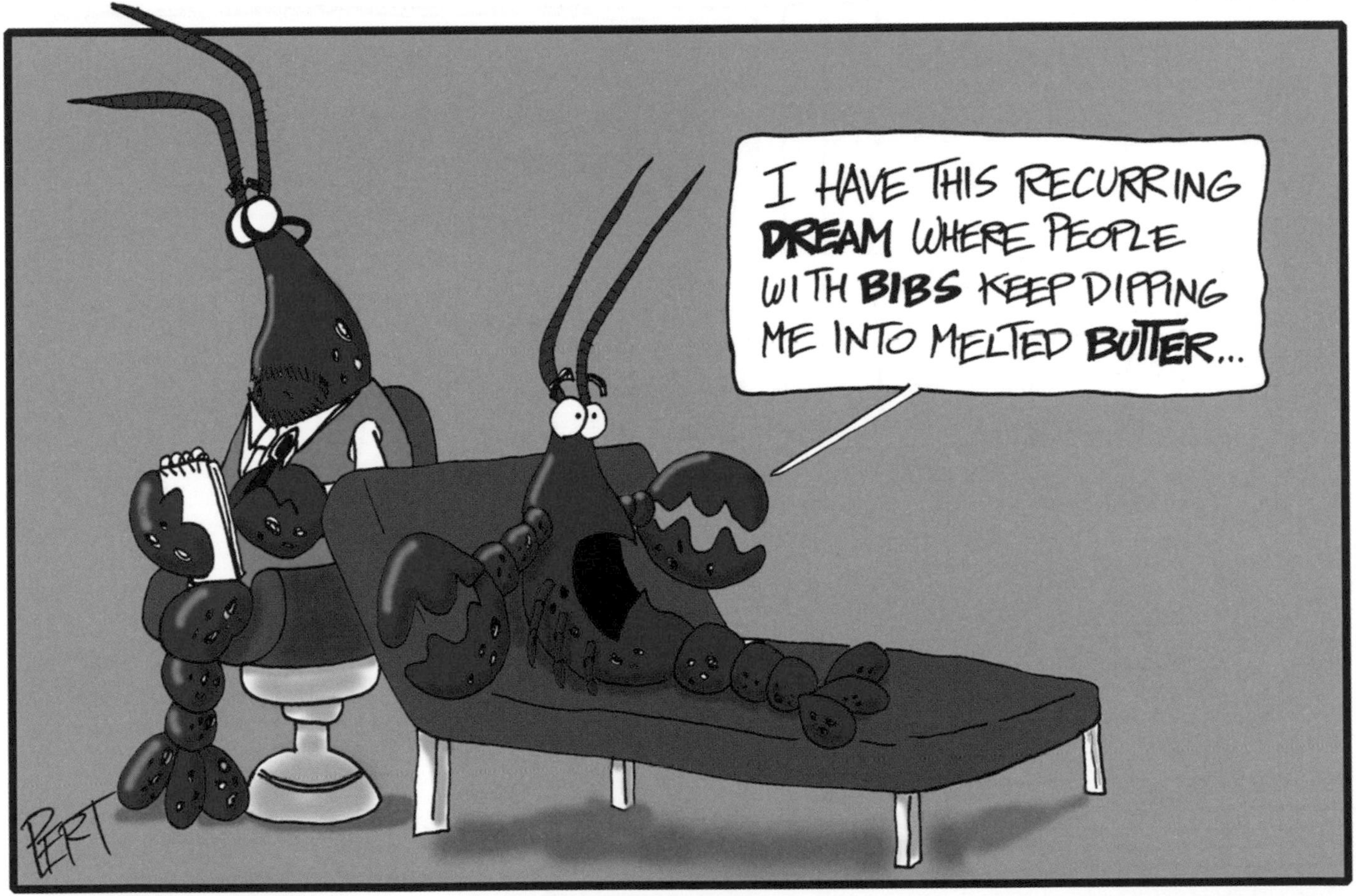
I HAVE THIS RECURRING **DREAM** WHERE PEOPLE WITH **BIBS** KEEP DIPPING ME INTO MELTED **BUTTER**...
PEERT

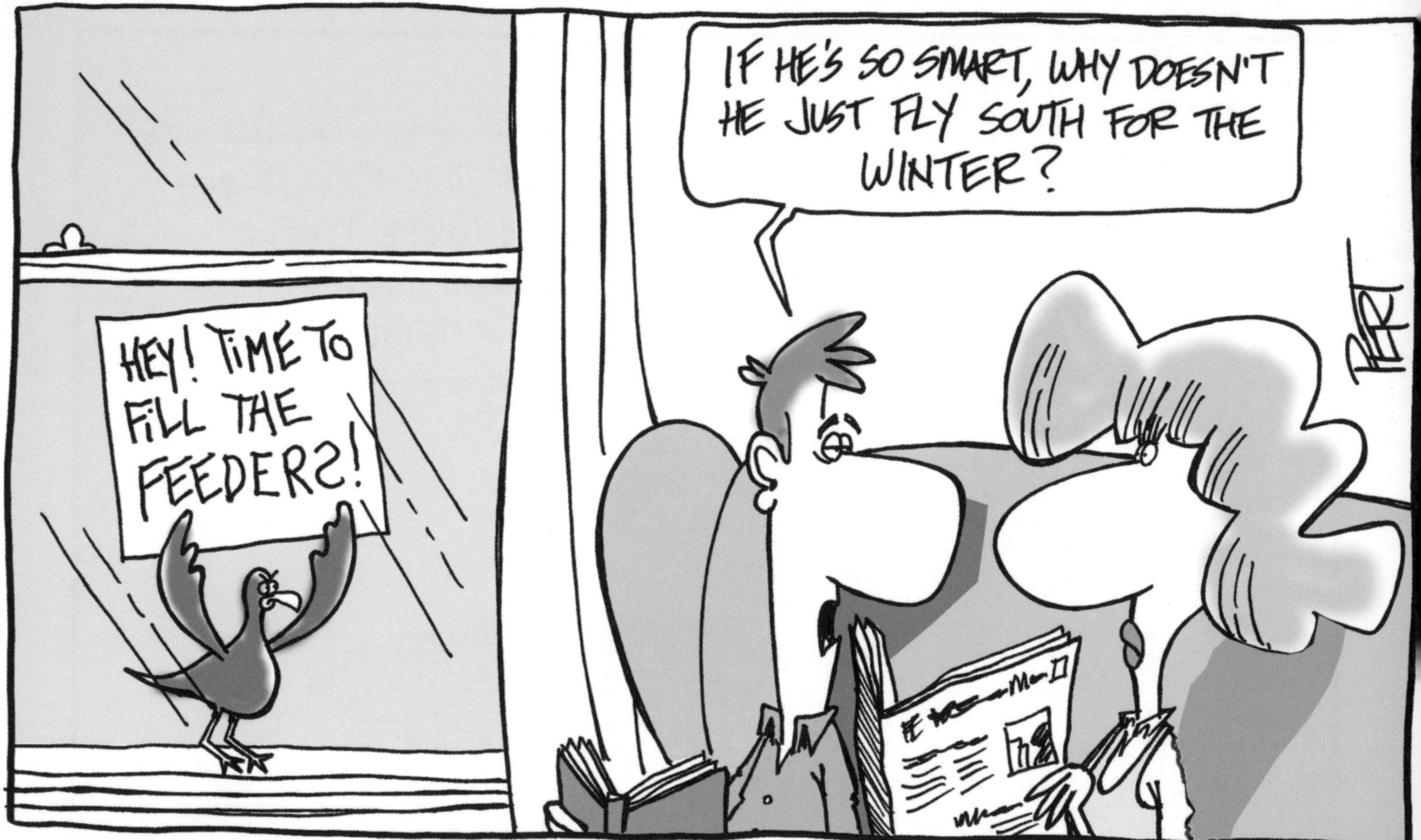
HEY! TIME TO FILL THE FEEDERS!
IF HE'S SO SMART, WHY DOESN'T HE JUST FLY SOUTH FOR THE WINTER?

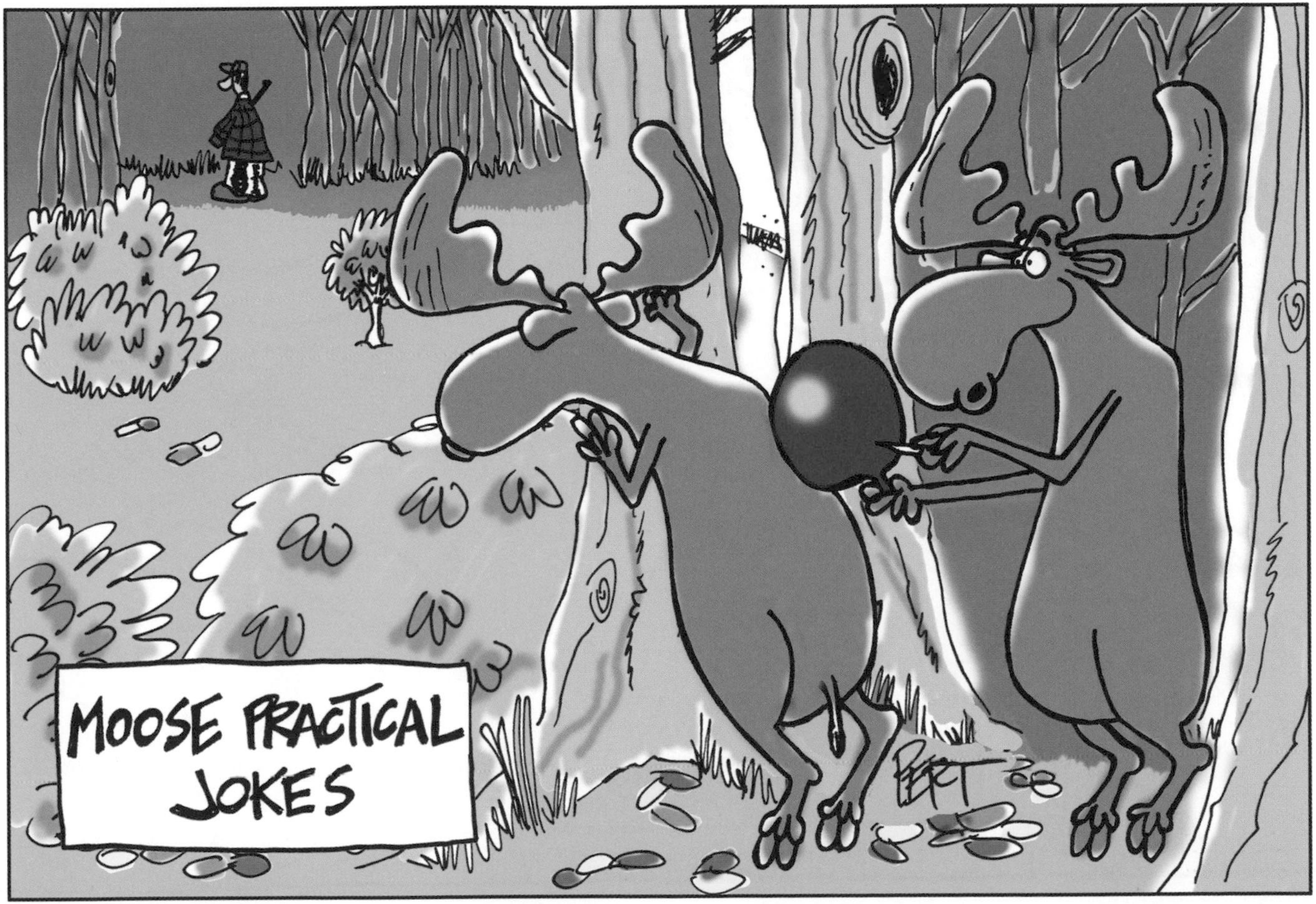
MOOSE PRACTICAL JOKES
BERT

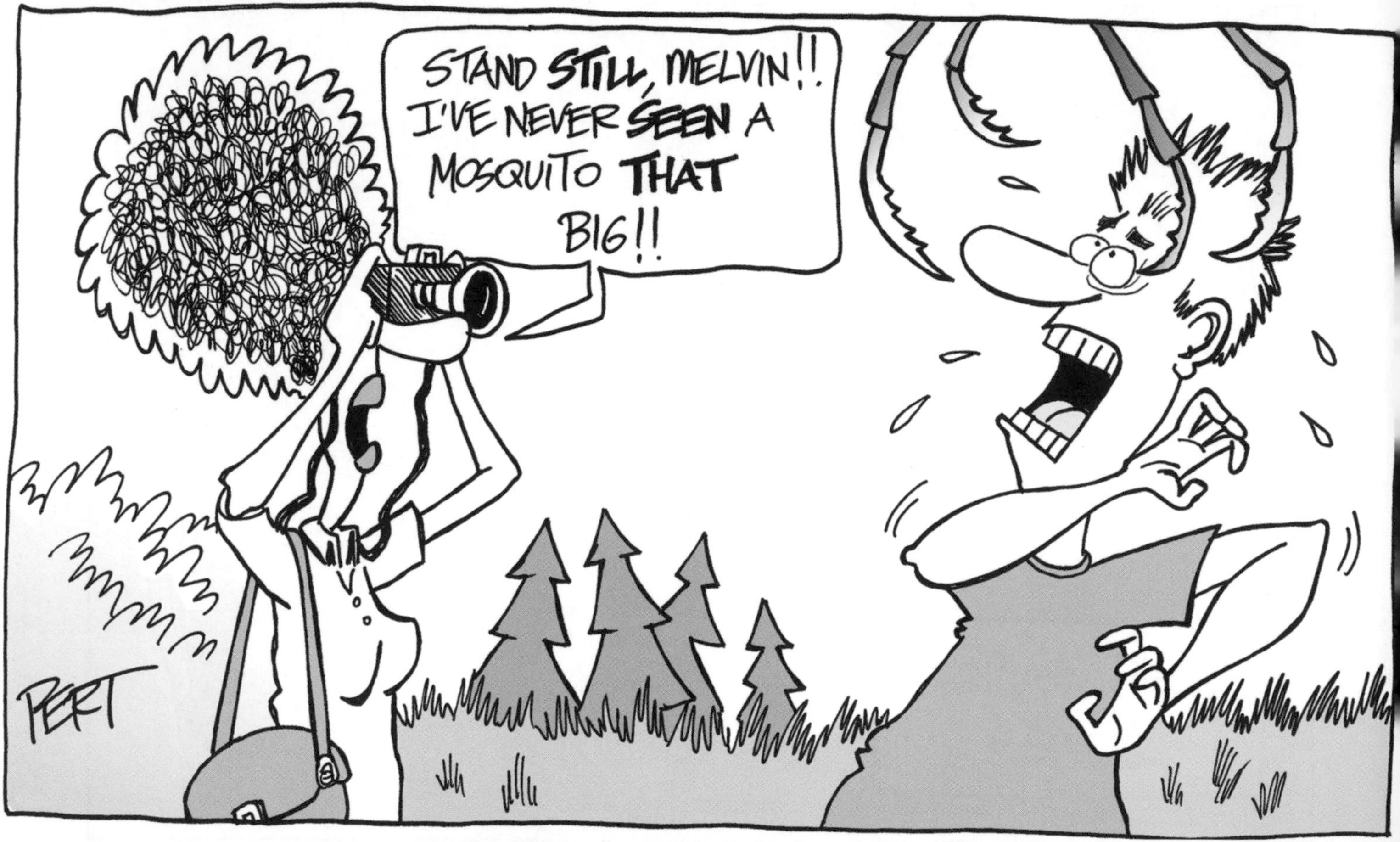
STAND STILL, MELVIN!! I'VE NEVER SEEN A MOSQUITO THAT BIG!!
PERT

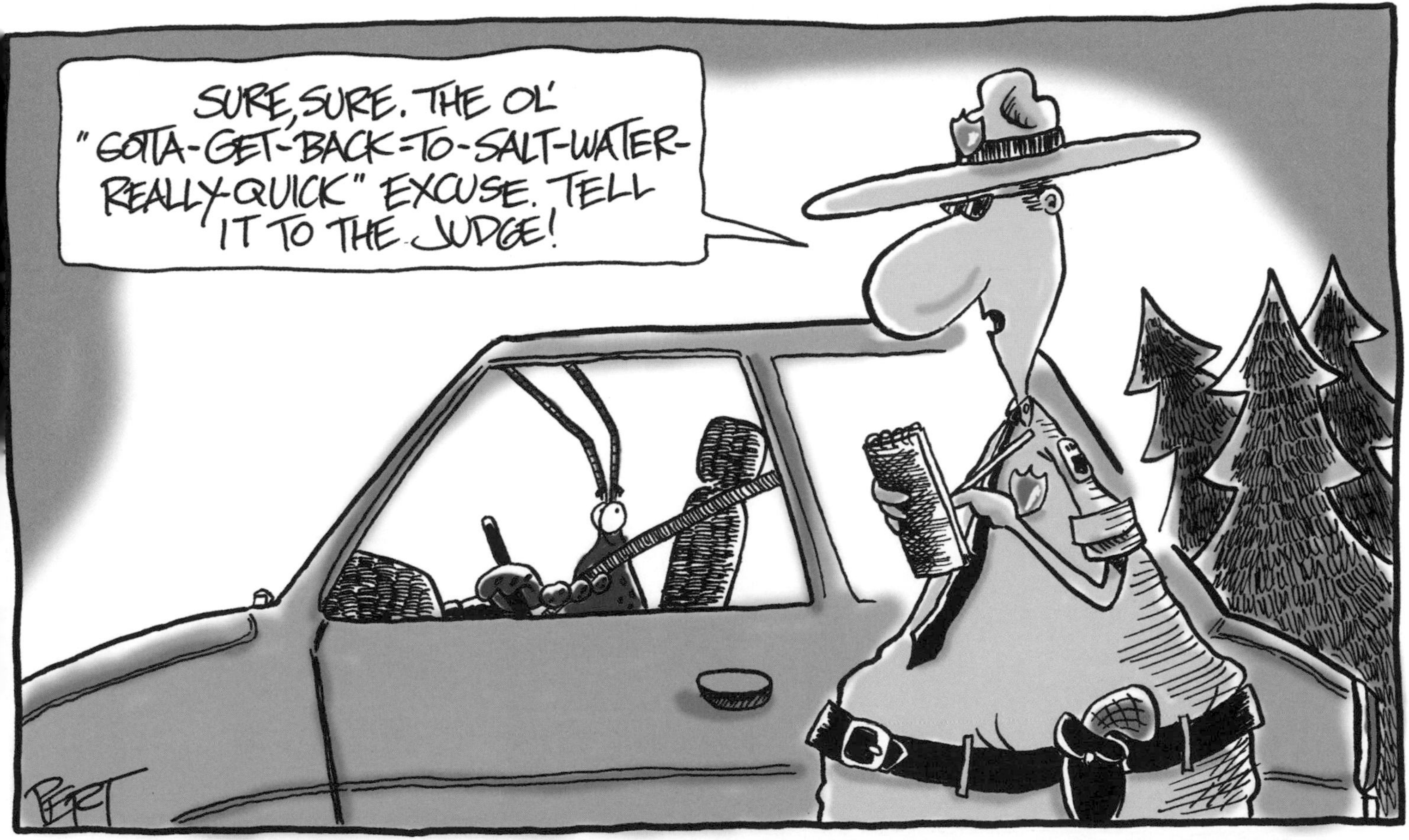
SURE, SURE. THE OL' "GOTTA-GET-BACK-TO-SALT-WATER-REALLY-QUICK" EXCUSE. TELL IT TO THE JUDGE!
PEGET

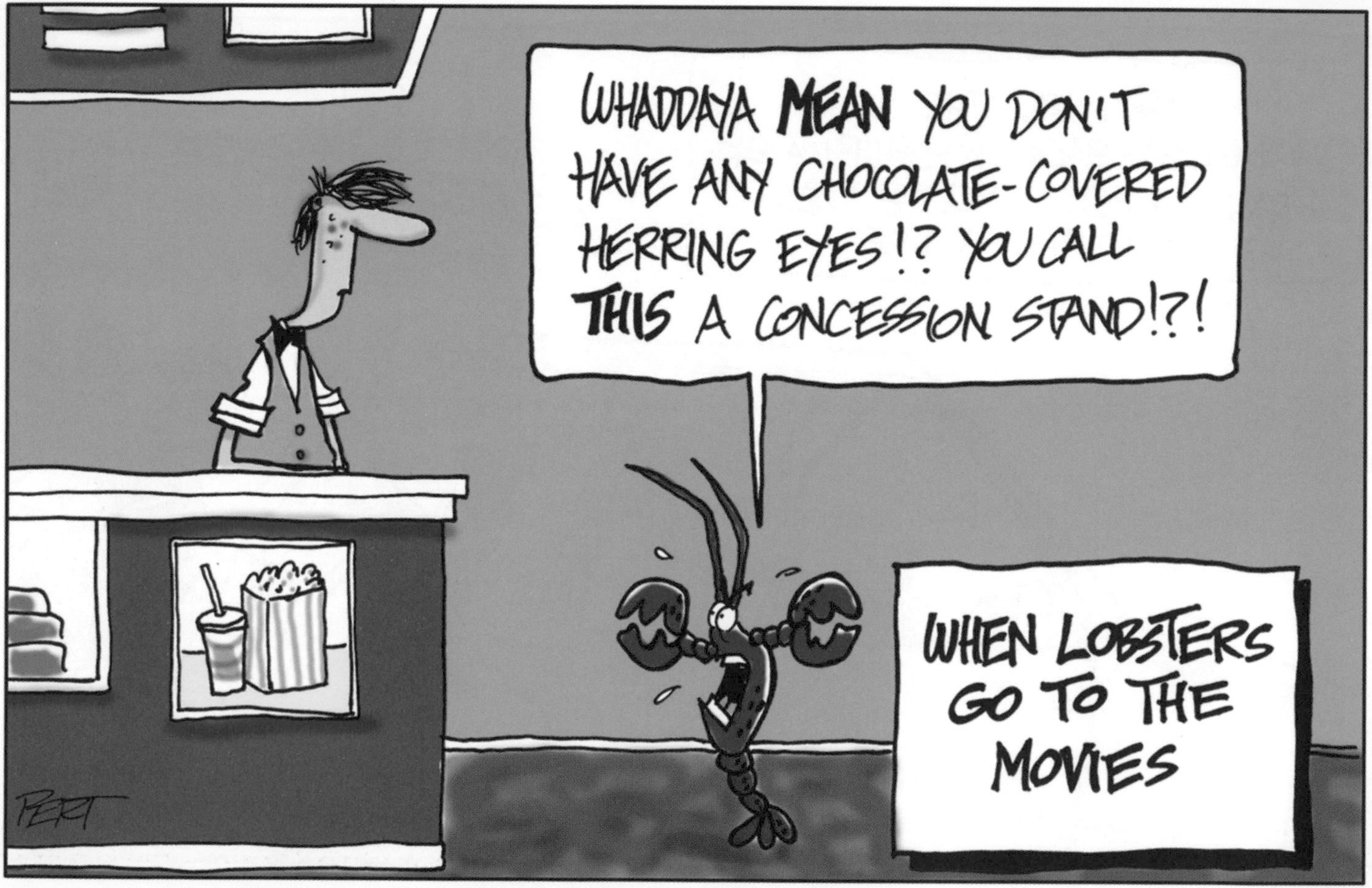
WHADDAYA MEAN YOU DON'T HAVE ANY CHOCOLATE-COVERED HERRING EYES!? YOU CALL THIS A CONCESSION STAND!?!
WHEN LOBSTERS GO TO THE MOVIES
PERT

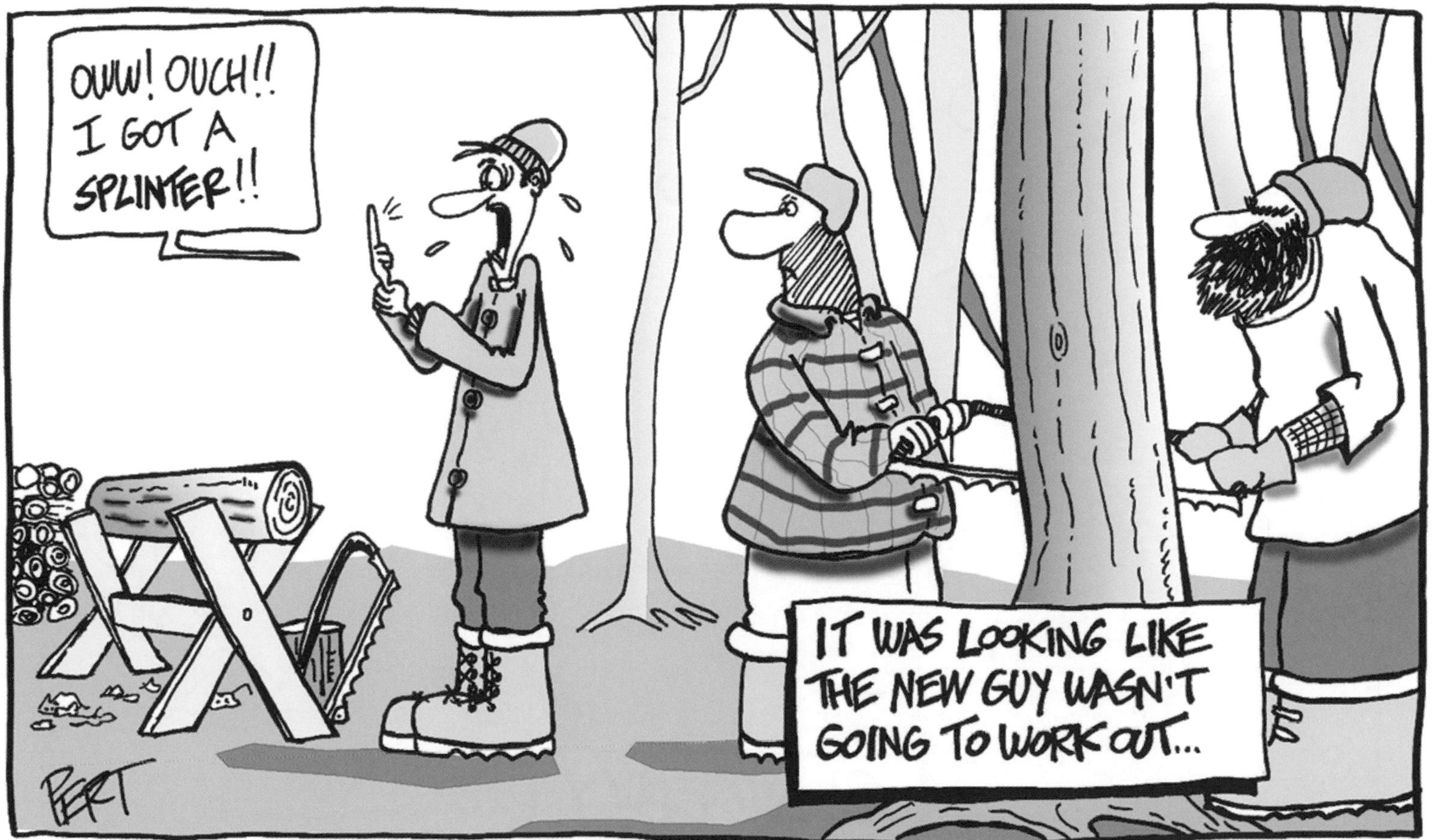
OWW! OUCH!! I GOT A SPLINTER!!
IT WAS LOOKING LIKE THE NEW GUY WASN'T GOING TO WORK OUT...
PERT

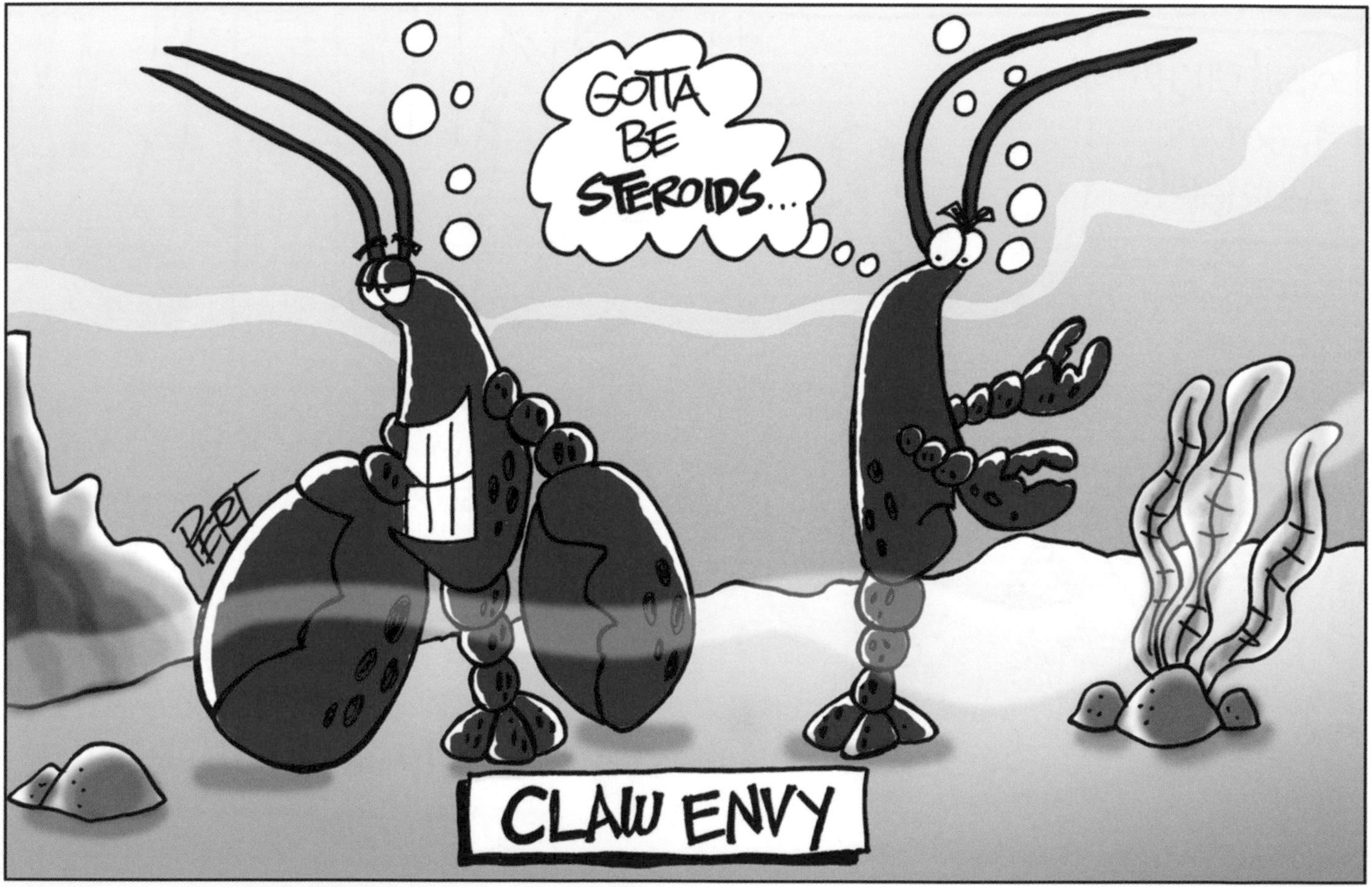
GOTTA BE STEROIDS...
PERT
CLAW ENVY

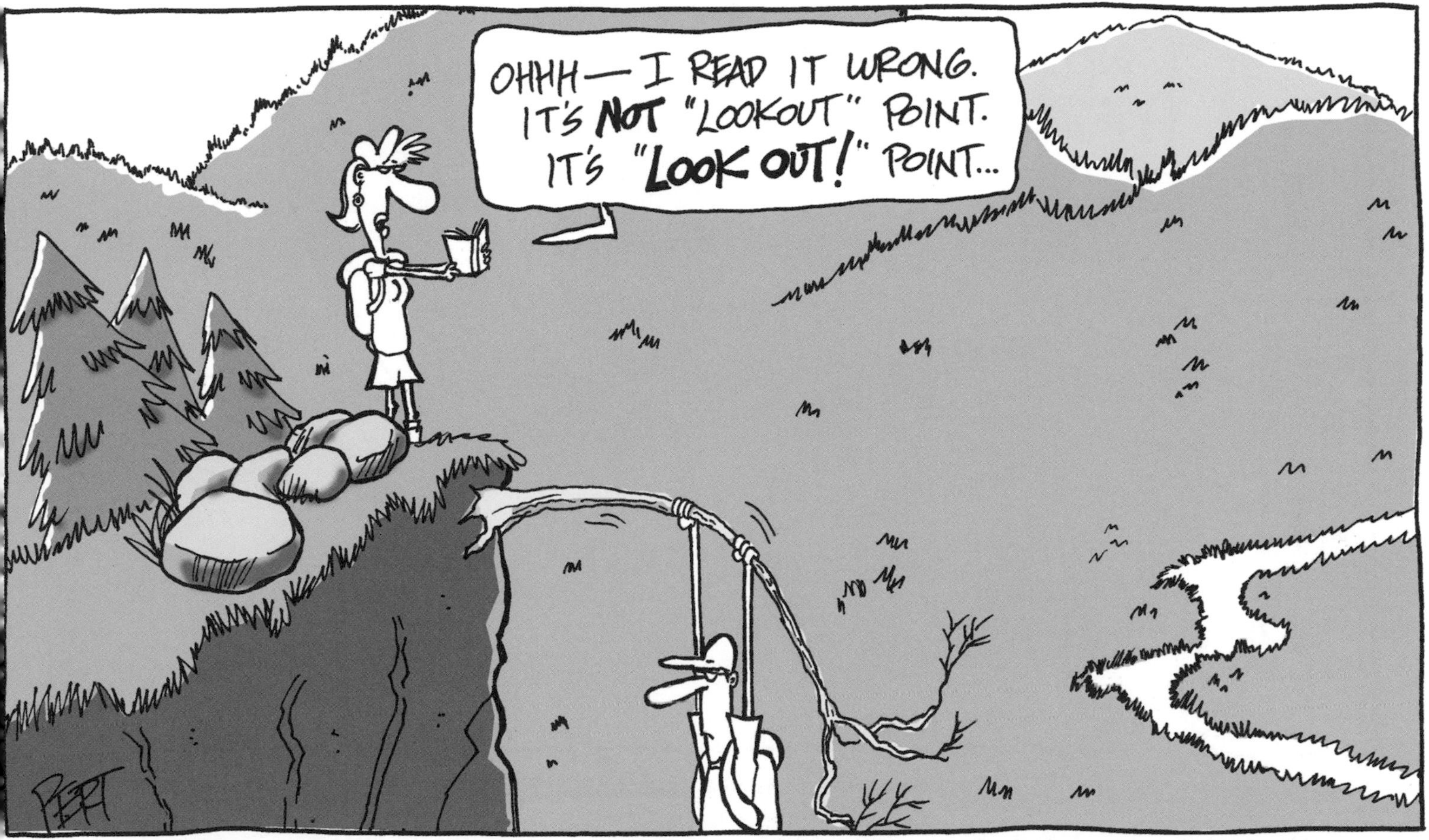
OHHH— I READ IT WRONG. IT'S **NOT** "LOOKOUT" POINT. IT'S "**LOOK OUT!**" POINT...
PEART

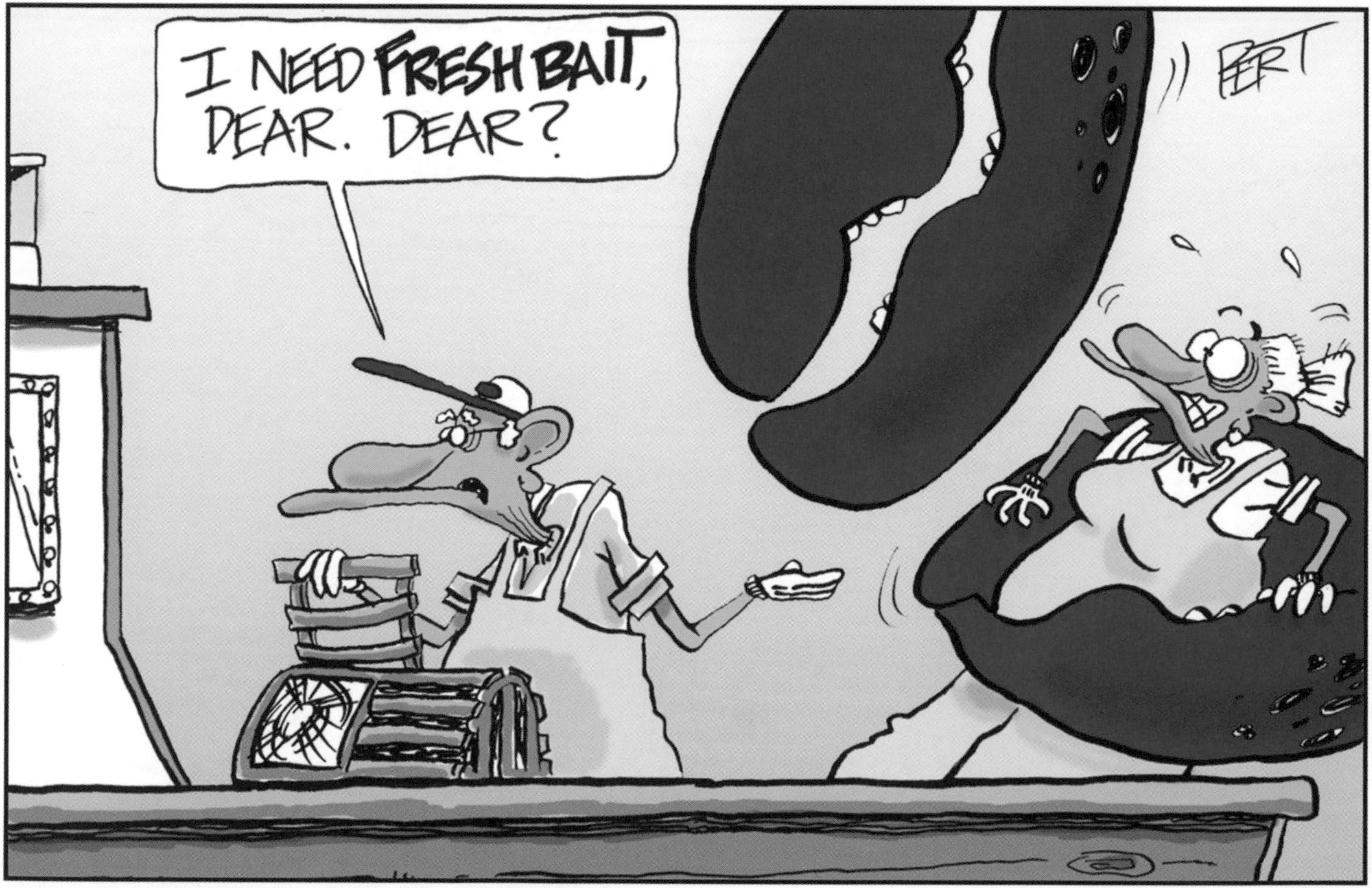
I NEED FRESH BAIT, DEAR. DEAR?
BERT

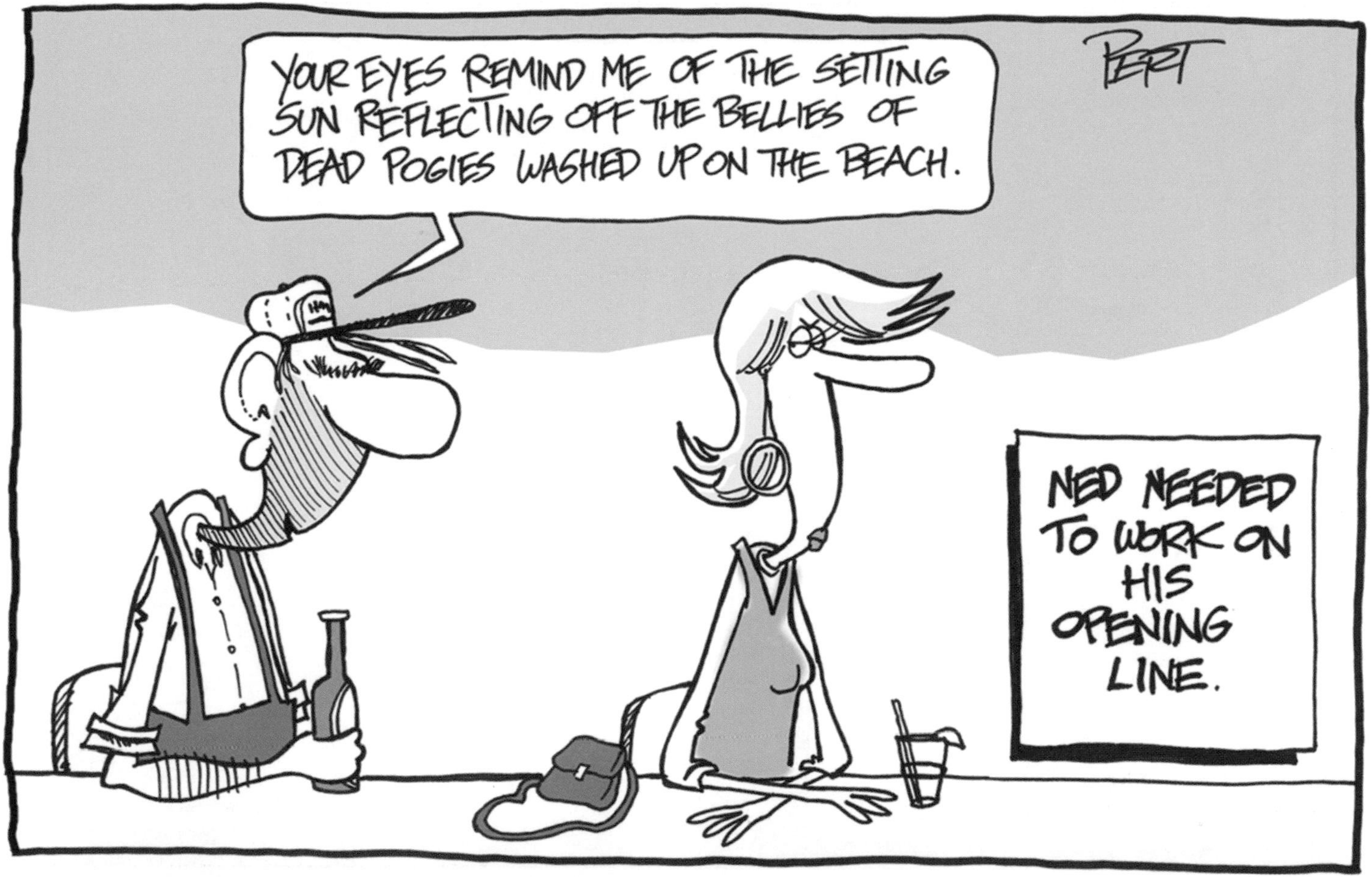
YOUR EYES REMIND ME OF THE SETTING SUN REFLECTING OFF THE BELLIES OF DEAD POGIES WASHED UP ON THE BEACH.
PERT
NED NEEDED TO WORK ON HIS OPENING LINE.

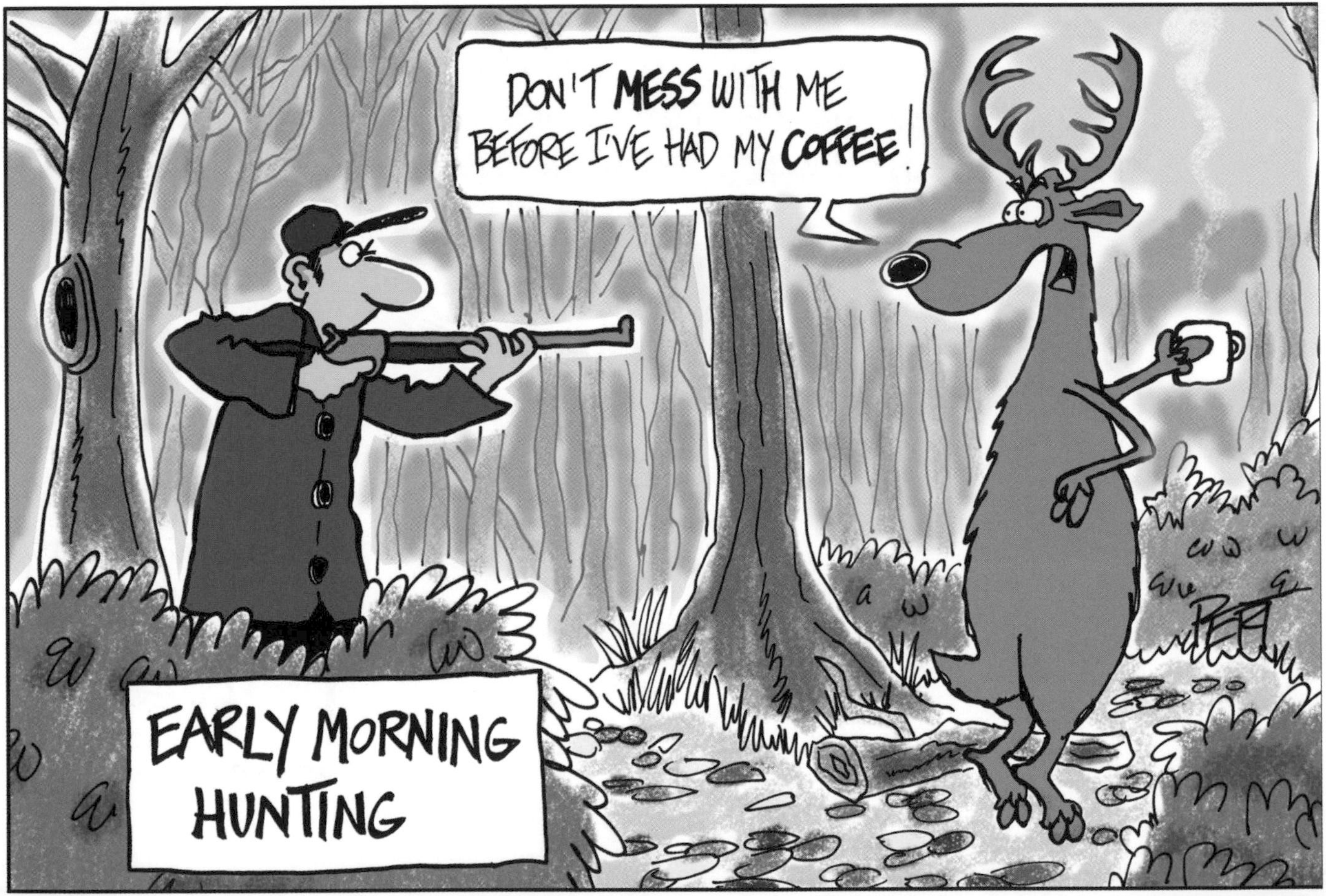
DON'T MESS WITH ME BEFORE I'VE HAD MY COFFEE!
EARLY MORNING HUNTING

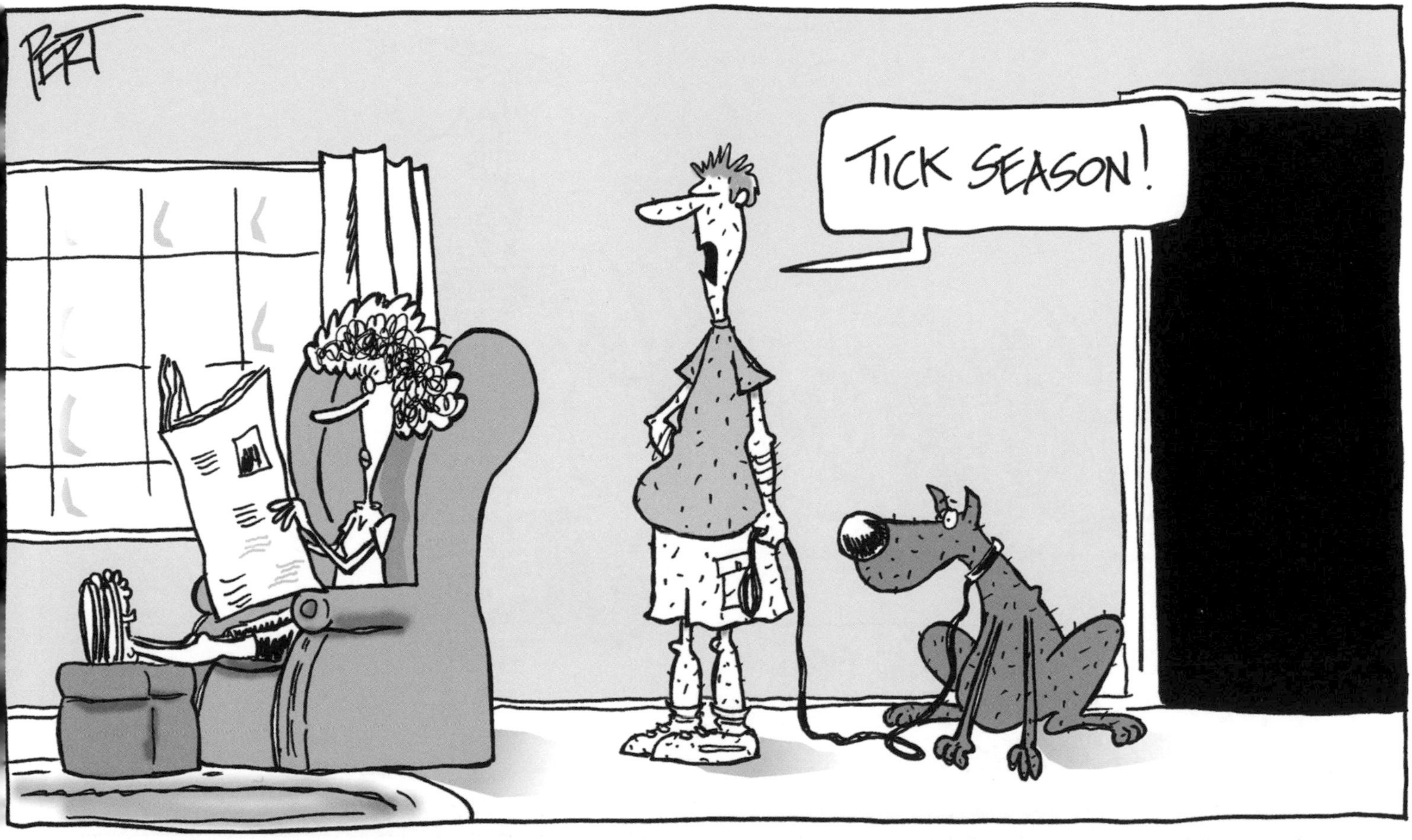

PERT
TICK SEASON!

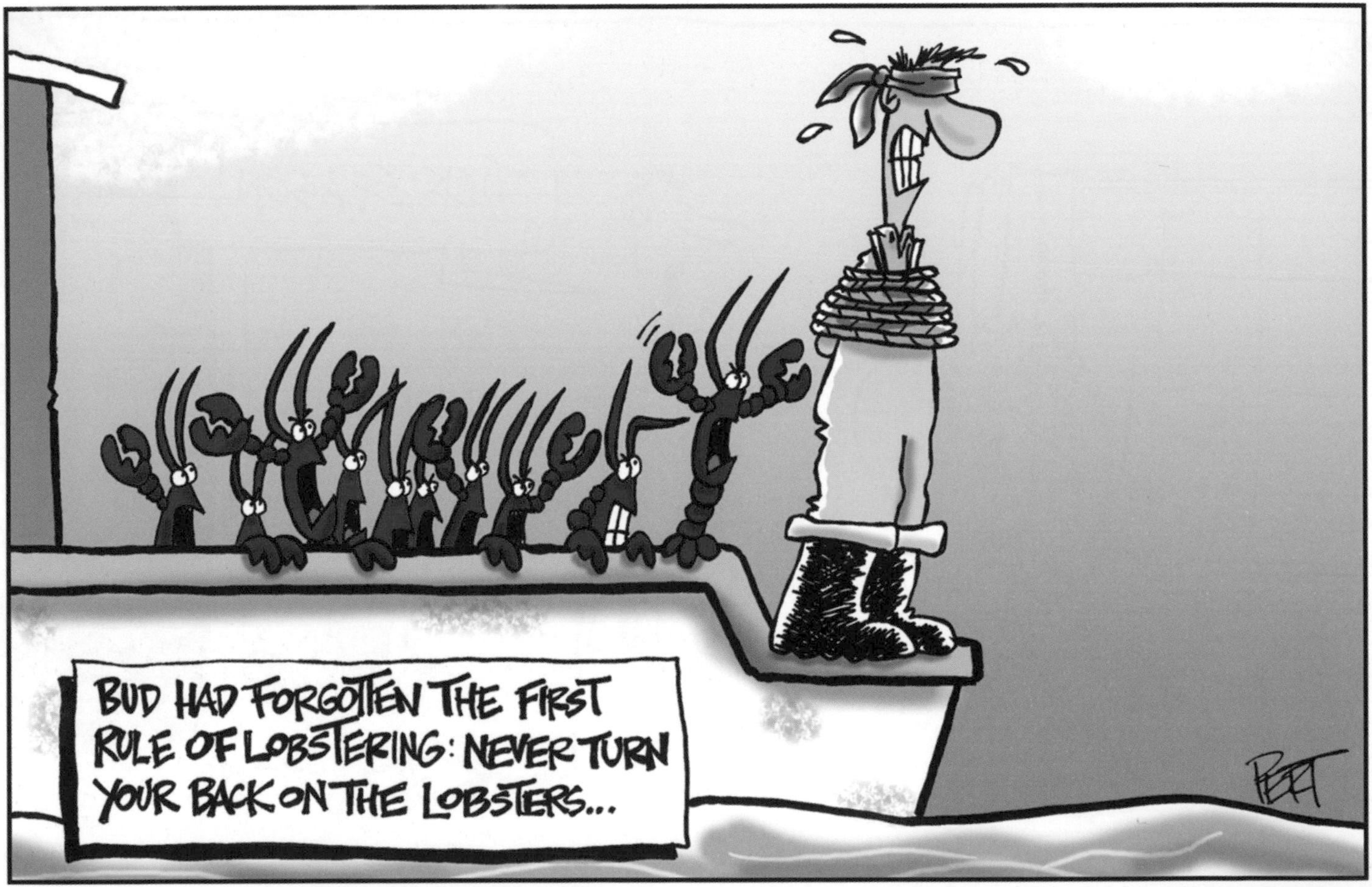
BUD HAD FORGOTTEN THE FIRST RULE OF LOBSTERING: NEVER TURN YOUR BACK ON THE LOBSTERS...
PEET

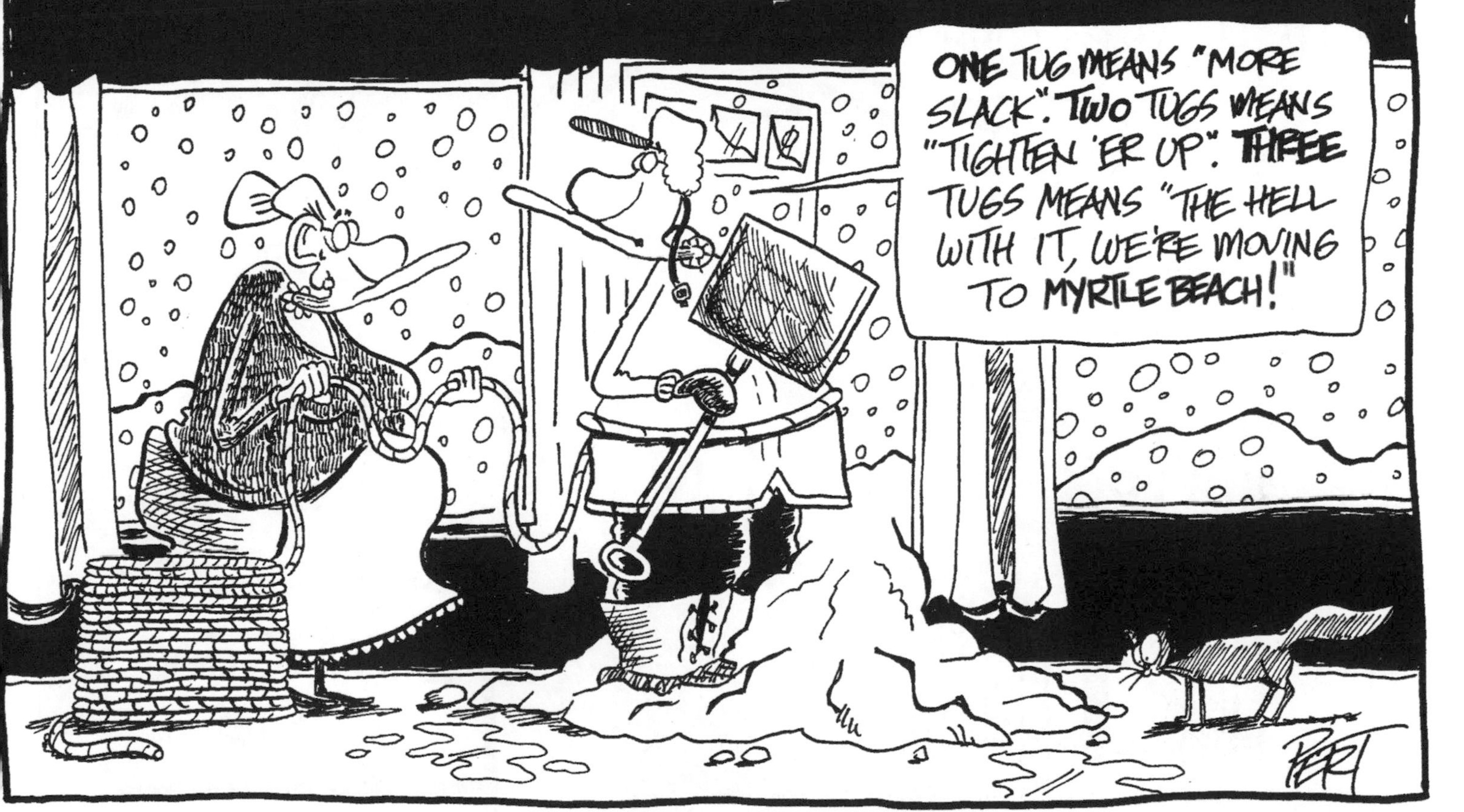
ONE TUG MEANS "MORE SLACK". TWO TUGS MEANS "TIGHTEN 'ER UP". THREE TUGS MEANS "THE HELL WITH IT, WE'RE MOVING TO MYRTLE BEACH!"
PERI

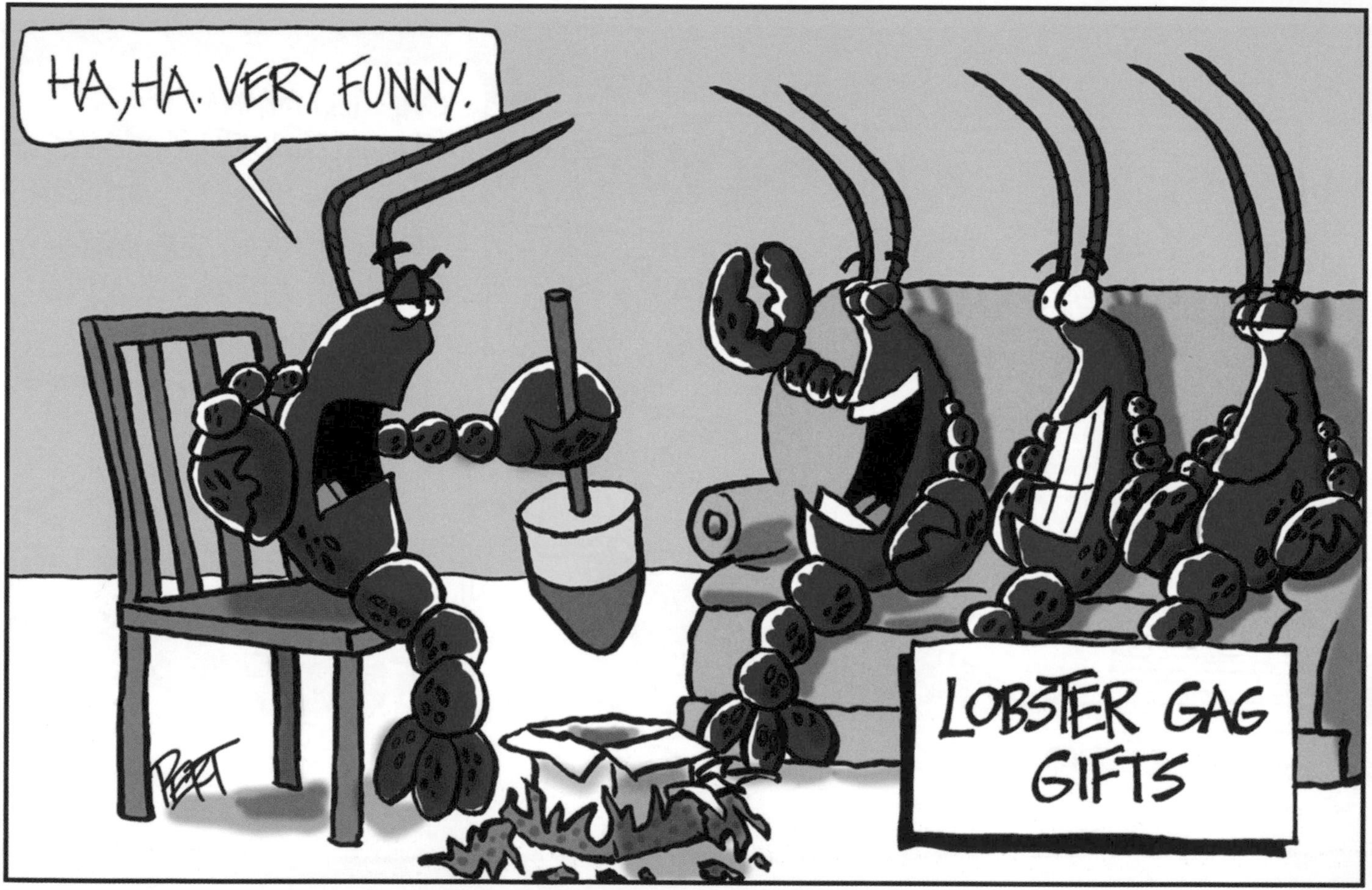
HA, HA. VERY FUNNY.
LOBSTER GAG GIFTS
BERT

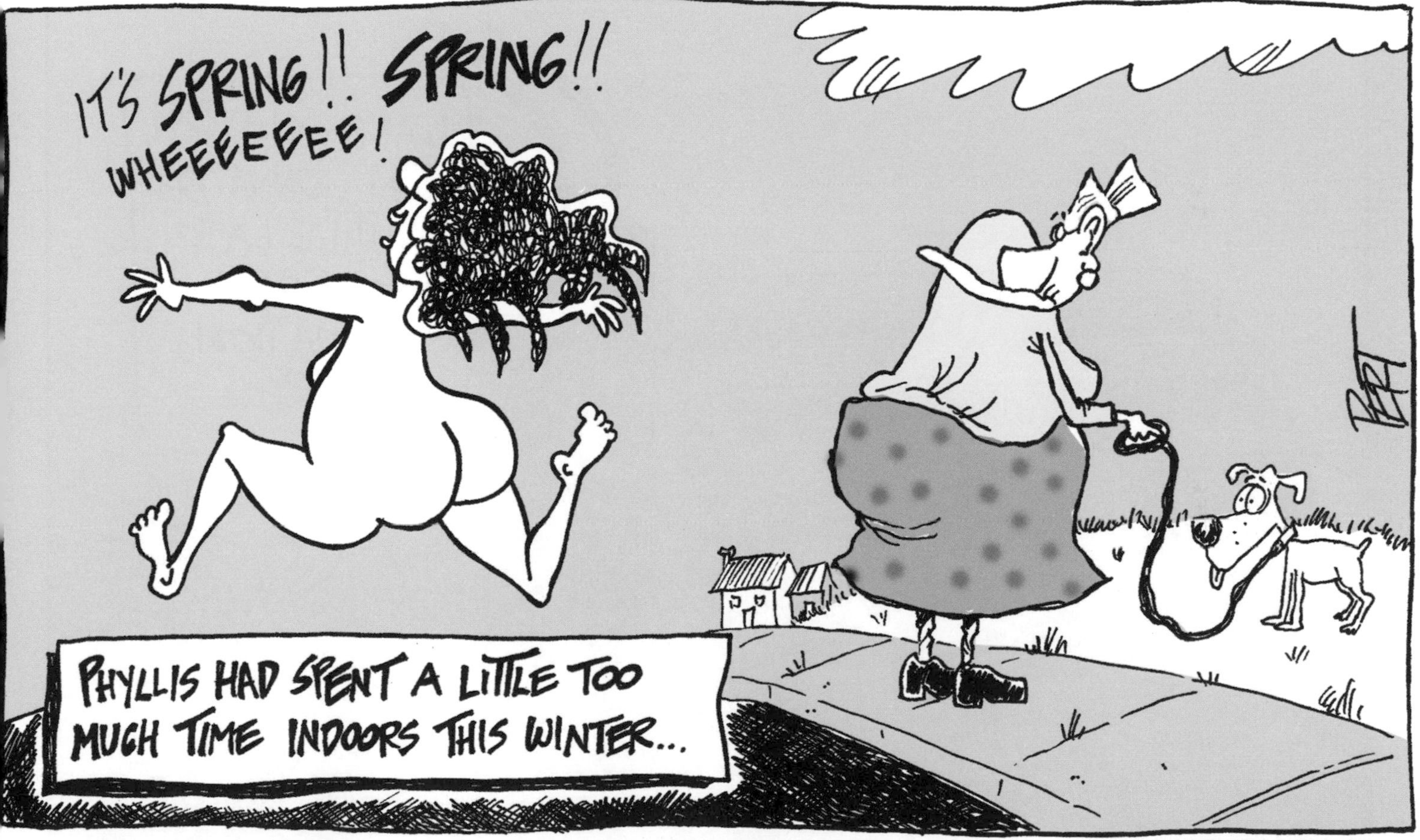
IT'S SPRING!! SPRING!! WHEEEEEEE!
PHYLLIS HAD SPENT A LITTLE TOO MUCH TIME INDOORS THIS WINTER...

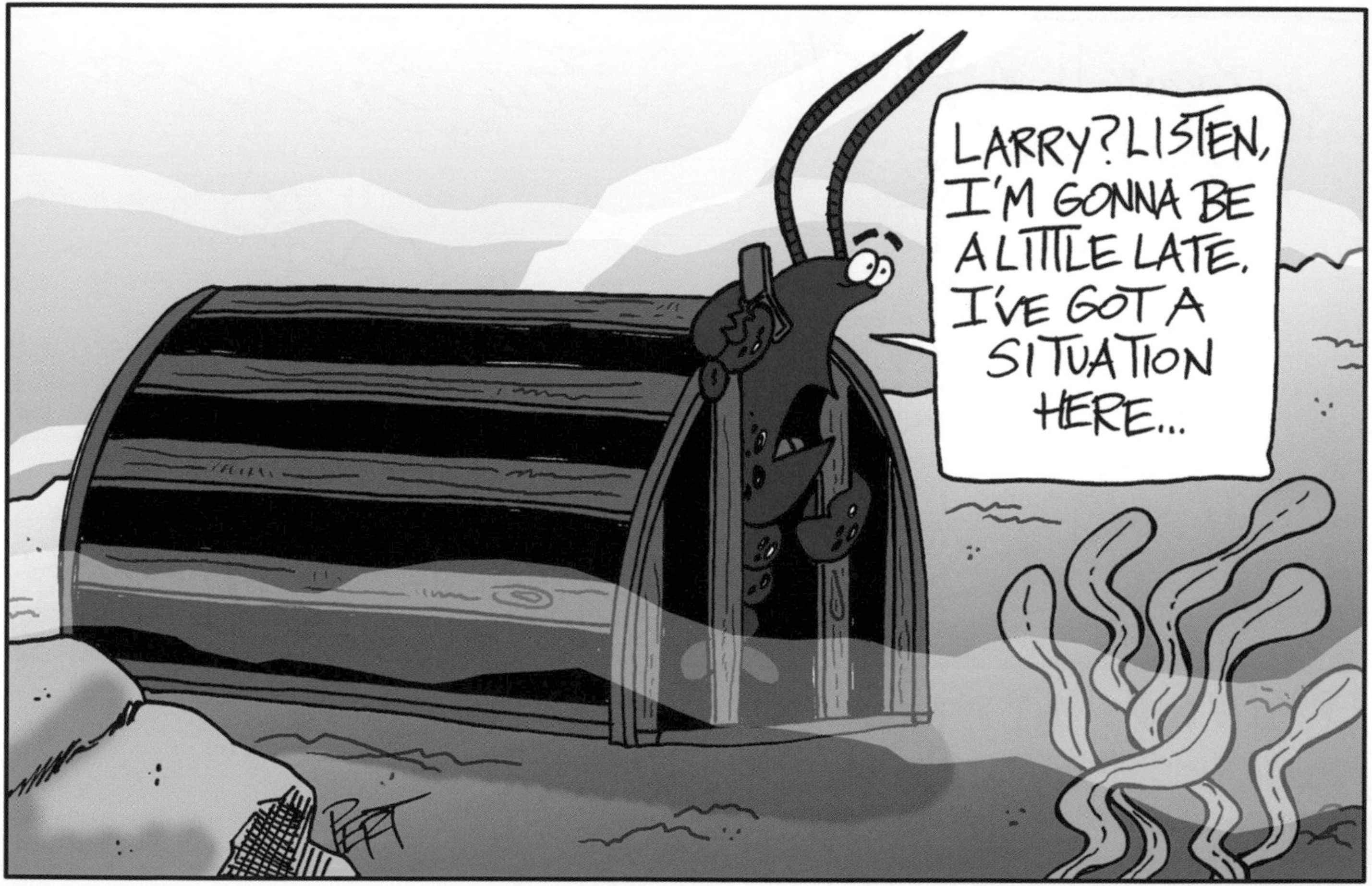
LARRY? LISTEN, I'M GONNA BE A LITTLE LATE. I'VE GOT A SITUATION HERE...
PEET

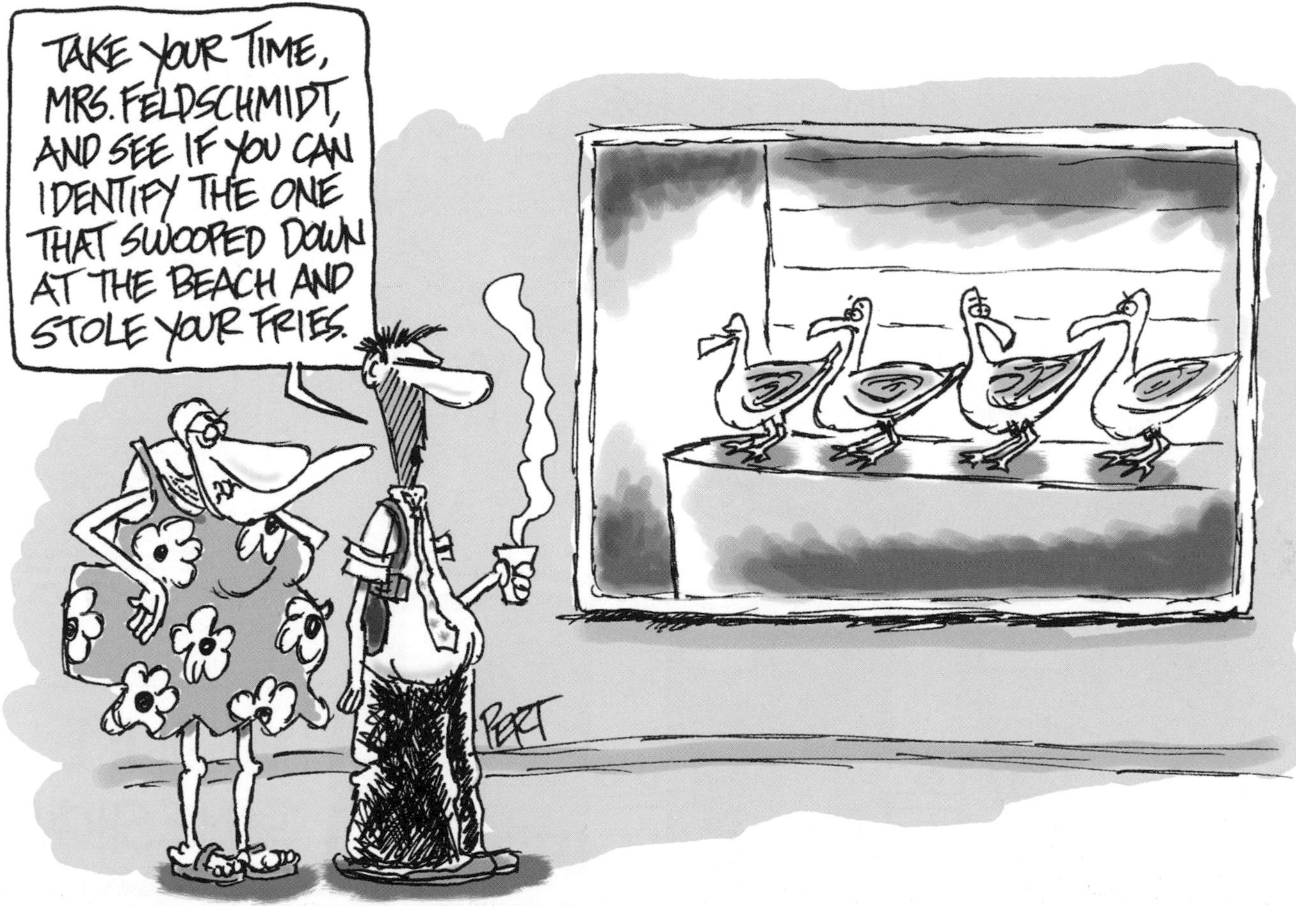
TAKE YOUR TIME, MRS. FELDSCHMIDT, AND SEE IF YOU CAN IDENTIFY THE ONE THAT SWOOPED DOWN AT THE BEACH AND STOLE YOUR FRIES.
PEART

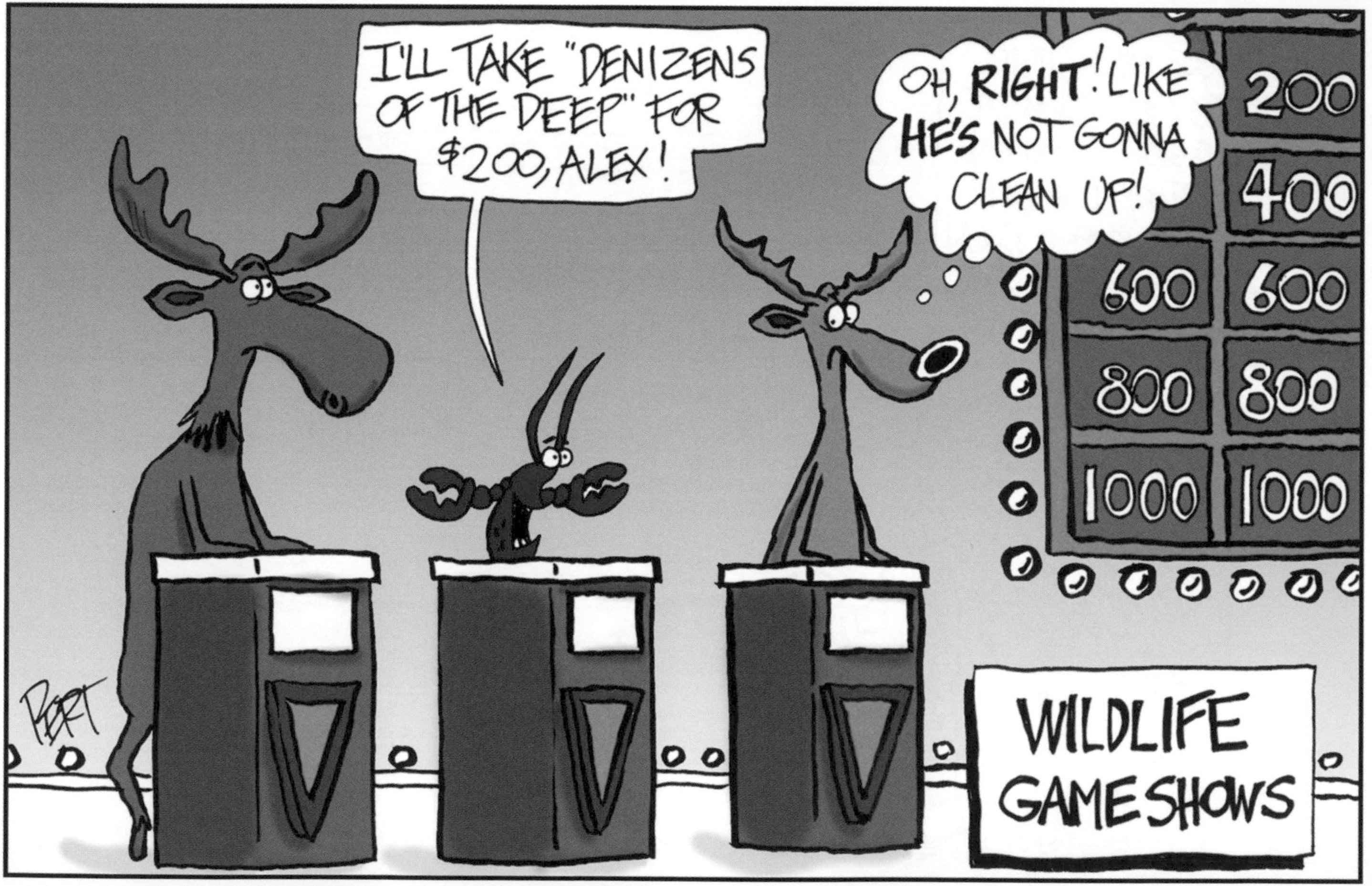
I'LL TAKE "DENIZENS OF THE DEEP" FOR $200, ALEX!
OH, **RIGHT**! LIKE **HE'S** NOT GONNA CLEAN UP!
200
400
600
600
800
800
1000
1000
WILDLIFE GAME SHOWS
BERT

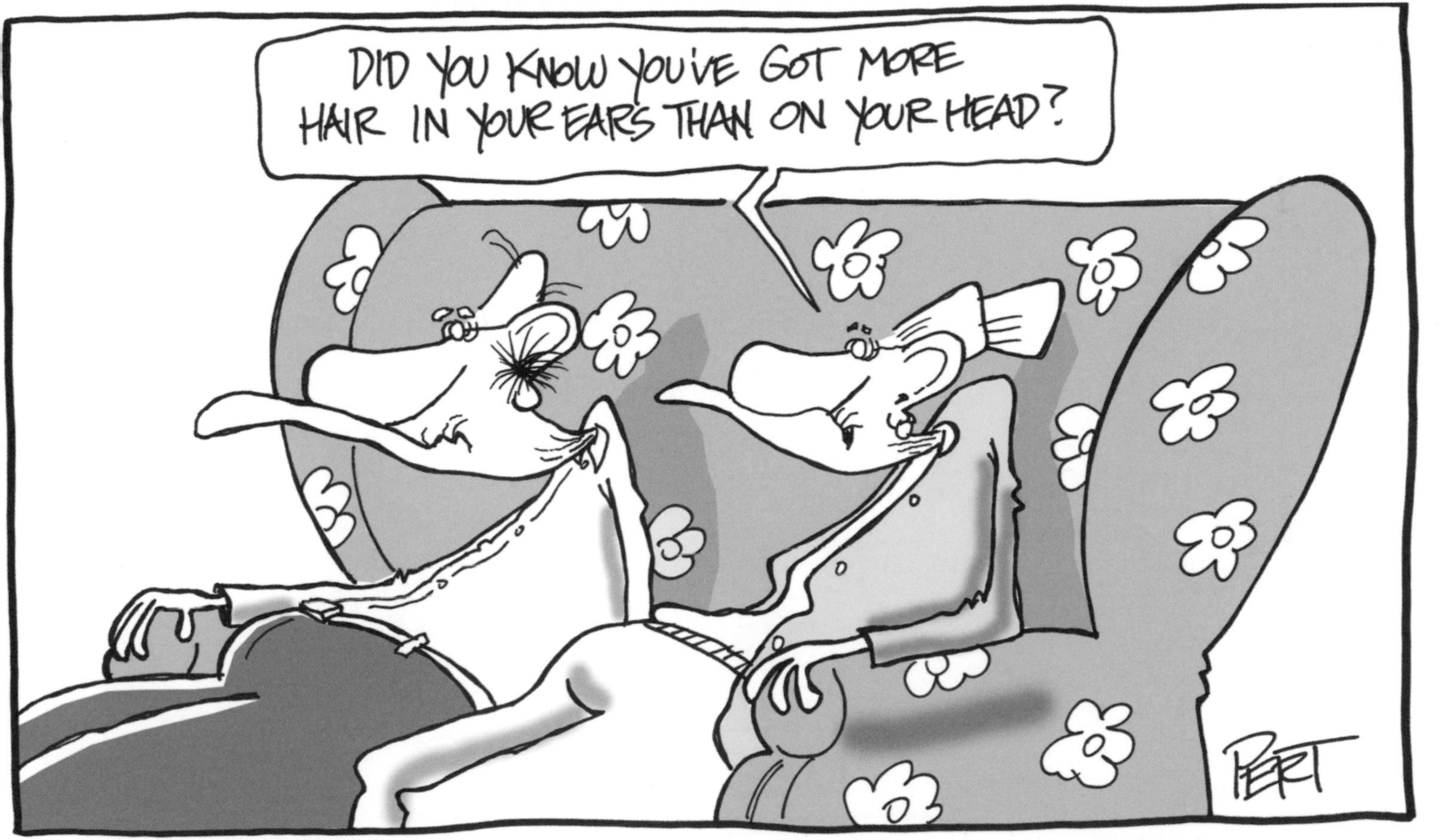
DID YOU KNOW YOU'VE GOT MORE HAIR IN YOUR EARS THAN ON YOUR HEAD?
PEARCE

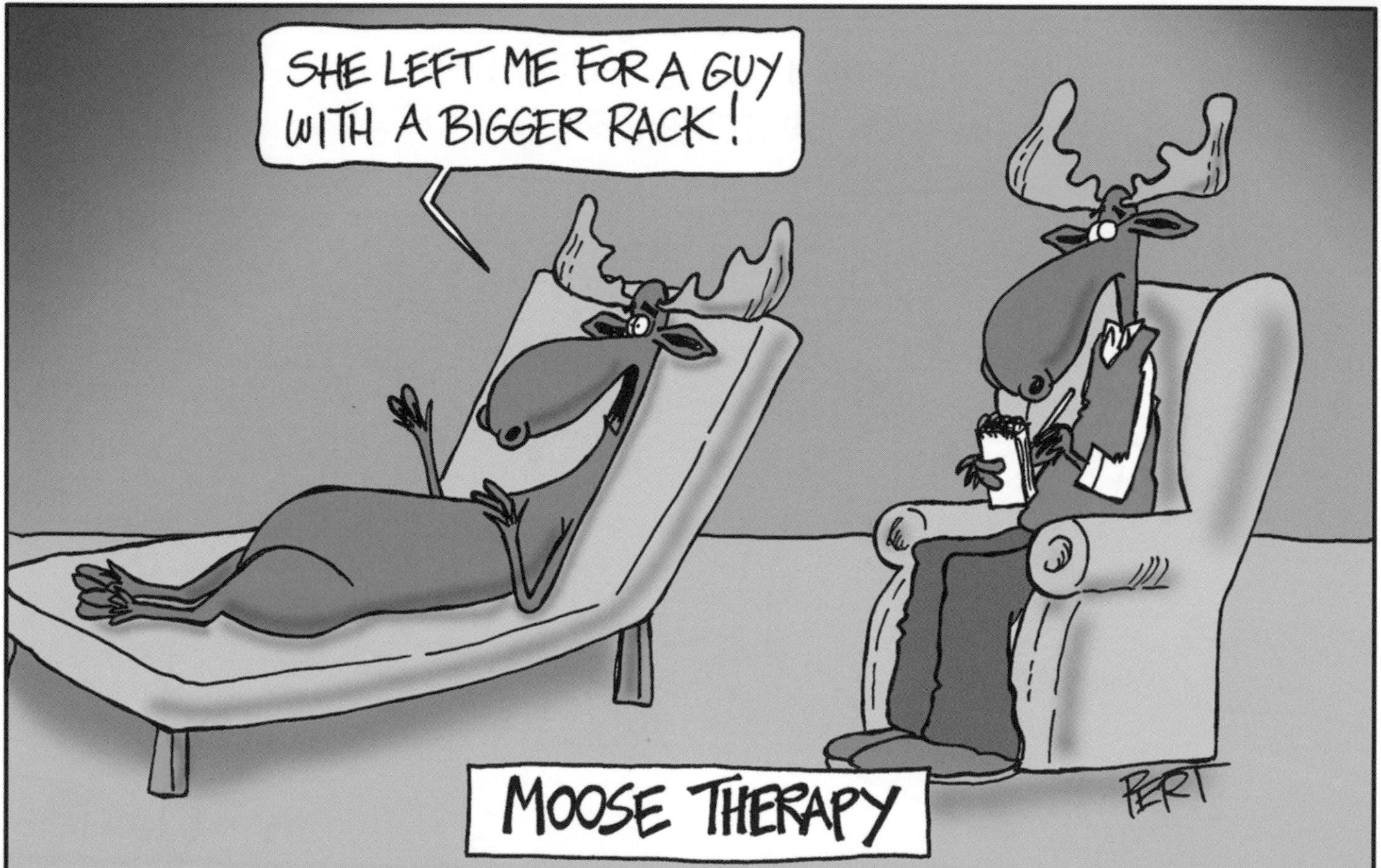
SHE LEFT ME FOR A GUY WITH A BIGGER RACK!
MOOSE THERAPY
PERT

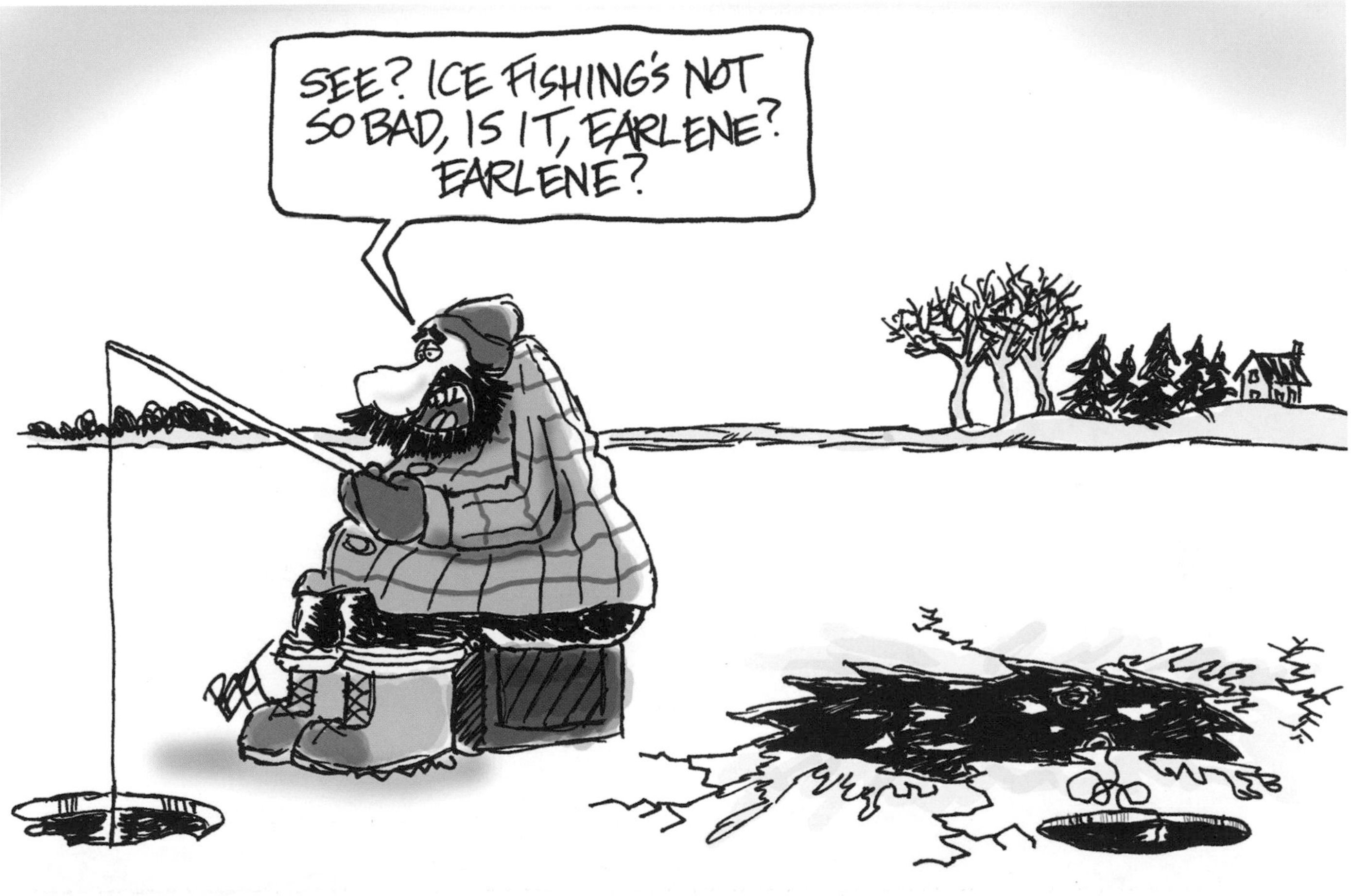
SEE? ICE FISHING'S NOT SO BAD, IS IT, EARLENE? EARLENE?

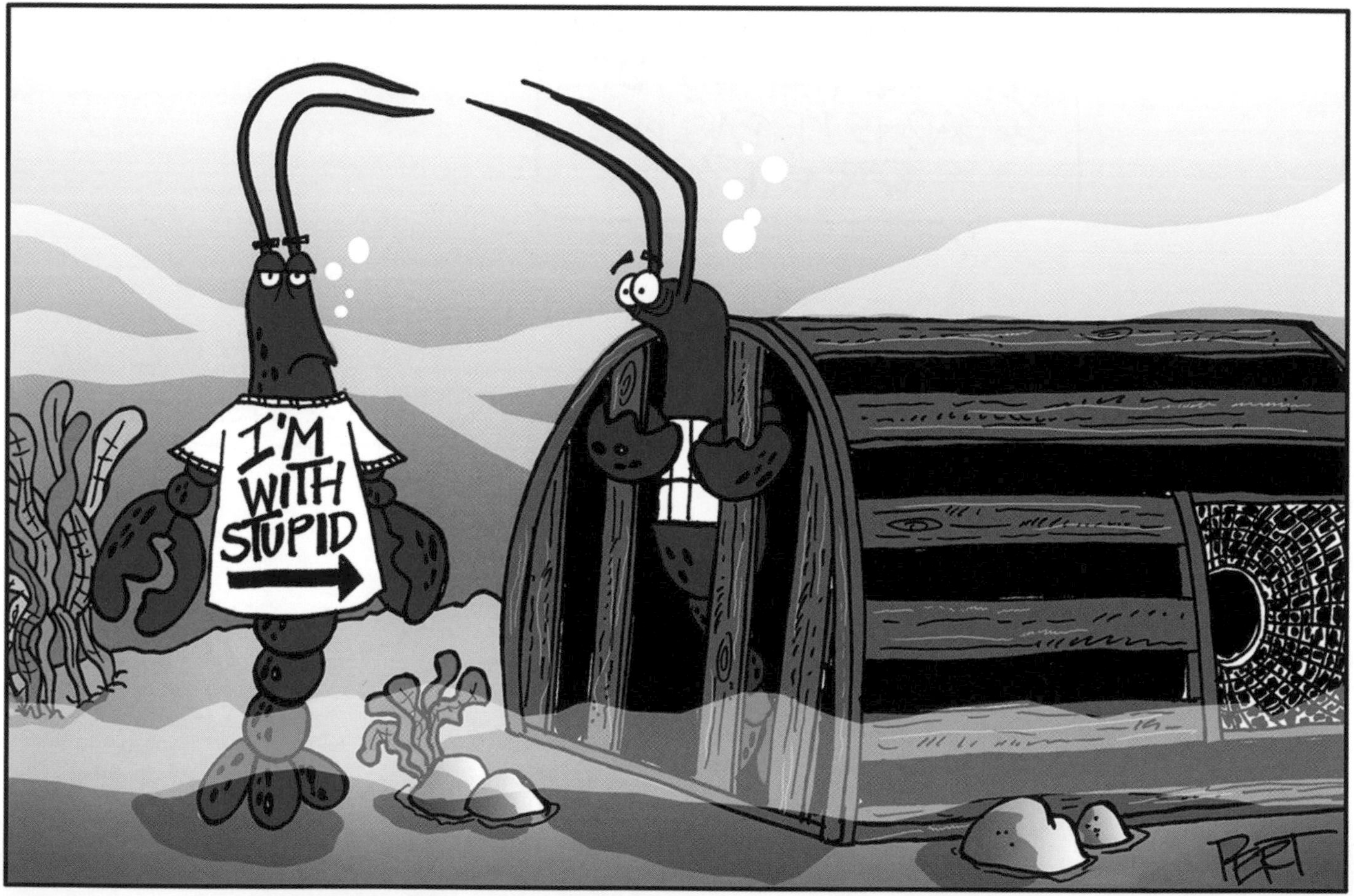
I'M
WITH
STUPID
BERT

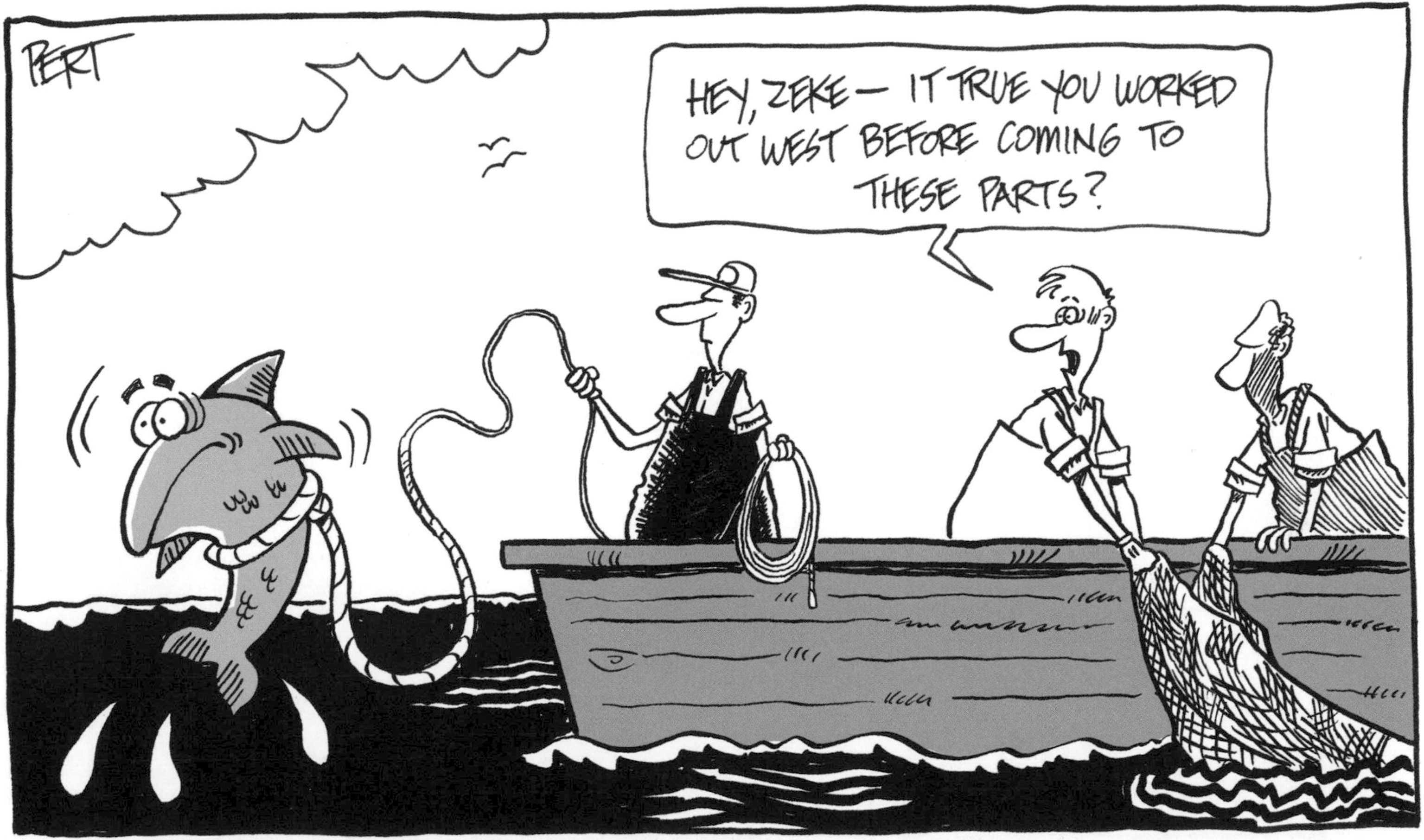
PERT
HEY, ZEKE— IT TRUE YOU WORKED OUT WEST BEFORE COMING TO THESE PARTS?

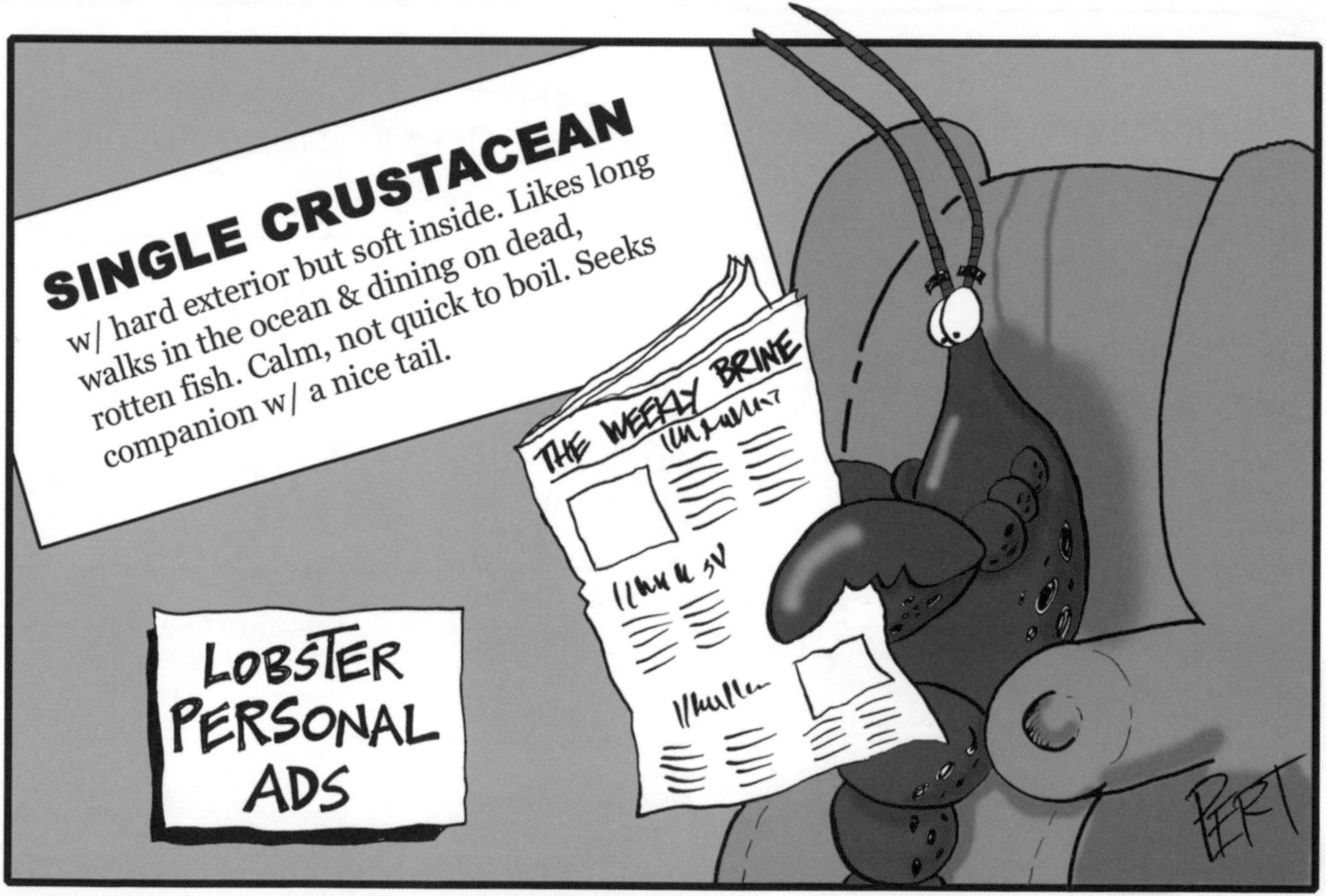
SINGLE CRUSTACEAN
w/ hard exterior but soft inside. Likes long walks in the ocean & dining on dead, rotten fish. Calm, not quick to boil. Seeks companion w/ a nice tail.
THE WEEKLY BRINE
LOBSTER PERSONAL ADS
PERT

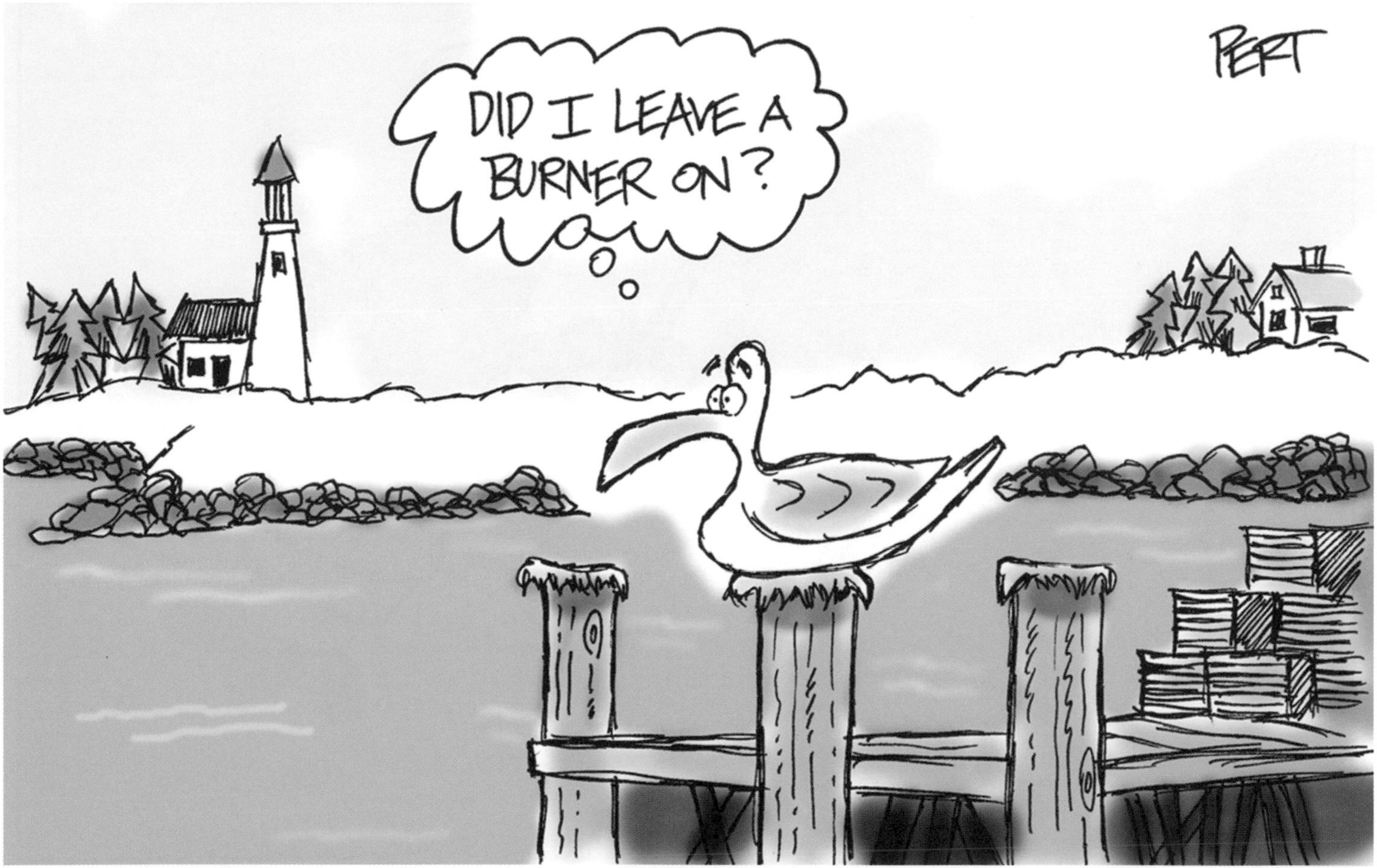
PERT
DID I LEAVE A BURNER ON?

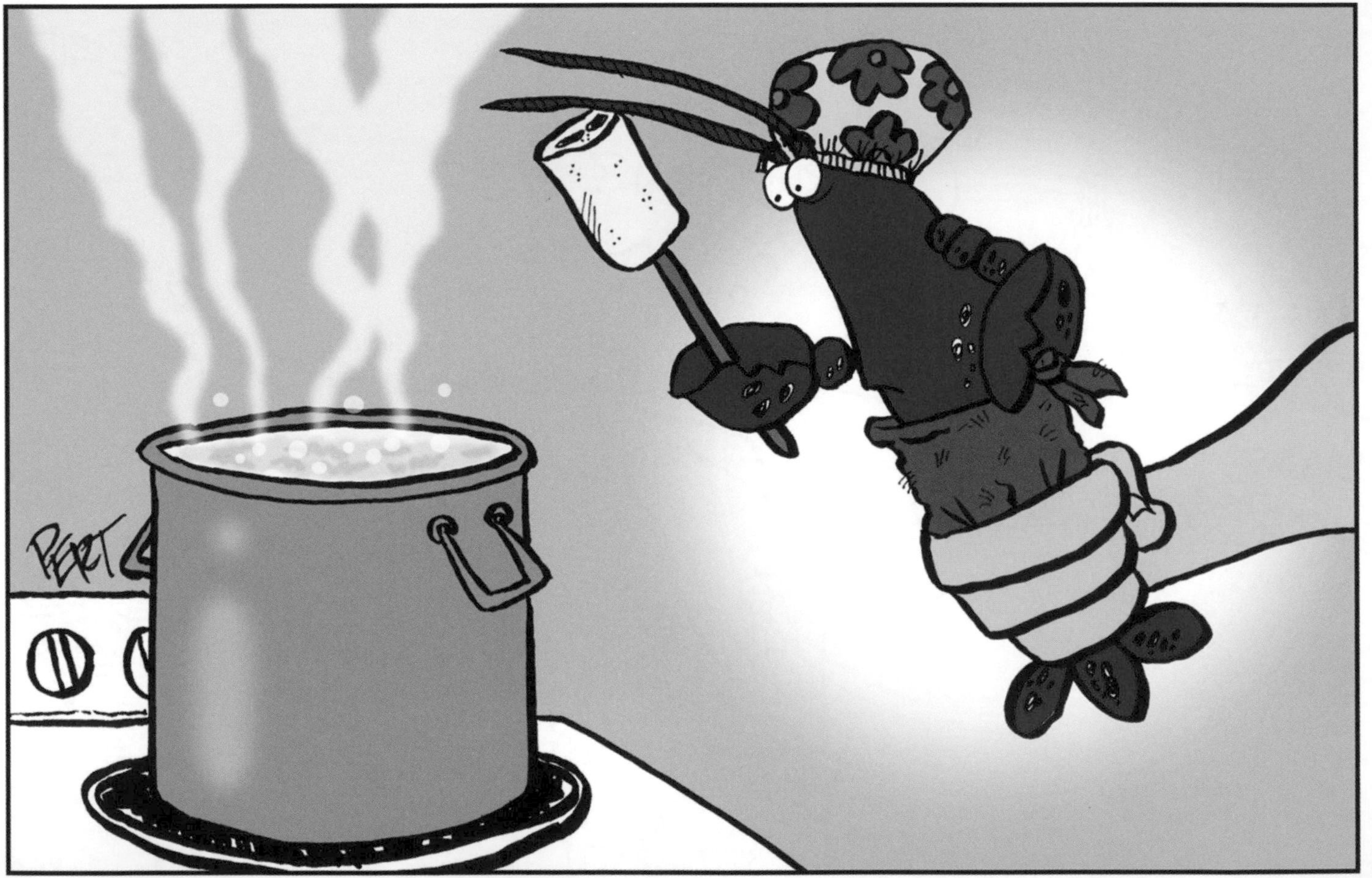
PEART

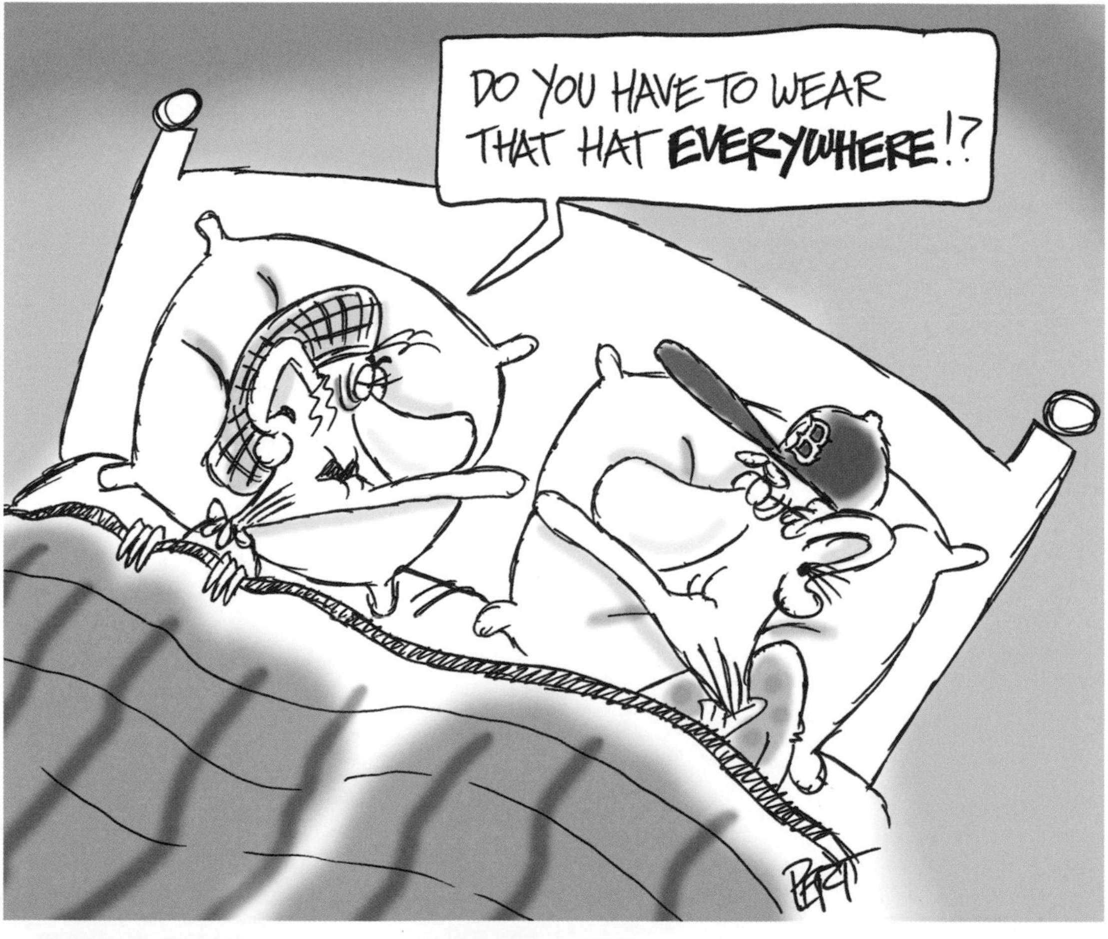
DO YOU HAVE TO WEAR THAT HAT EVERYWHERE!?

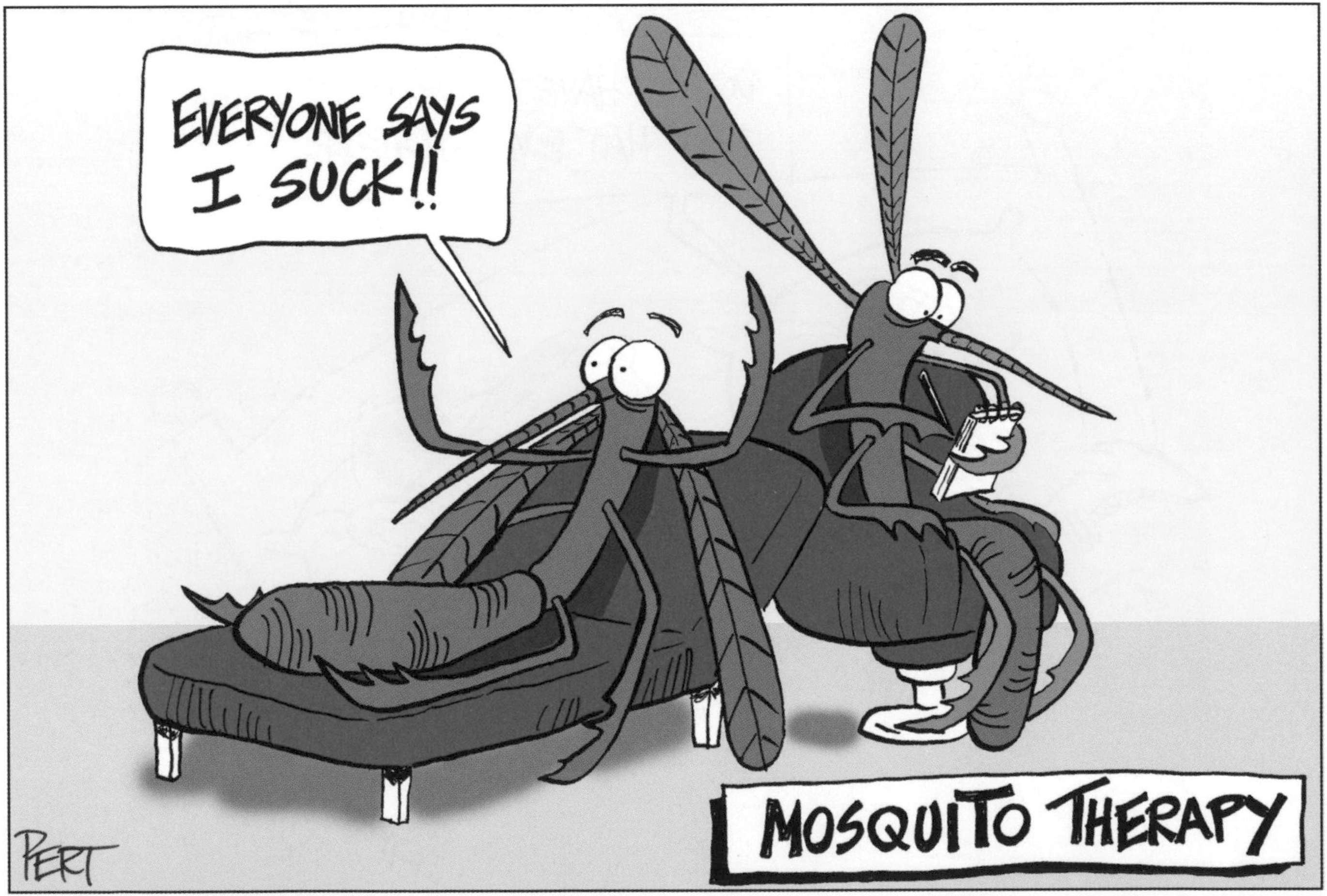
EVERYONE SAYS I SUCK!!
MOSQUITO THERAPY
PERT

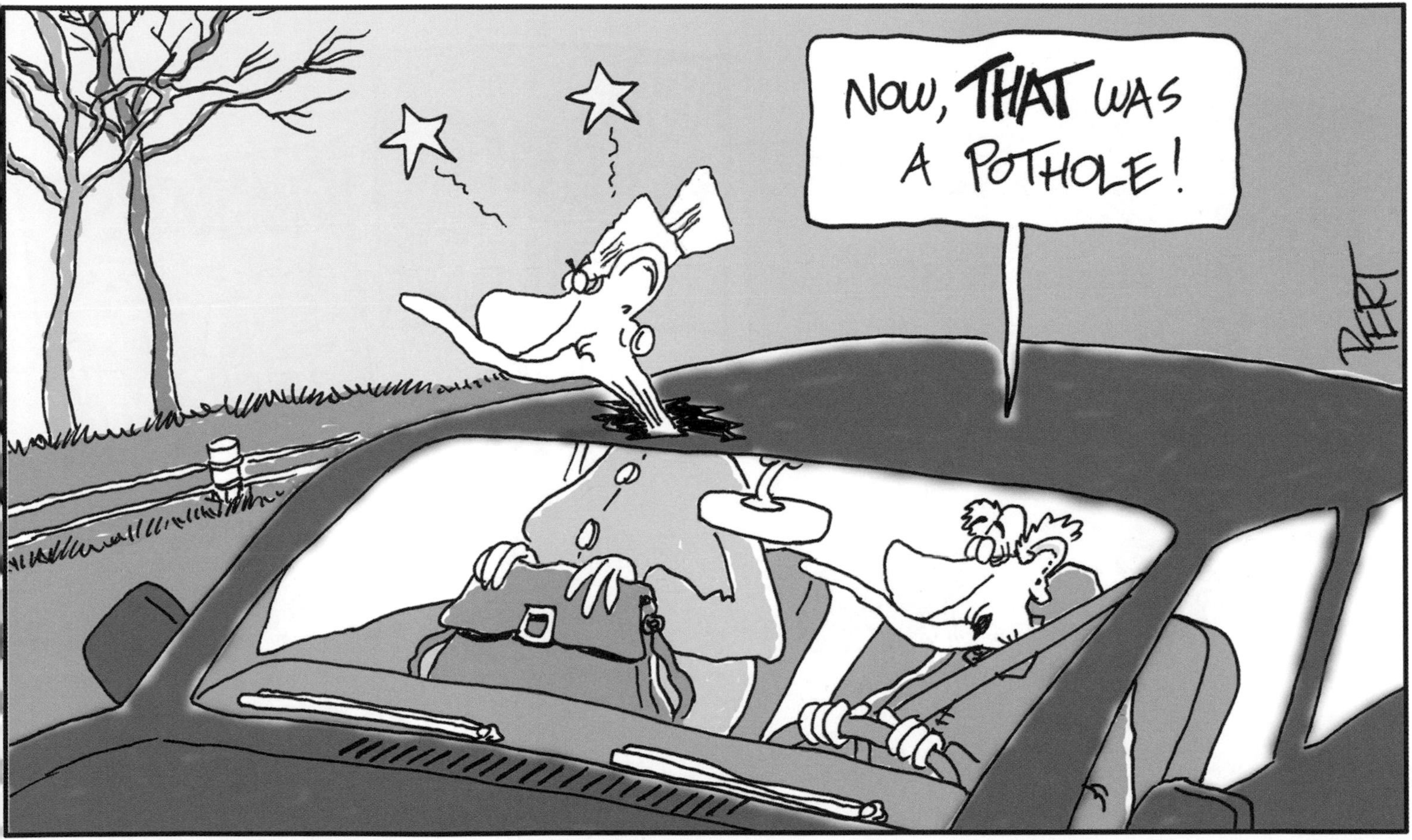
NOW, THAT WAS A POTHOLE!
PEET

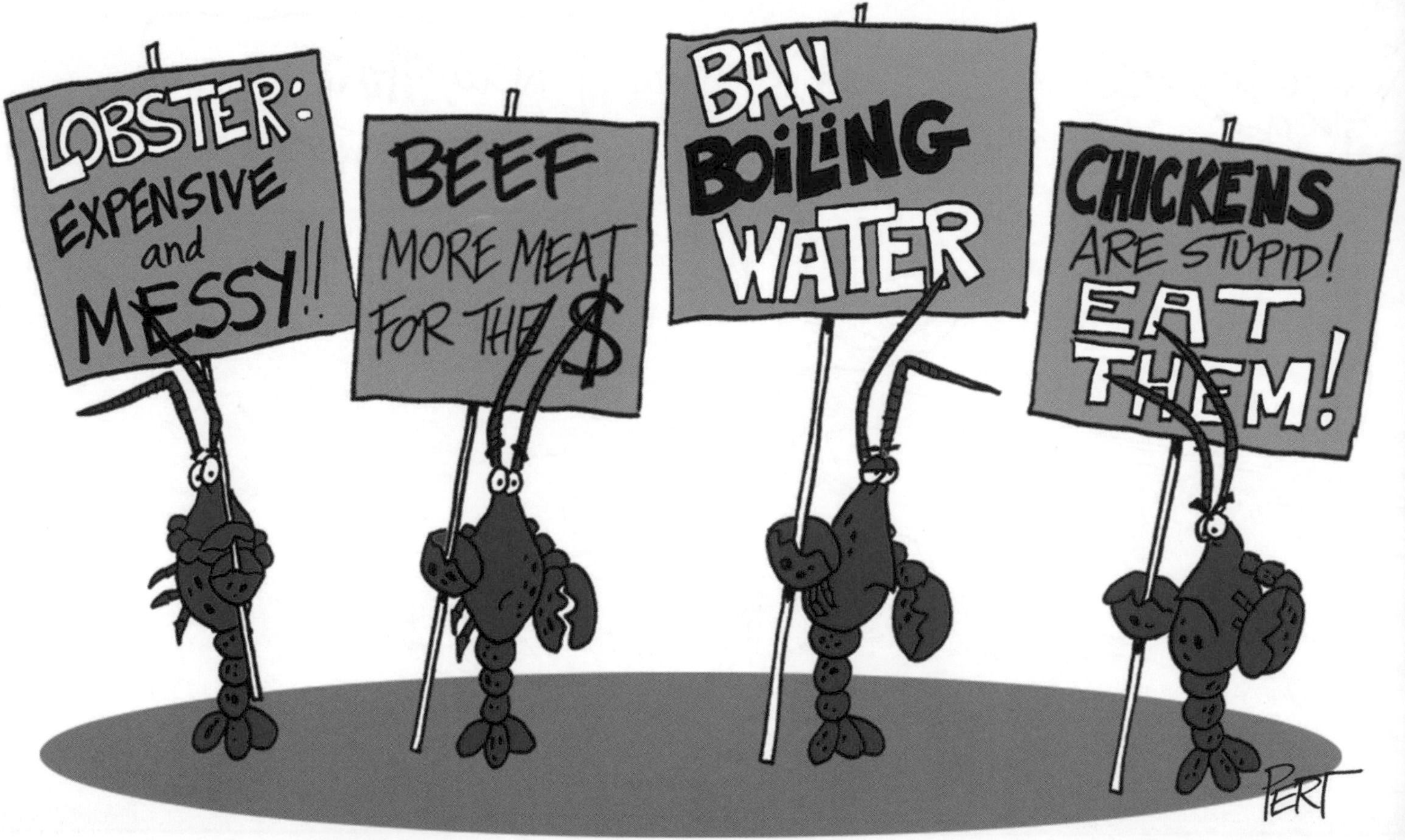
LOBSTER: EXPENSIVE and MESSY!!
BEEF MORE MEAT FOR THE $
BAN BOILING WATER
CHICKENS ARE STUPID! EAT THEM!
PERT

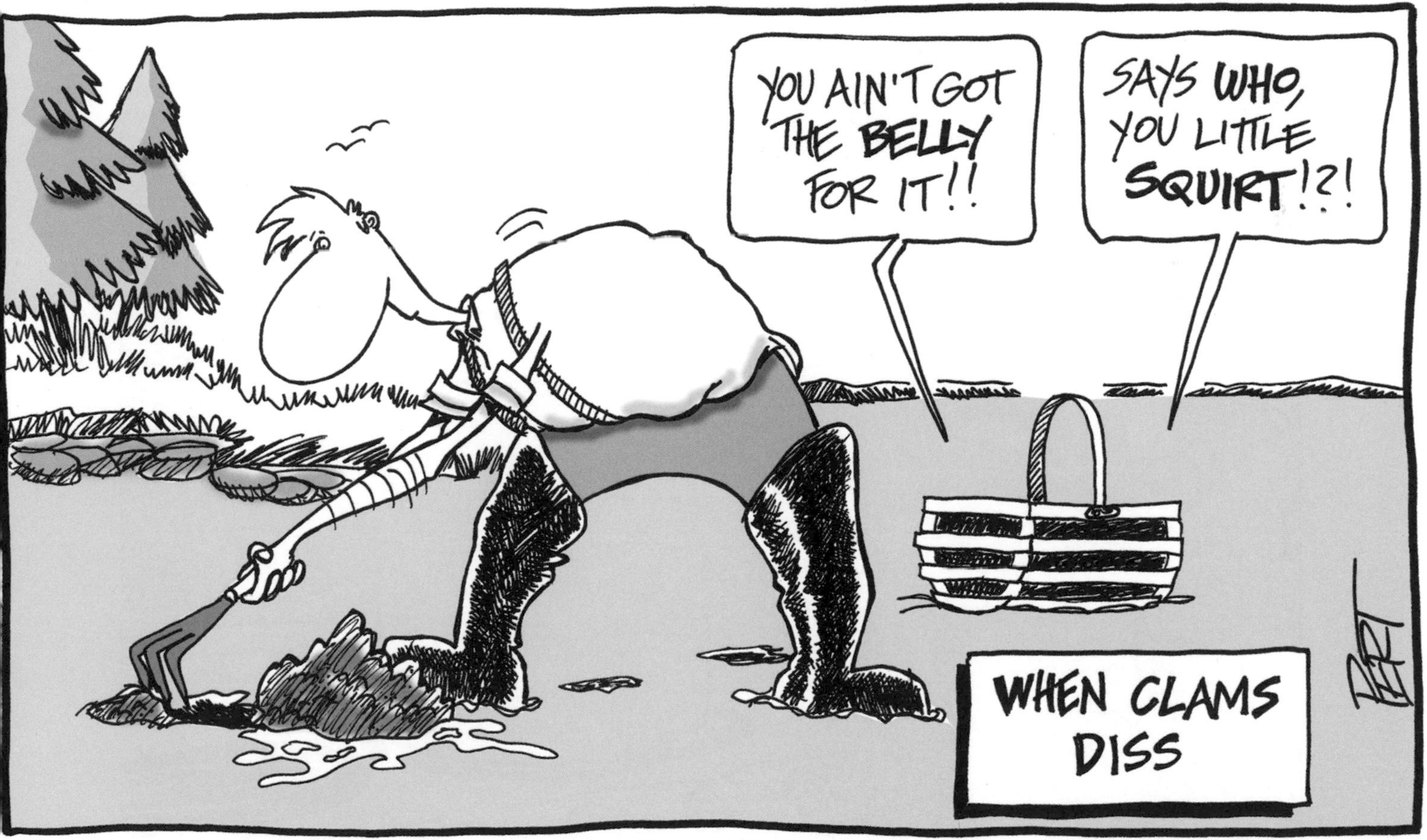
YOU AIN'T GOT THE BELLY FOR IT!!
SAYS WHO, YOU LITTLE SQUIRT!?!
WHEN CLAMS DISS

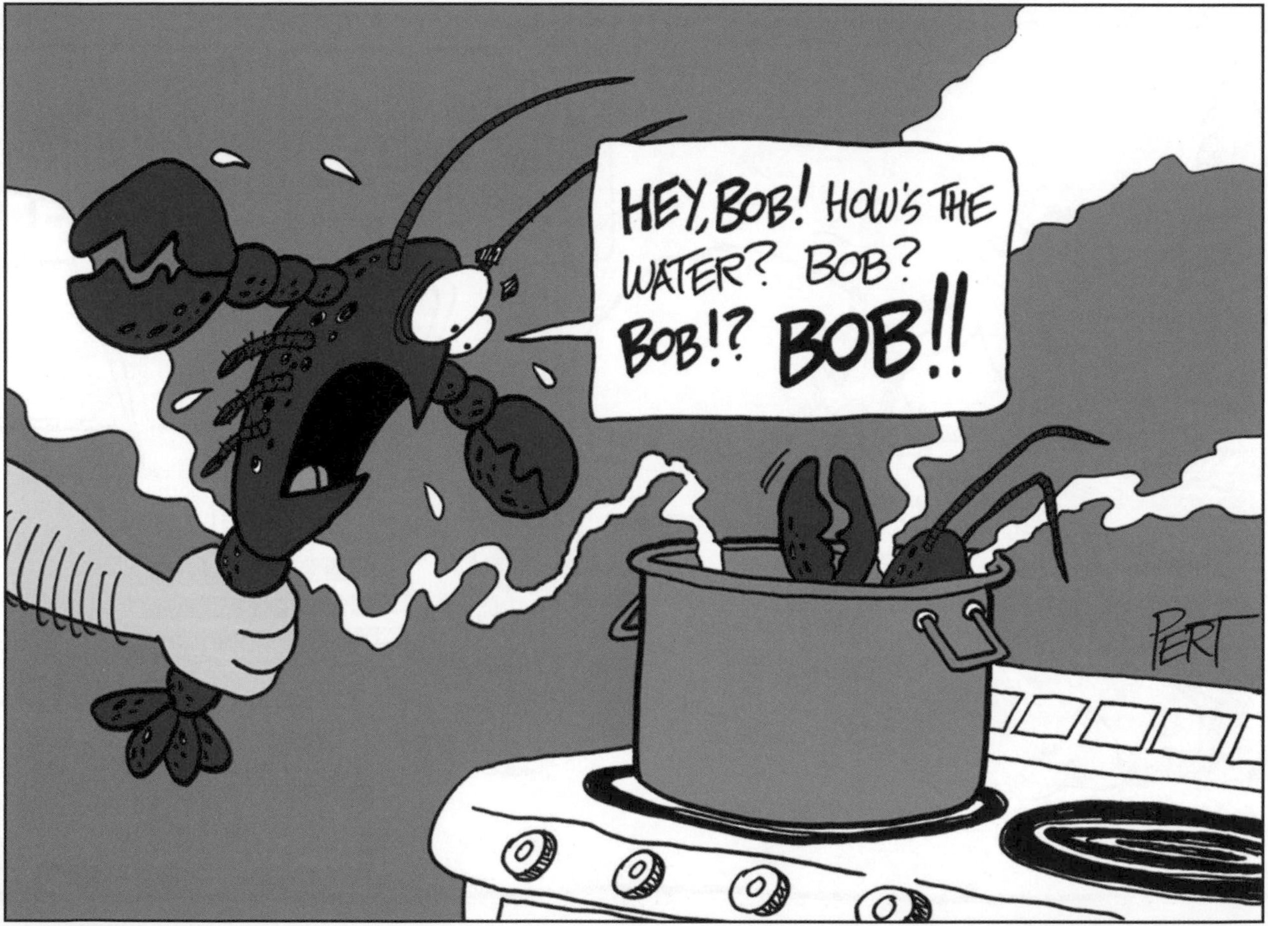
HEY, BOB! HOW'S THE WATER? BOB? BOB!? BOB!!
PERT

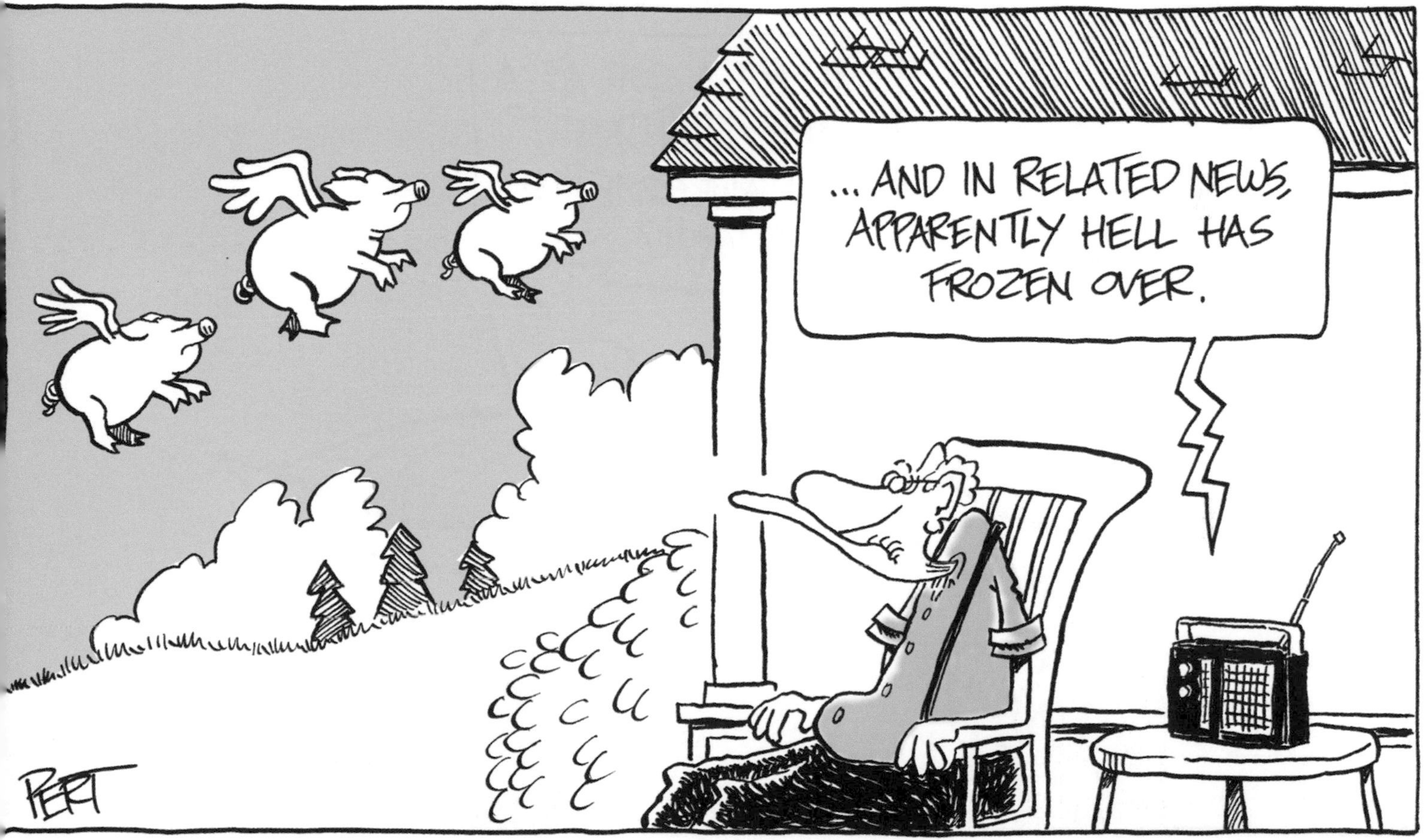
... AND IN RELATED NEWS, APPARENTLY HELL HAS FROZEN OVER.
PERT

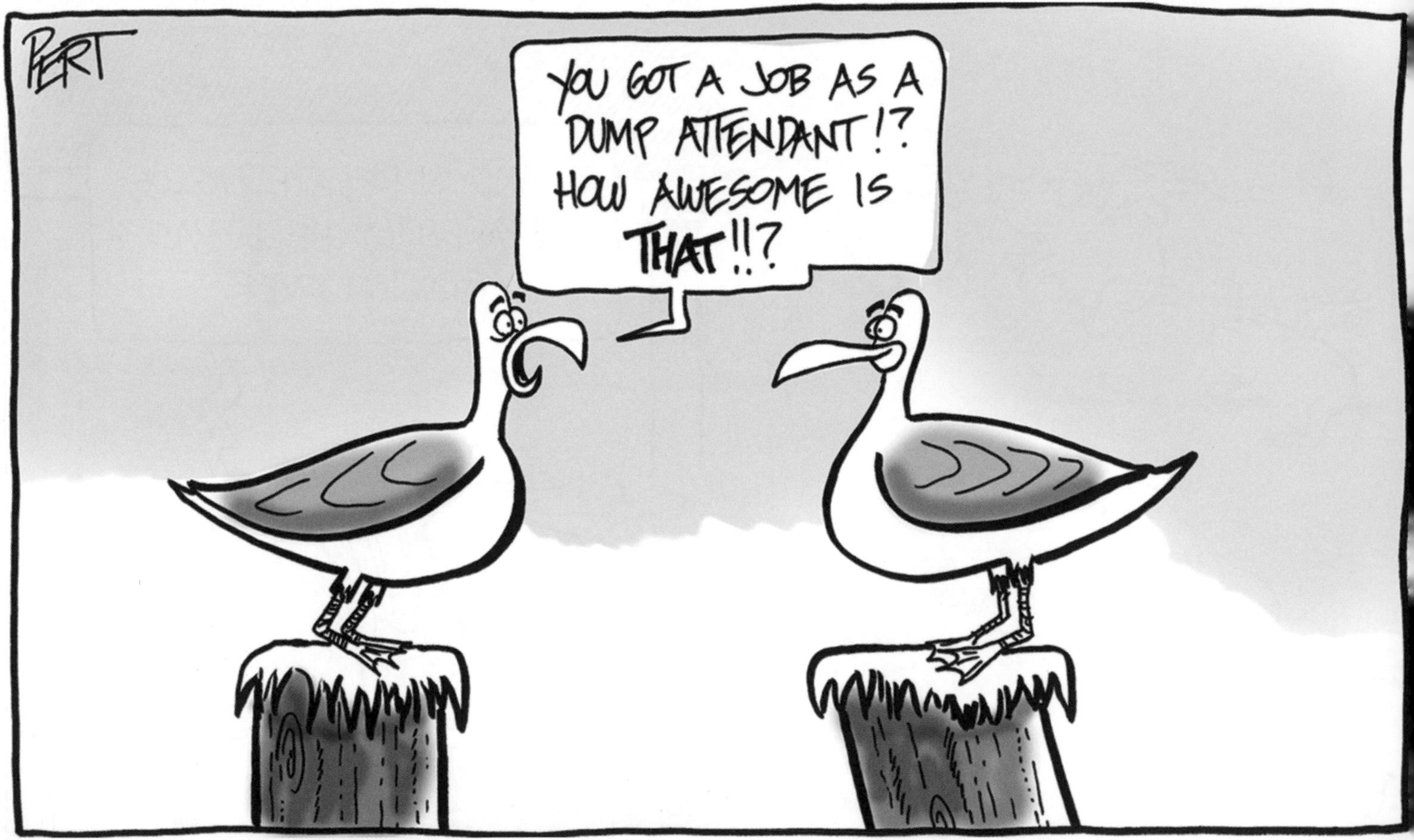
PERT
YOU GOT A JOB AS A DUMP ATTENDANT!? HOW AWESOME IS THAT!!?

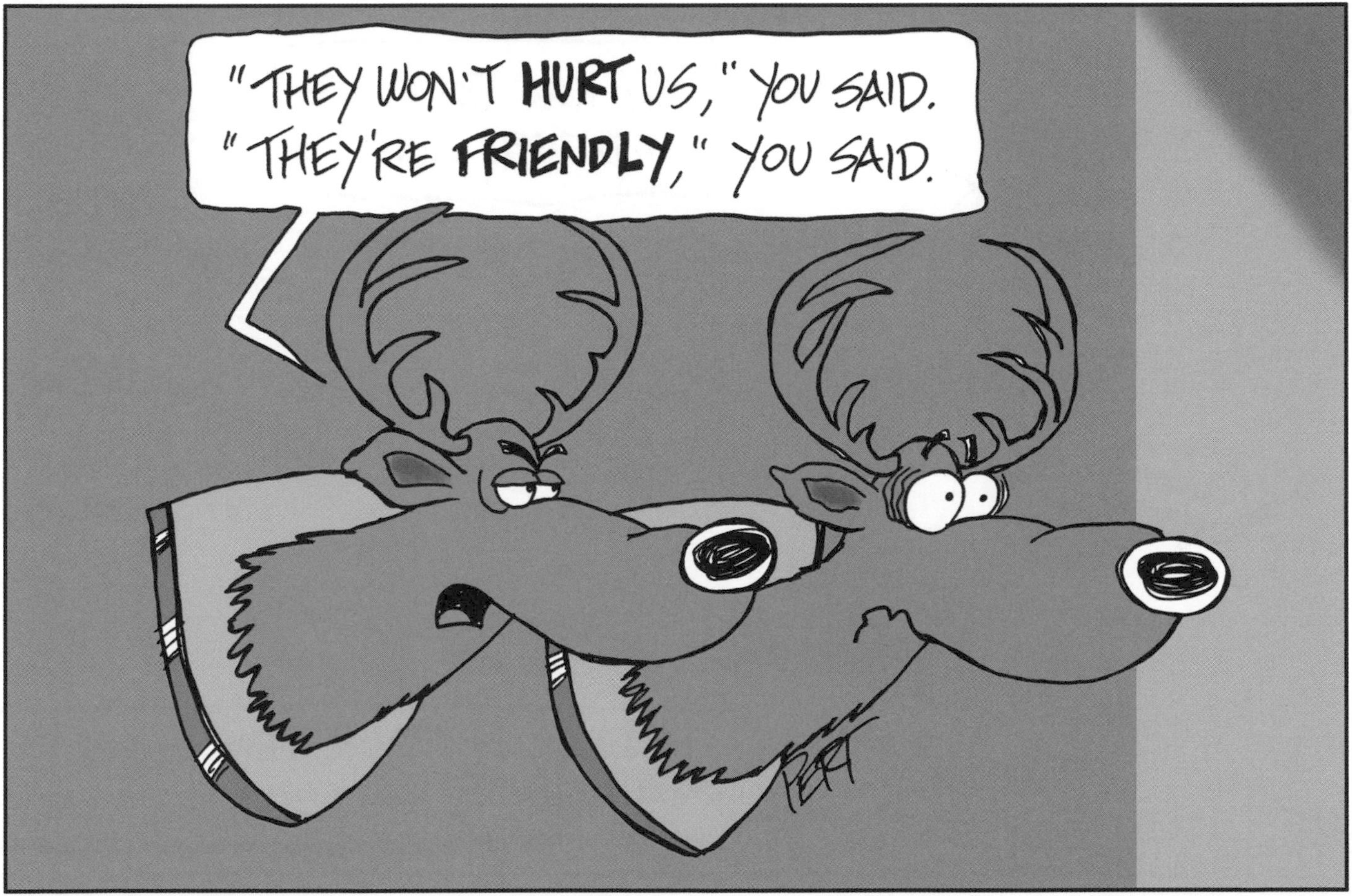
"THEY WON'T HURT US," YOU SAID. "THEY'RE FRIENDLY," YOU SAID.
PERT

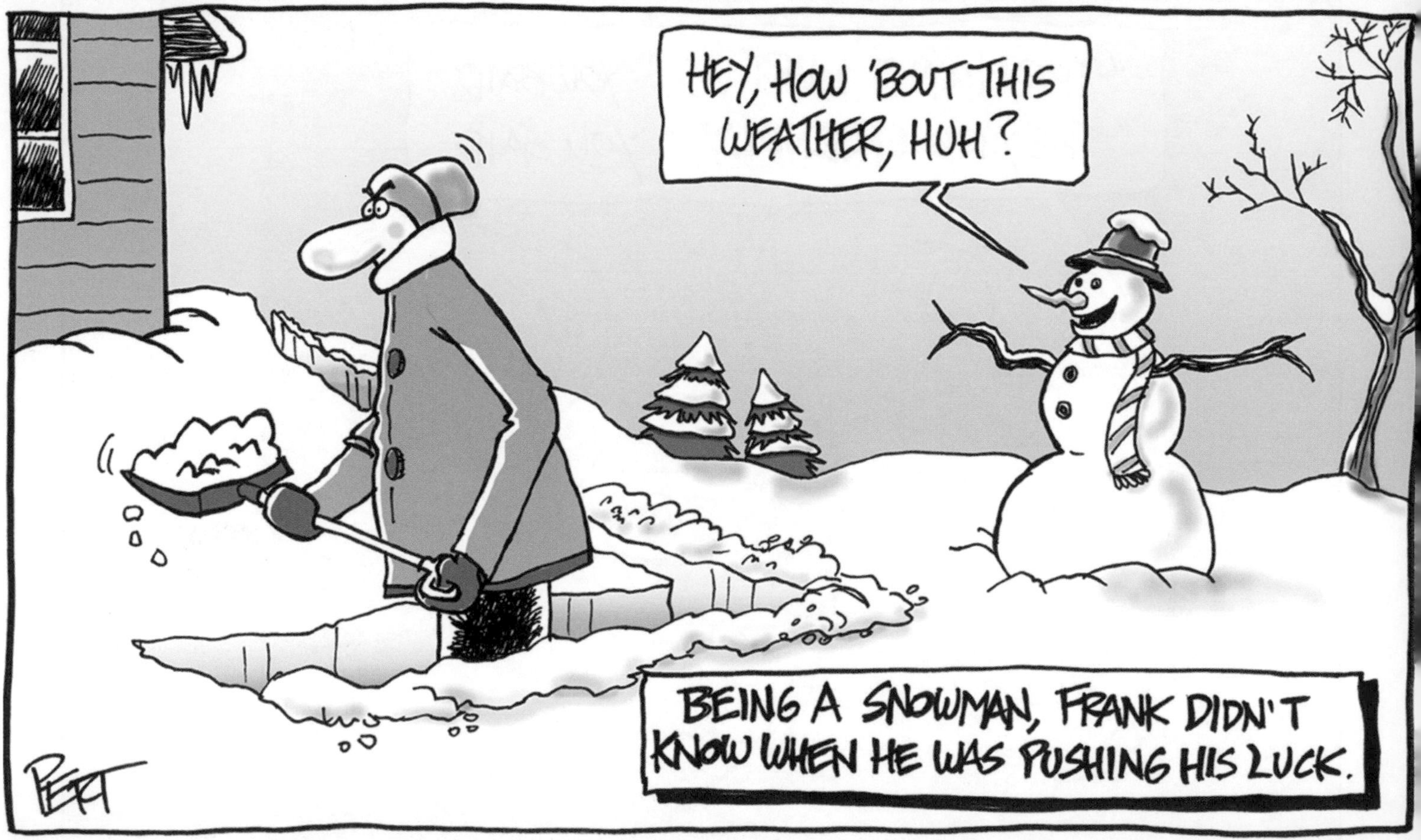
HEY, HOW 'BOUT THIS WEATHER, HUH?
BEING A SNOWMAN, FRANK DIDN'T KNOW WHEN HE WAS PUSHING HIS LUCK.
PEAT

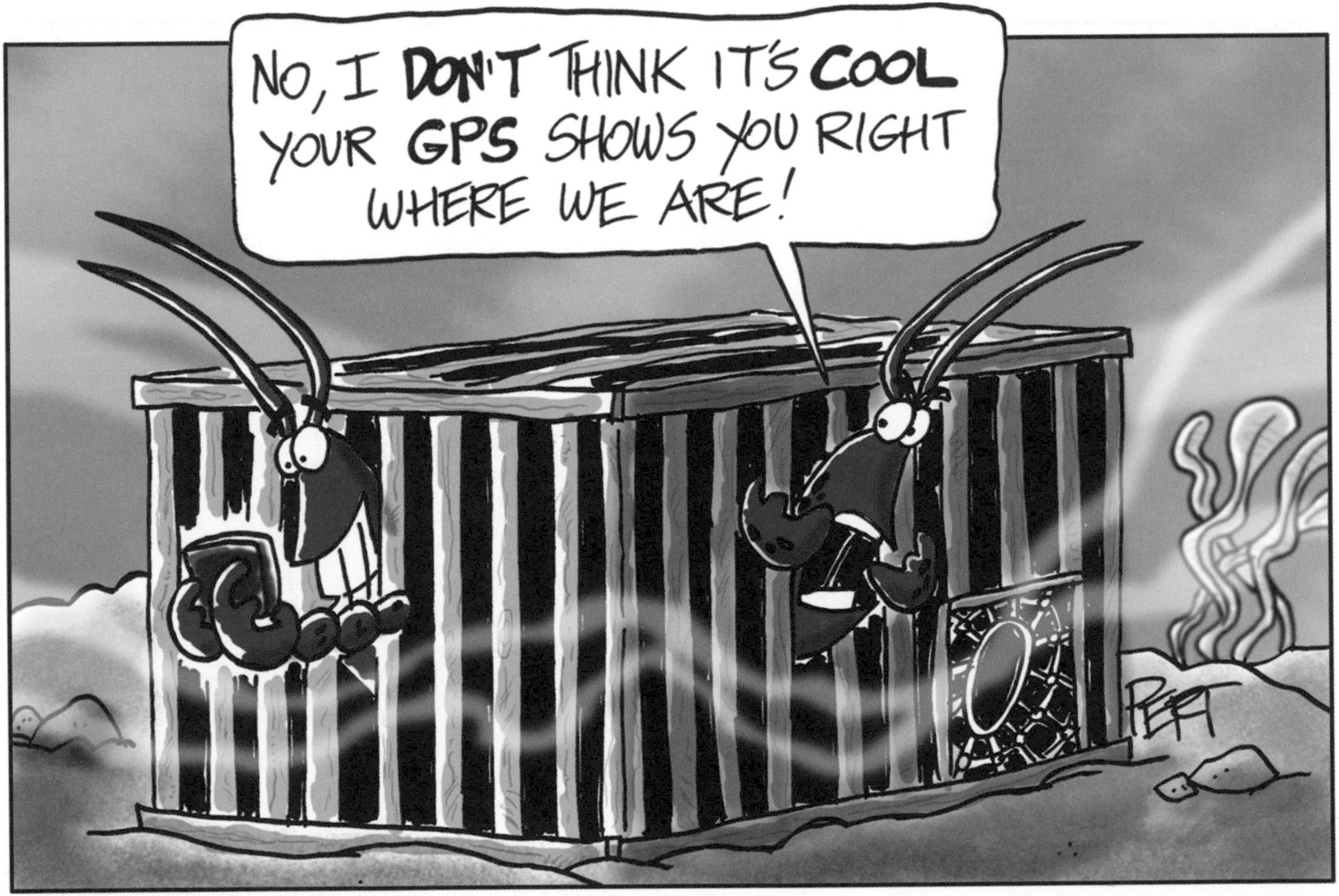
NO, I DON'T THINK IT'S COOL YOUR GPS SHOWS YOU RIGHT WHERE WE ARE!
PERT

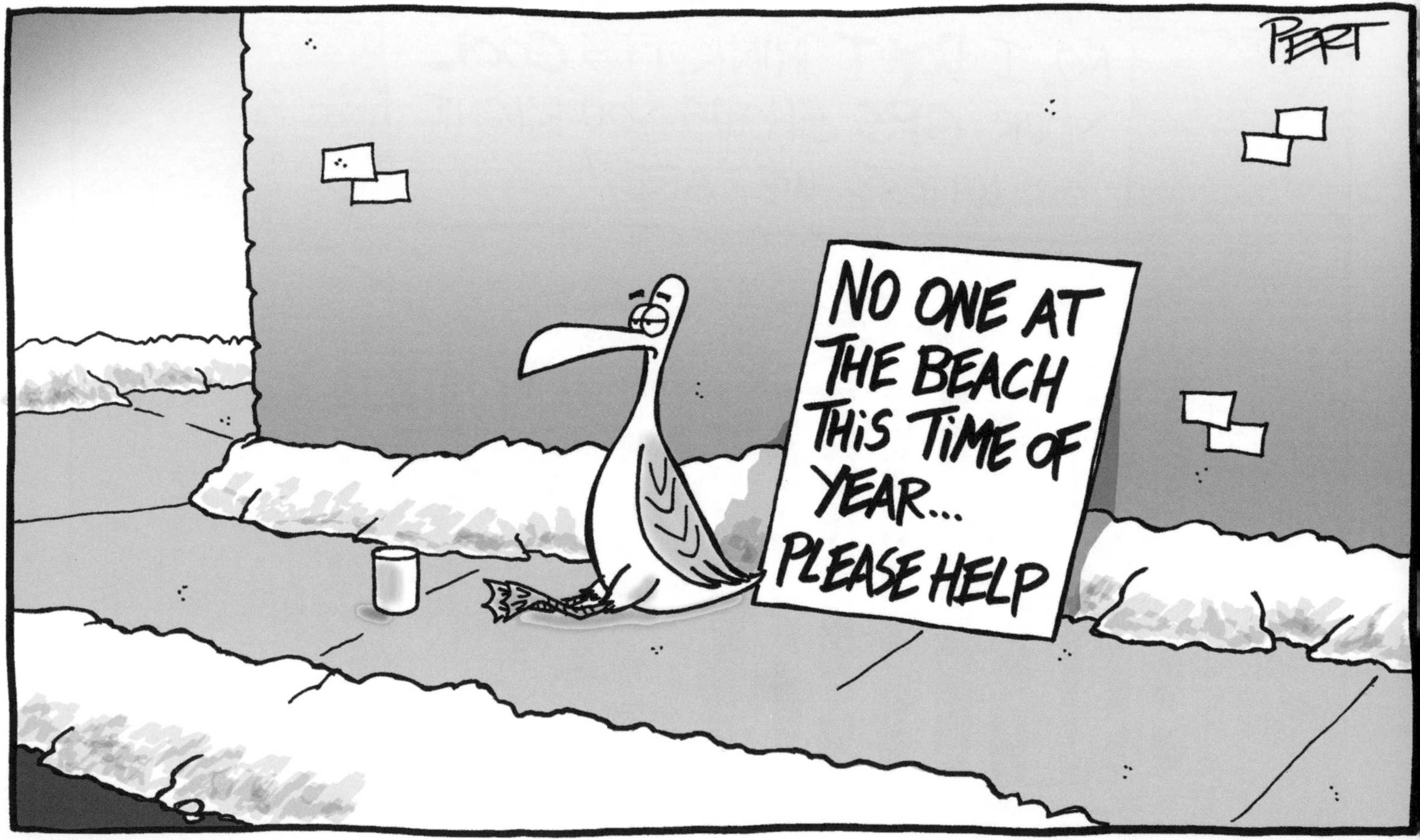
PERT
NO ONE AT THE BEACH THIS TIME OF YEAR... PLEASE HELP

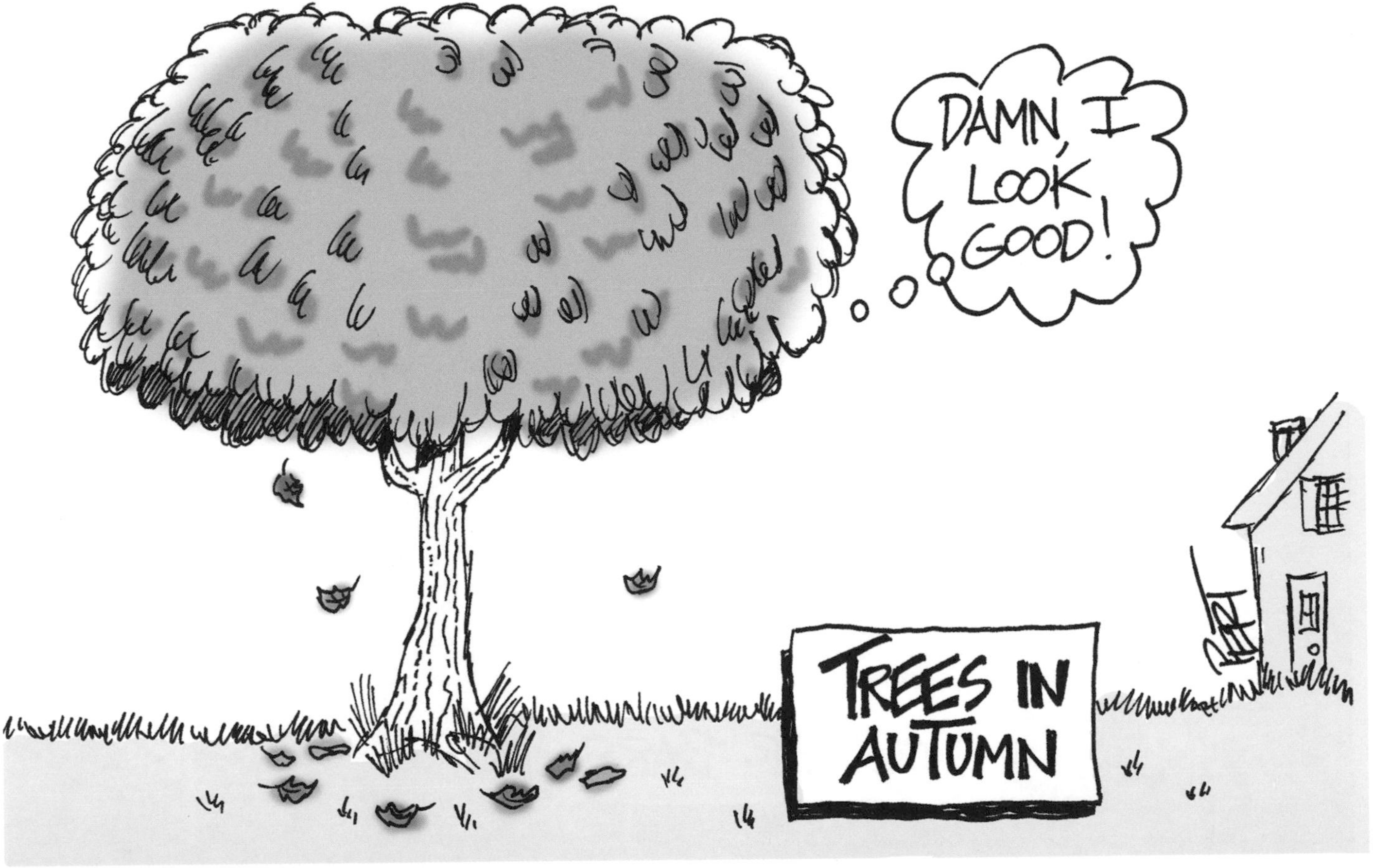
DAMN, I LOOK GOOD!
TREES IN AUTUMN

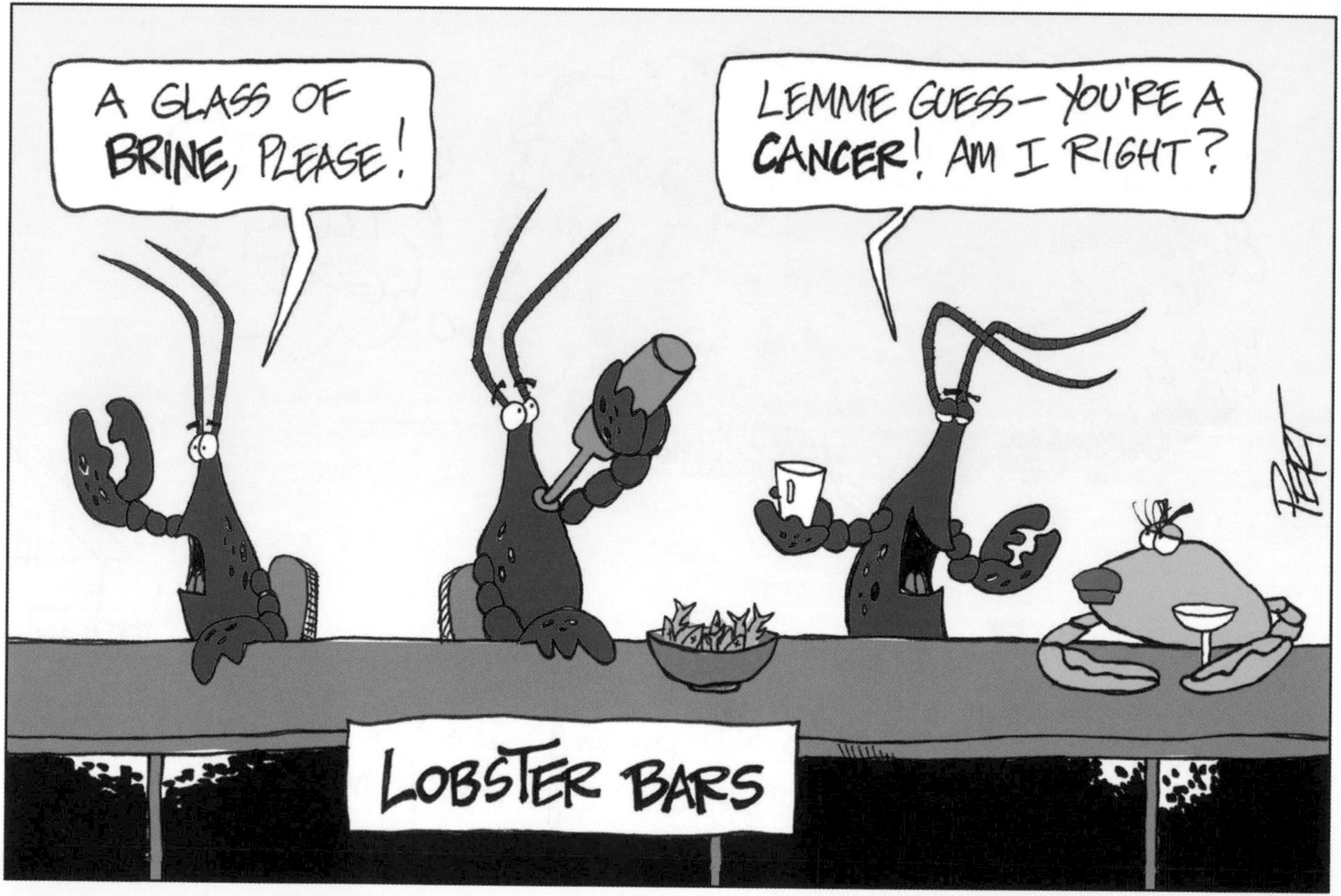
A GLASS OF BRINE, PLEASE!
LEMME GUESS— YOU'RE A CANCER! AM I RIGHT?
LOBSTER BARS

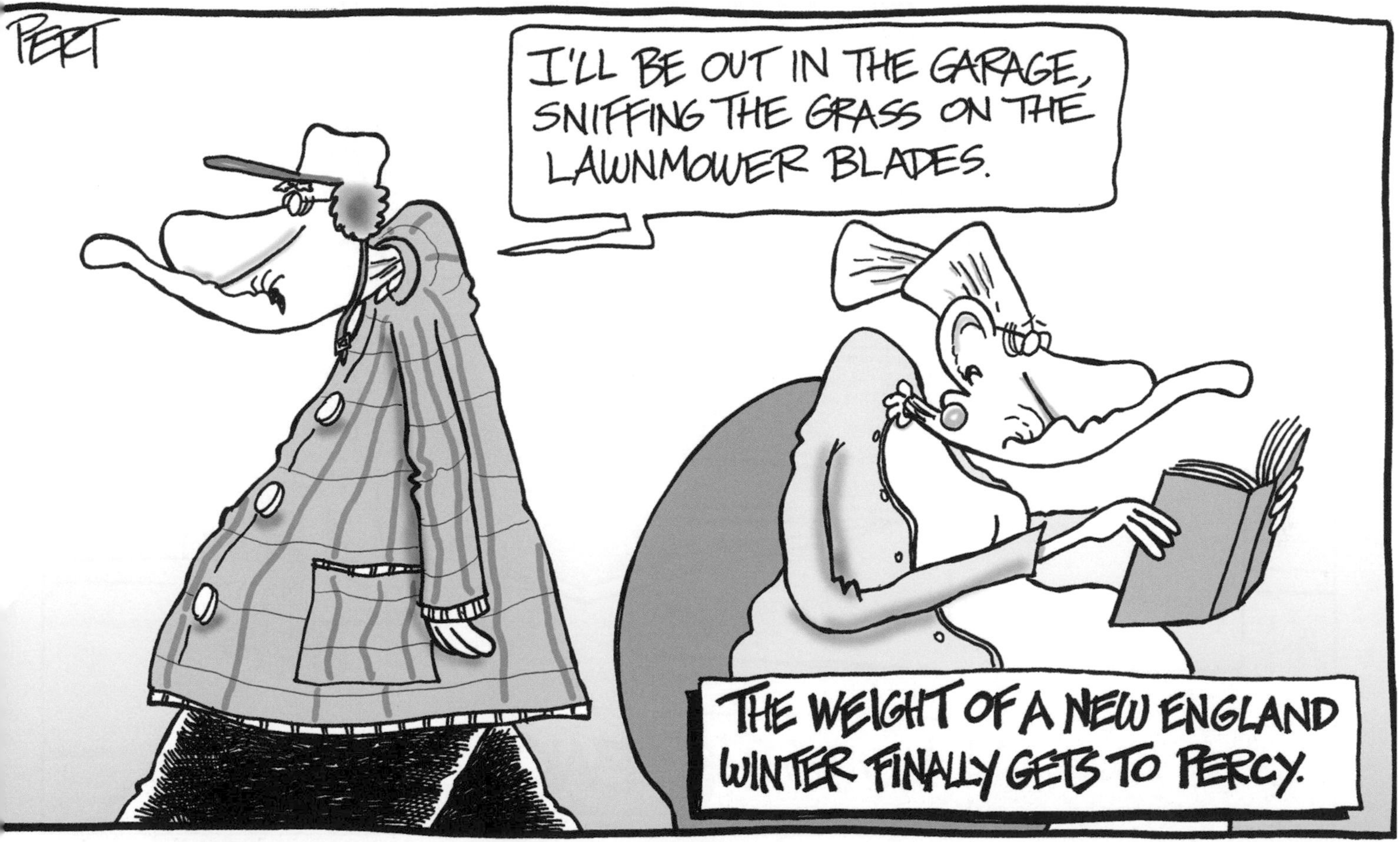
PERT
I'LL BE OUT IN THE GARAGE, SNIFFING THE GRASS ON THE LAWNMOWER BLADES.
THE WEIGHT OF A NEW ENGLAND WINTER FINALLY GETS TO PERCY.

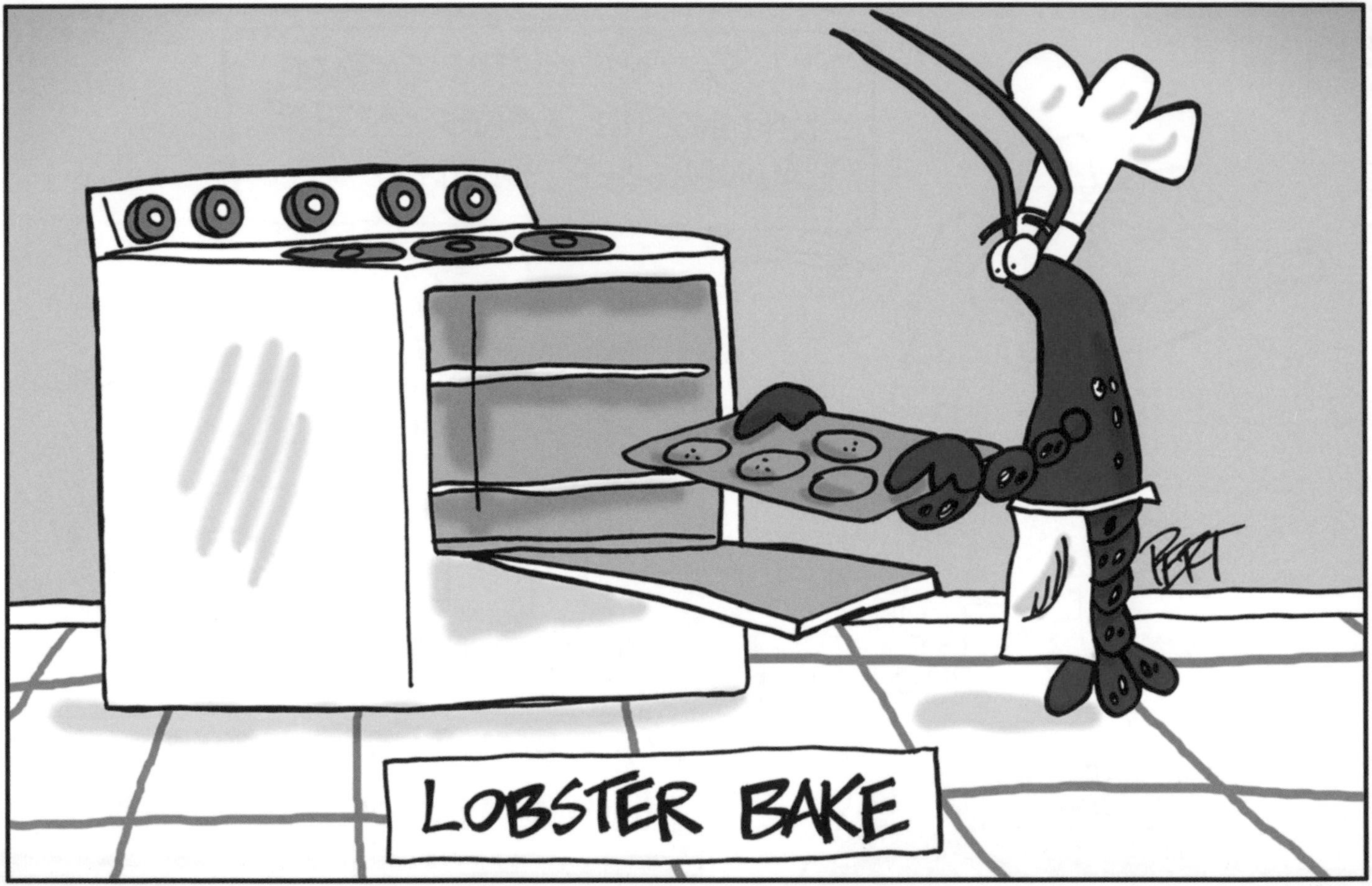
LOBSTER BAKE

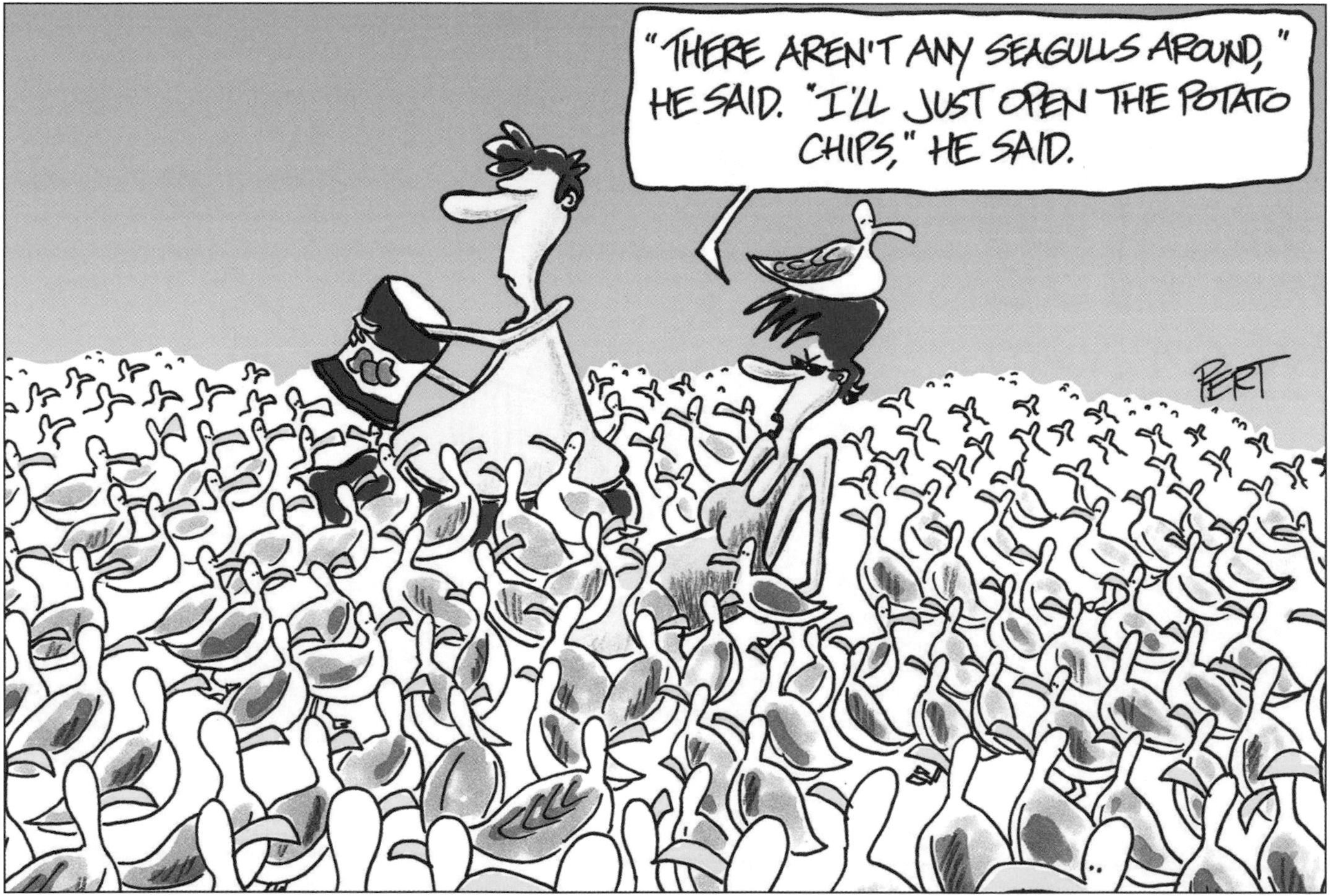
"THERE AREN'T ANY SEAGULLS AROUND," HE SAID. "I'LL JUST OPEN THE POTATO CHIPS," HE SAID.
PERT

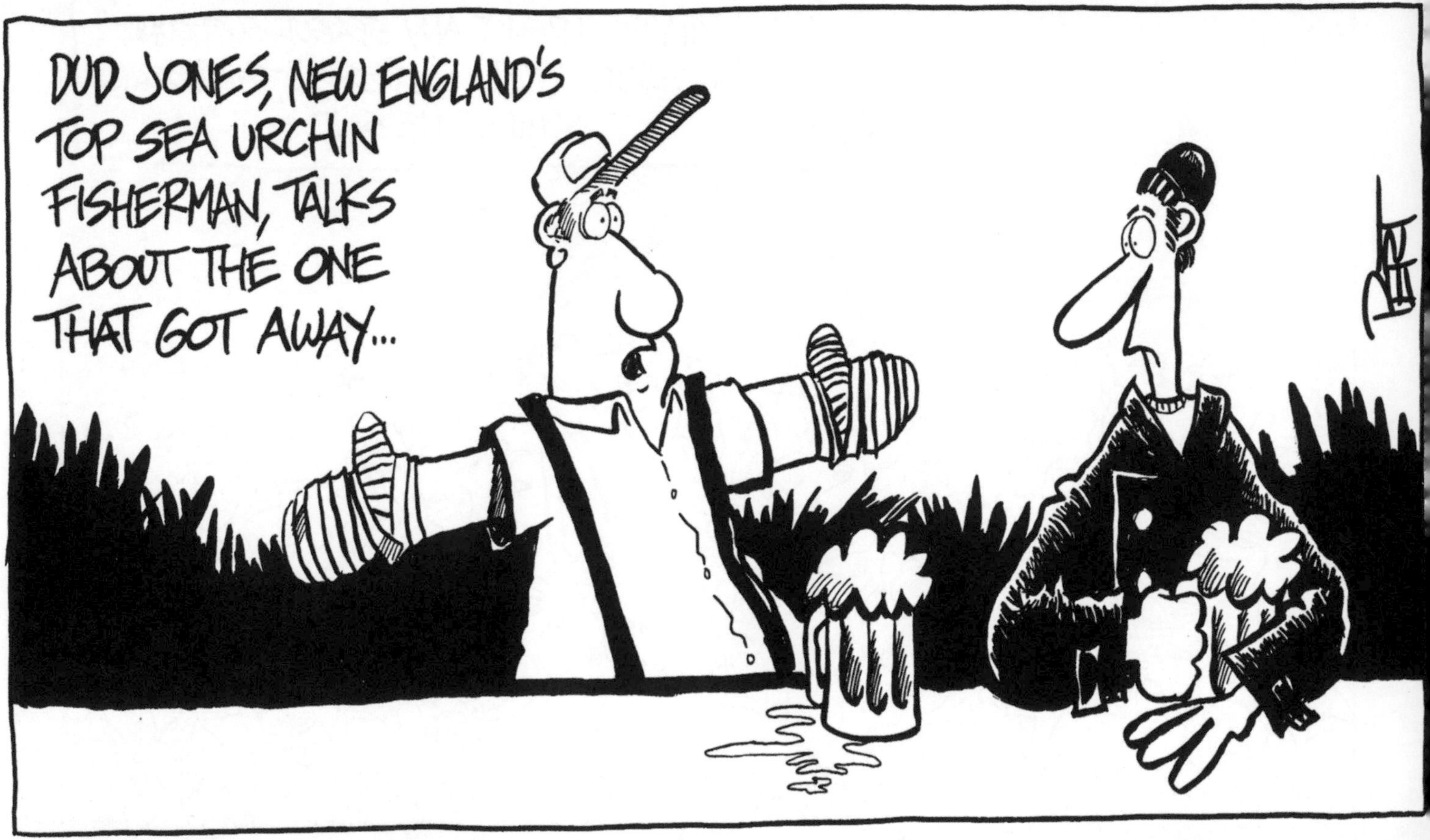
DUD JONES, NEW ENGLAND'S TOP SEA URCHIN FISHERMAN, TALKS ABOUT THE ONE THAT GOT AWAY...

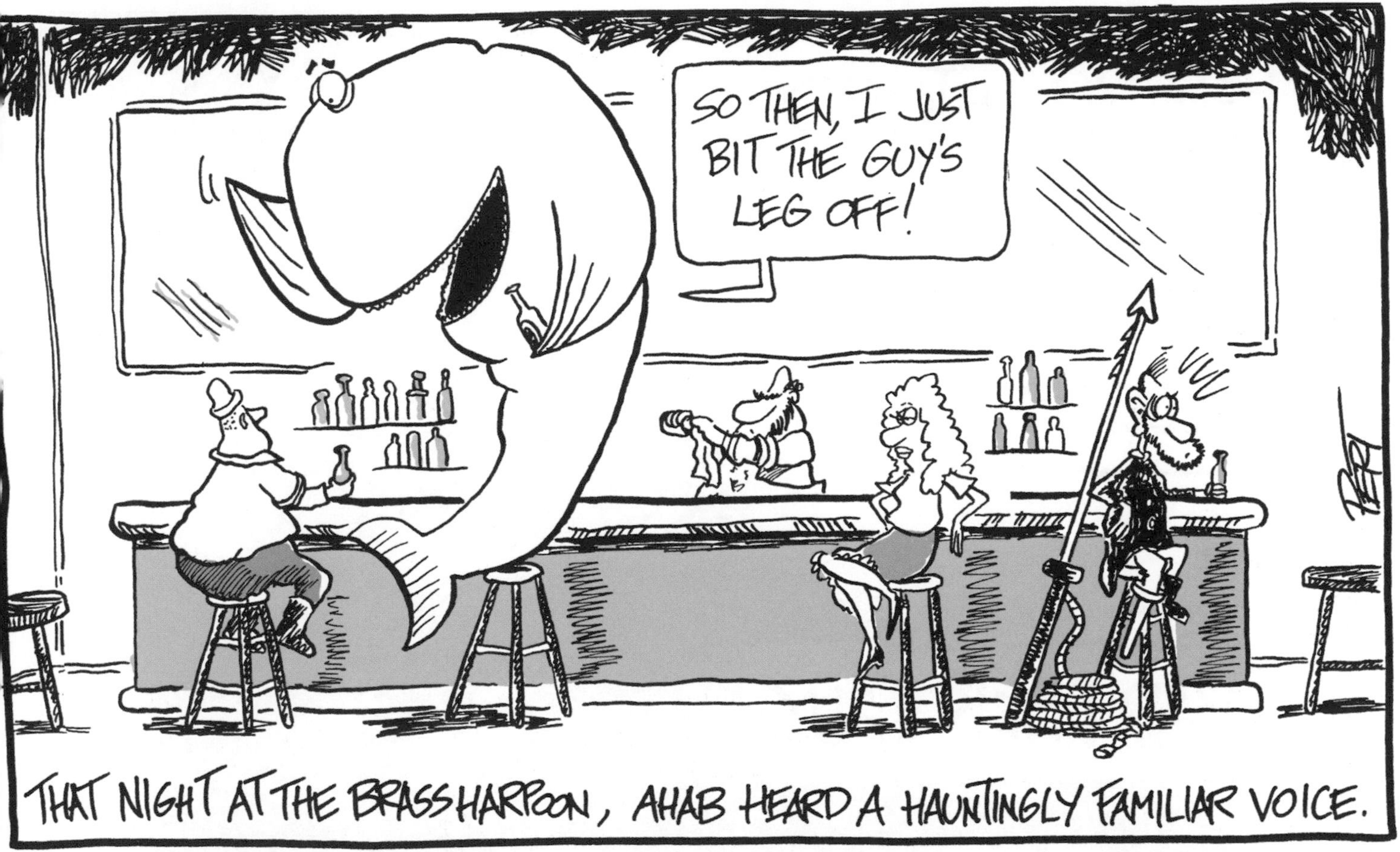
SO THEN, I JUST BIT THE GUY'S LEG OFF!
THAT NIGHT AT THE BRASS HARPOON, AHAB HEARD A HAUNTINGLY FAMILIAR VOICE.

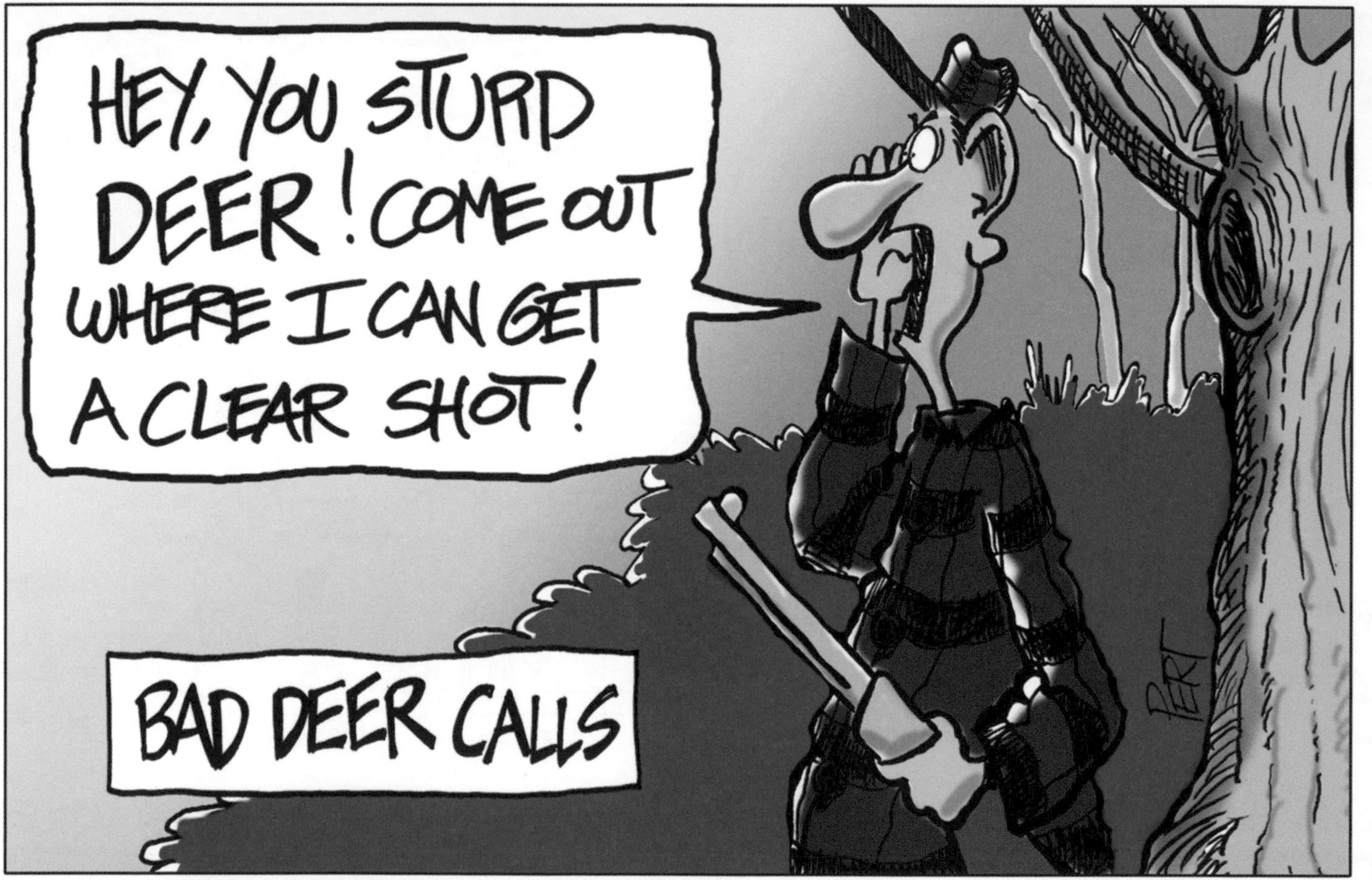
HEY, YOU STUPID DEER! COME OUT WHERE I CAN GET A CLEAR SHOT!
BAD DEER CALLS
BERT

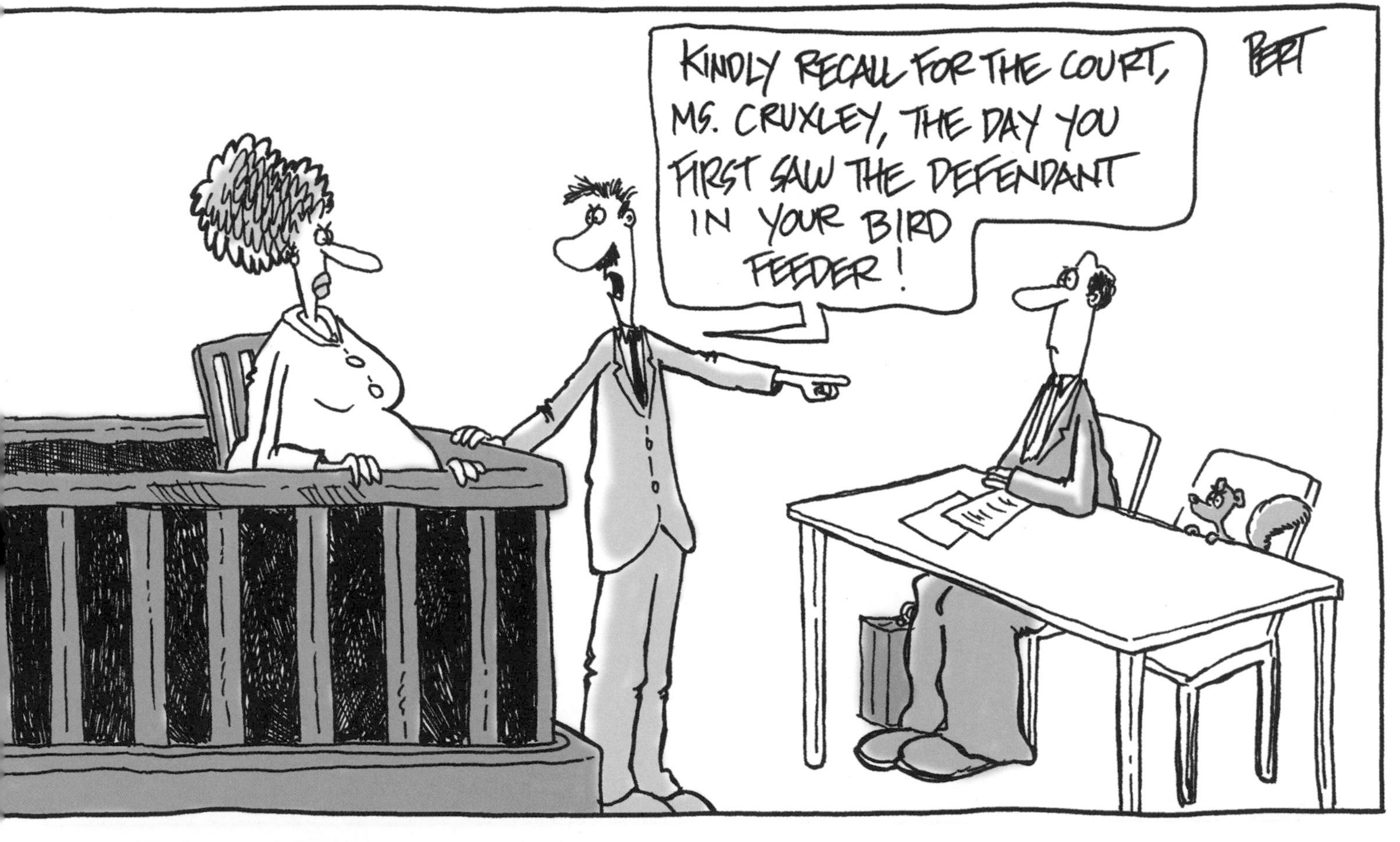
KINDLY RECALL FOR THE COURT, MS. CRUXLEY, THE DAY YOU FIRST SAW THE DEFENDANT IN YOUR BIRD FEEDER!
BERT

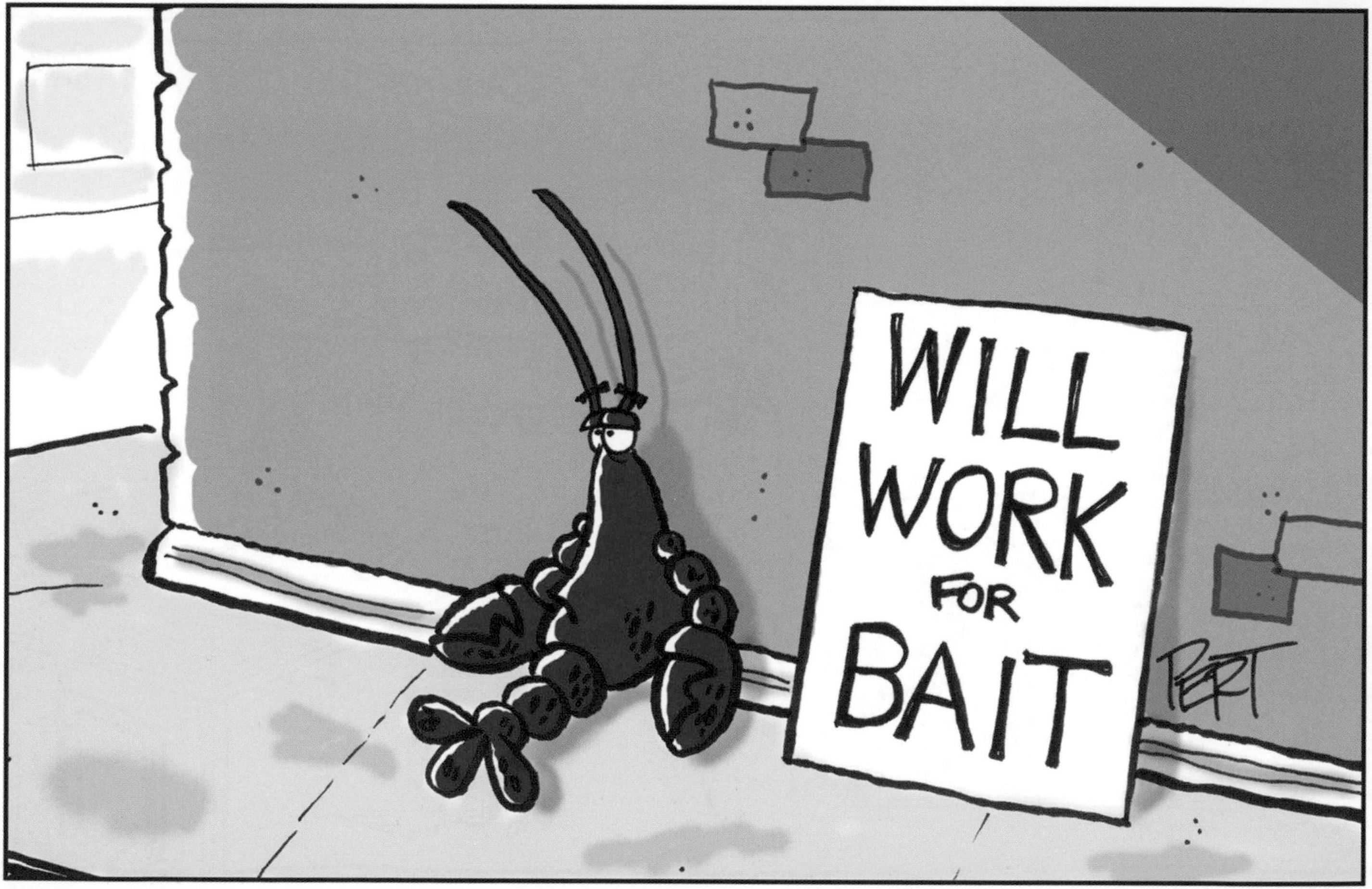
WILL WORK FOR BAIT
PERT

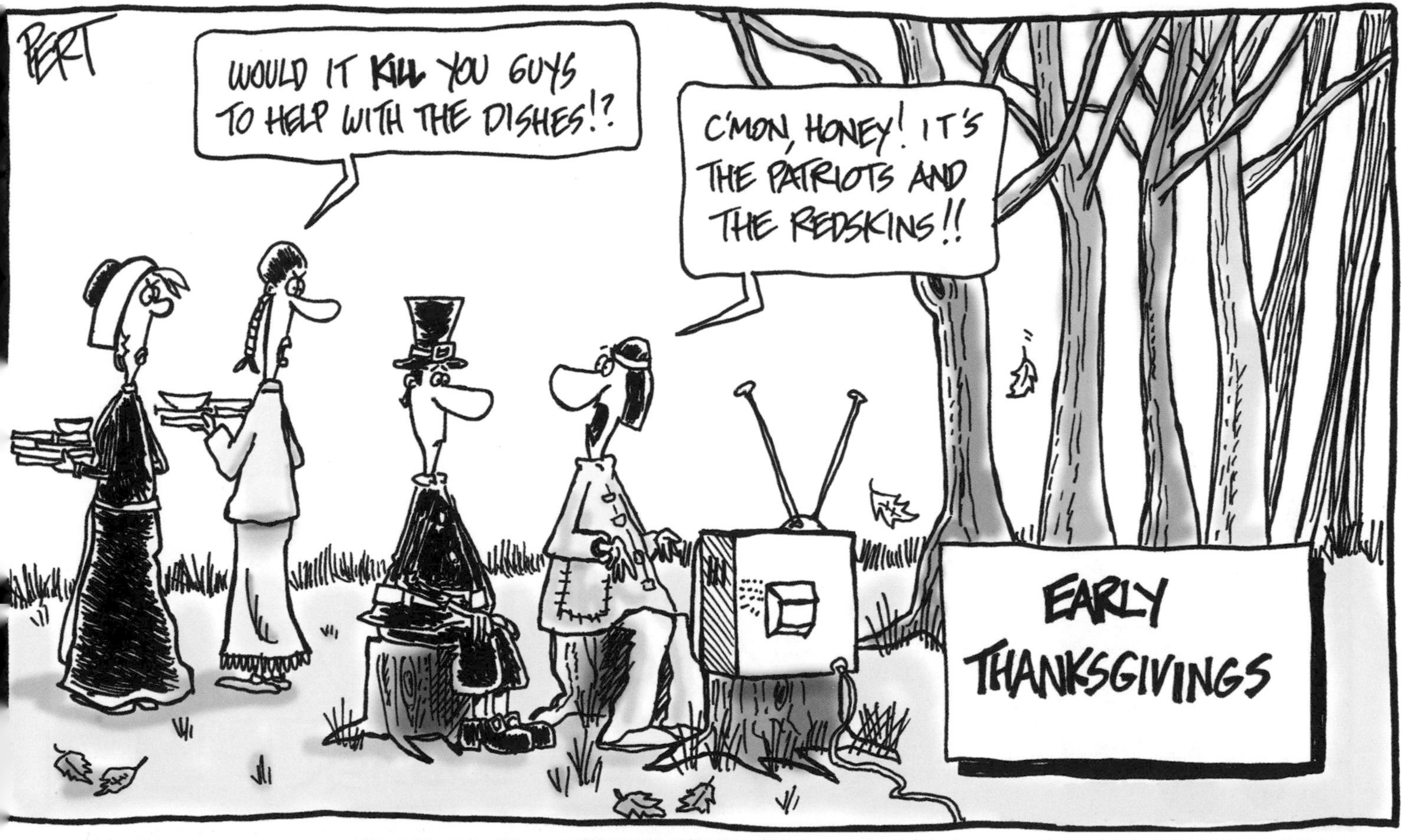
PERT
WOULD IT **KILL** YOU GUYS TO HELP WITH THE DISHES!?
C'MON, HONEY! IT'S THE PATRIOTS AND THE REDSKINS!!
EARLY THANKSGIVINGS

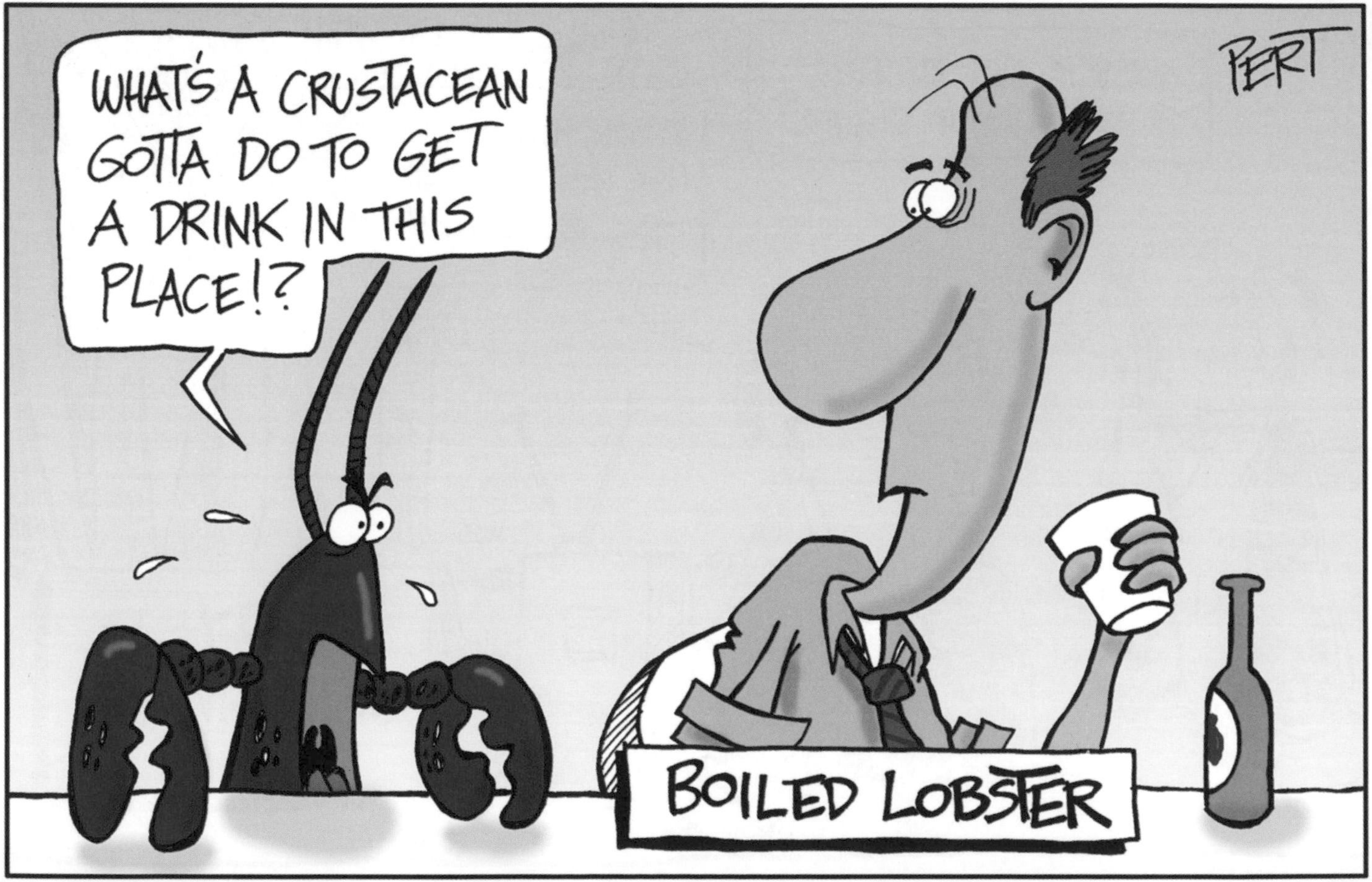
WHAT'S A CRUSTACEAN GOTTA DO TO GET A DRINK IN THIS PLACE!?
BOILED LOBSTER
PERT

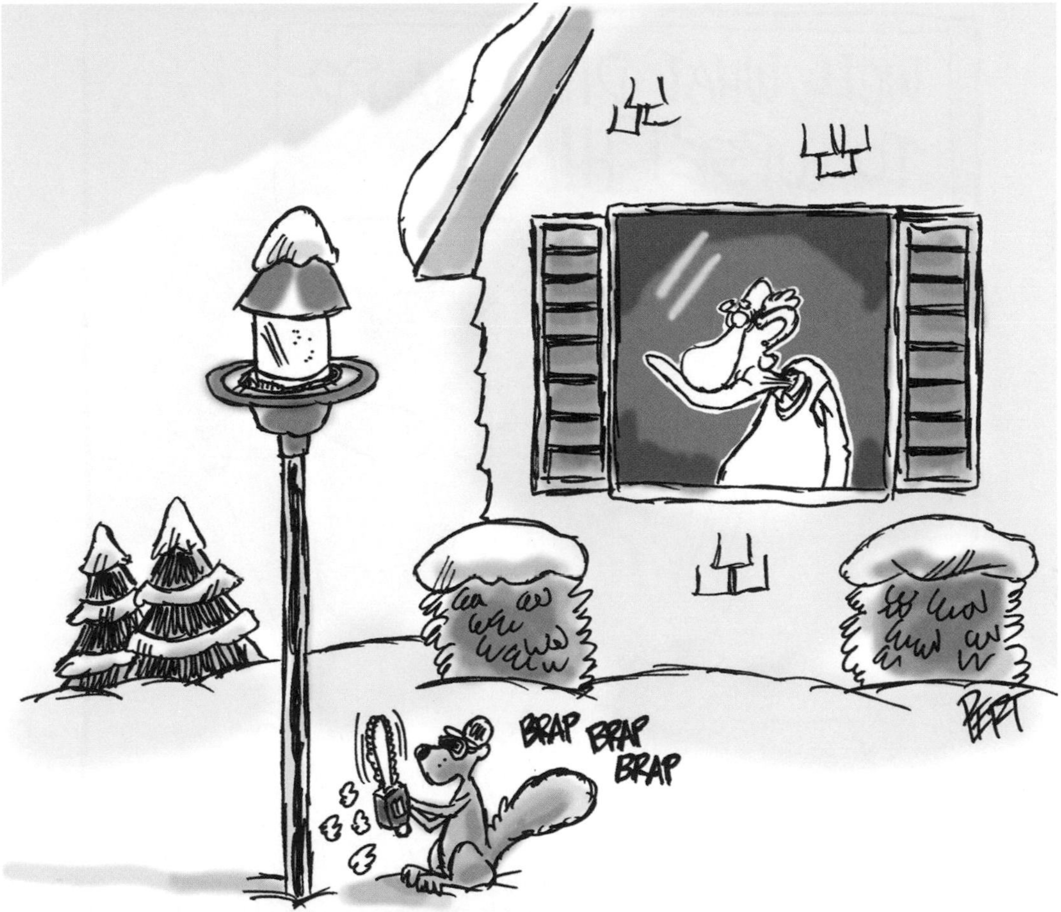
BRAP BRAP
BRAP
BERT

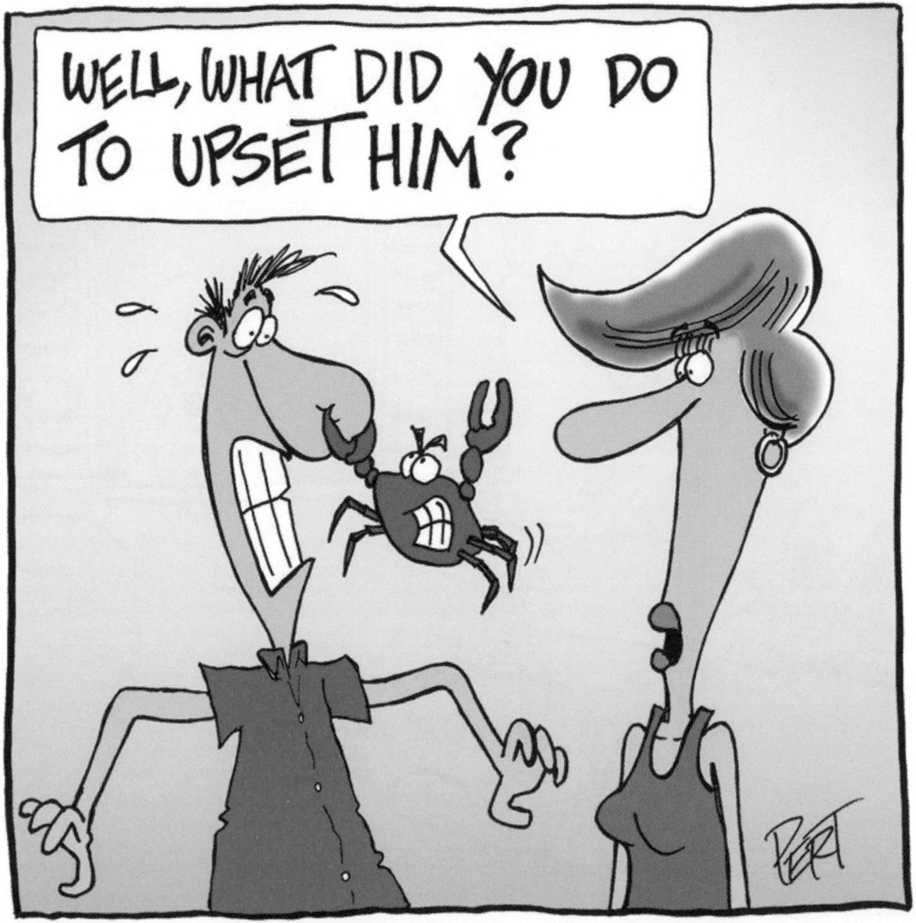
WELL, WHAT DID YOU DO TO UPSET HIM?
PERT

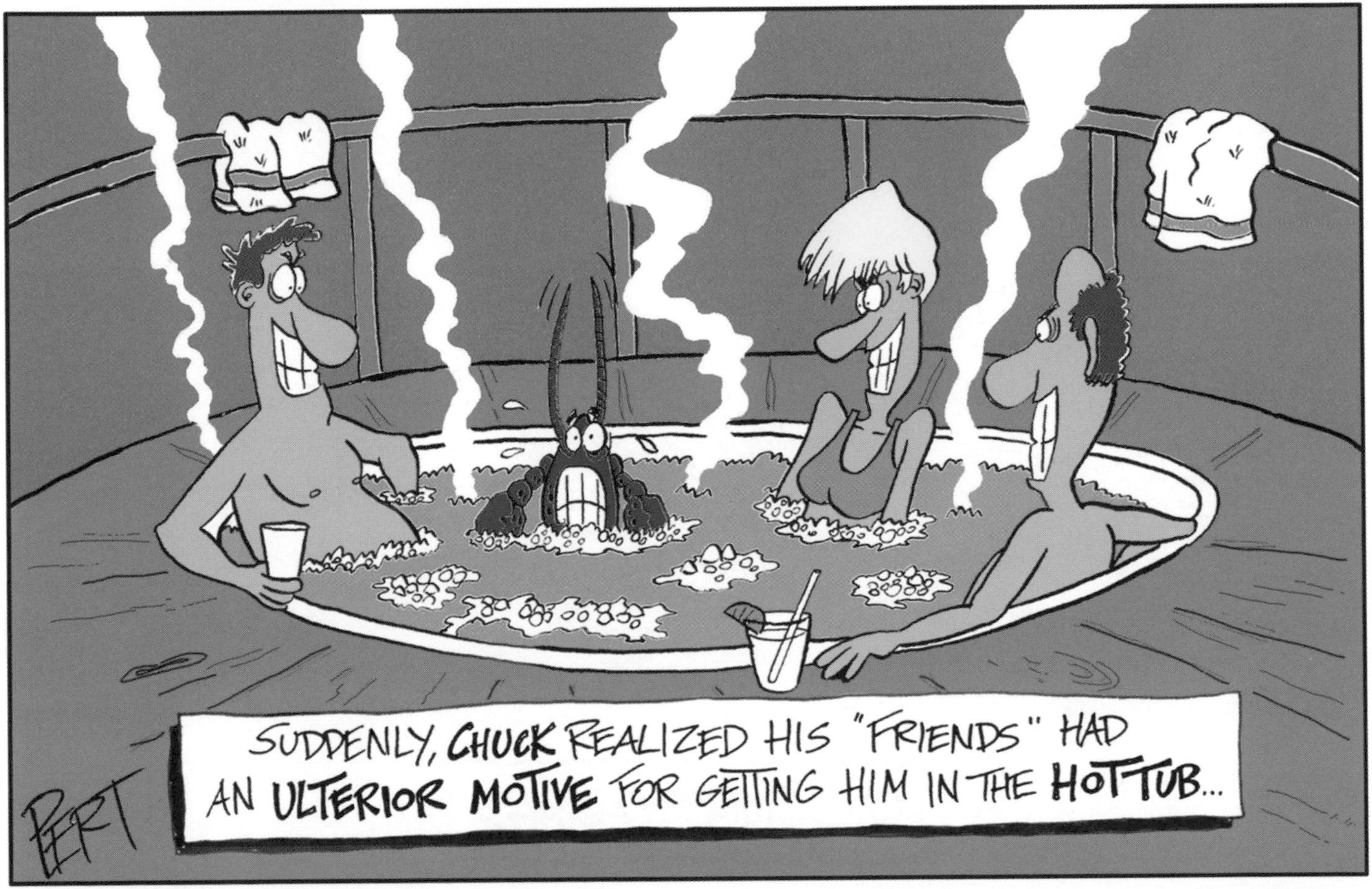
SUDDENLY, CHUCK REALIZED HIS "FRIENDS" HAD AN ULTERIOR MOTIVE FOR GETTING HIM IN THE HOT TUB...
PERT

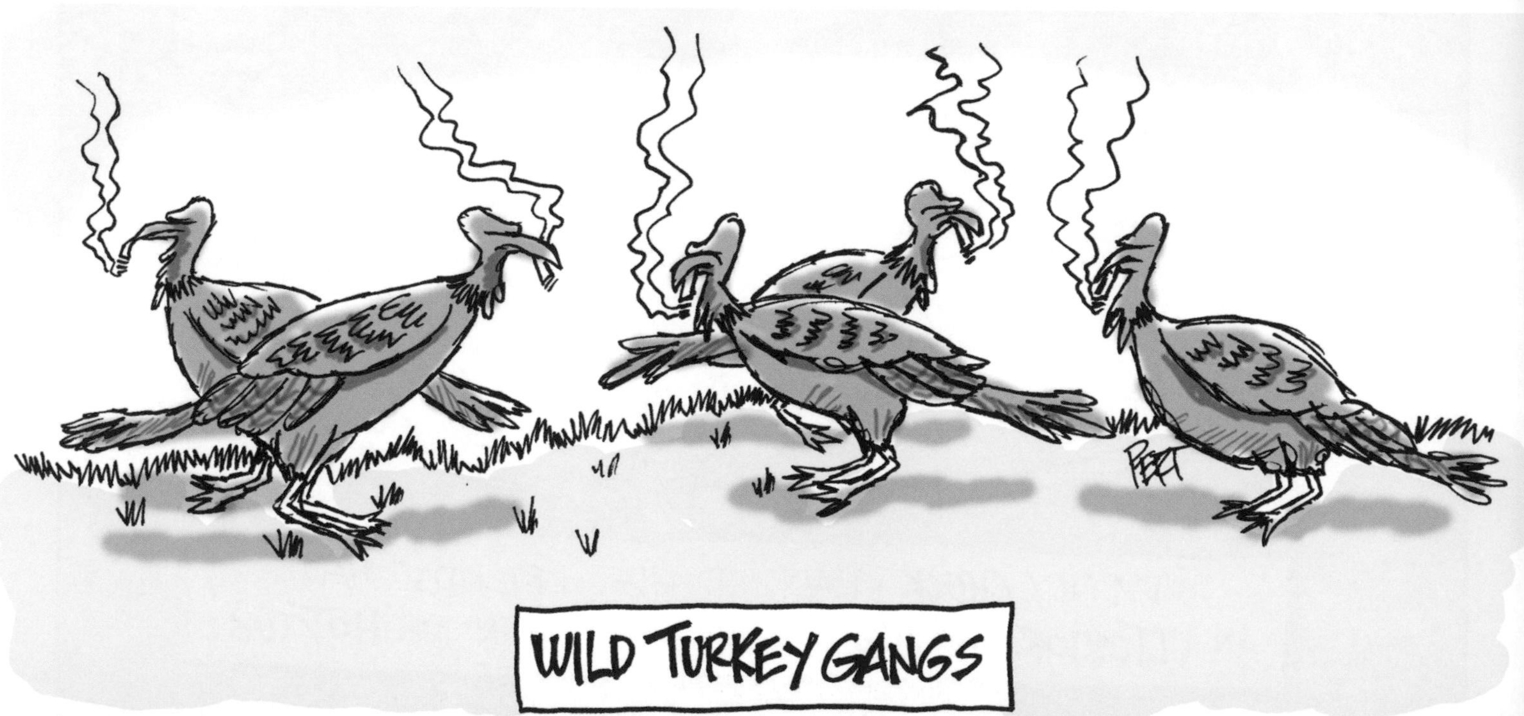
WILD TURKEY GANGS

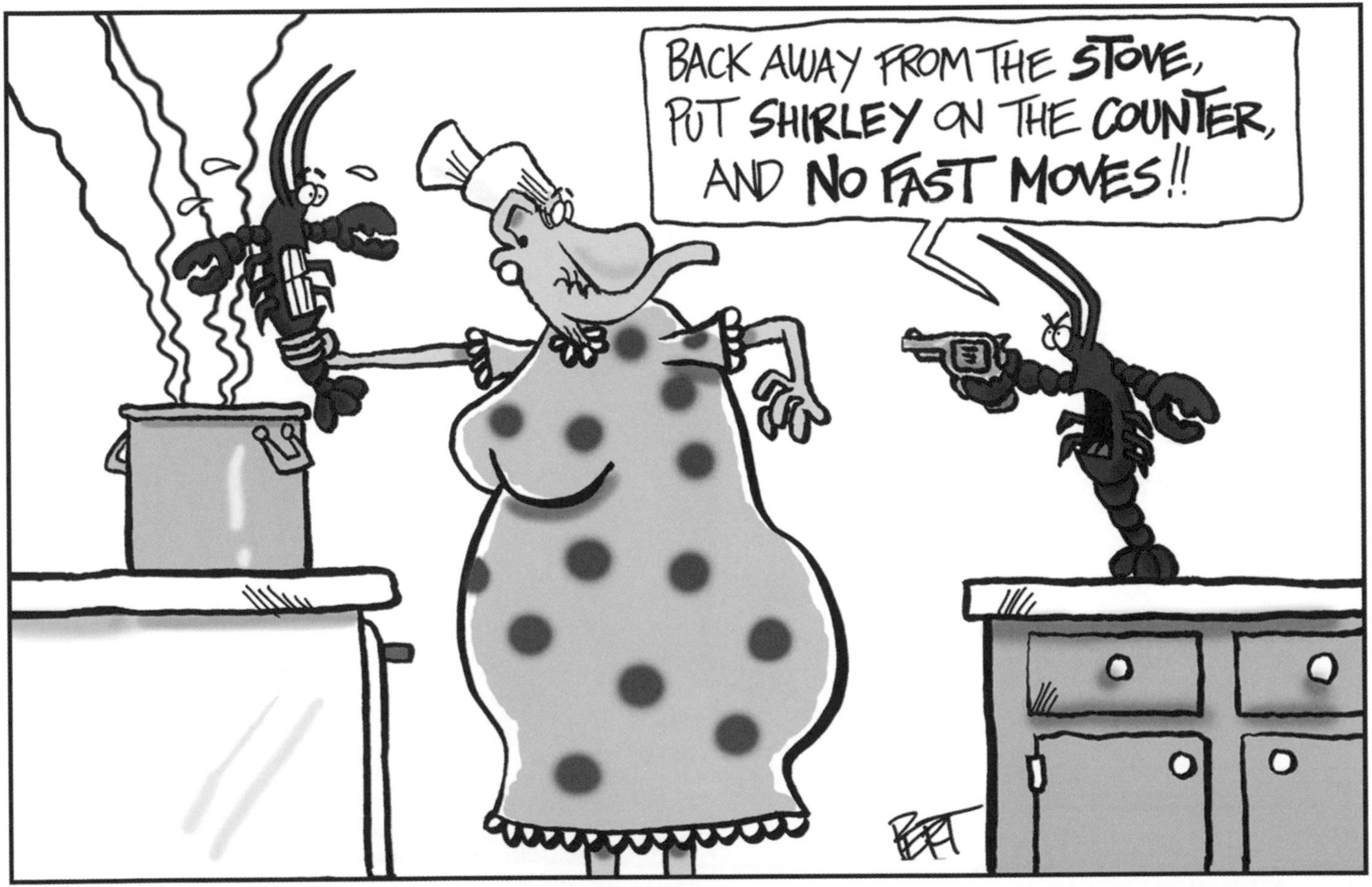
BACK AWAY FROM THE STOVE, PUT SHIRLEY ON THE COUNTER, AND NO FAST MOVES!!
BERT

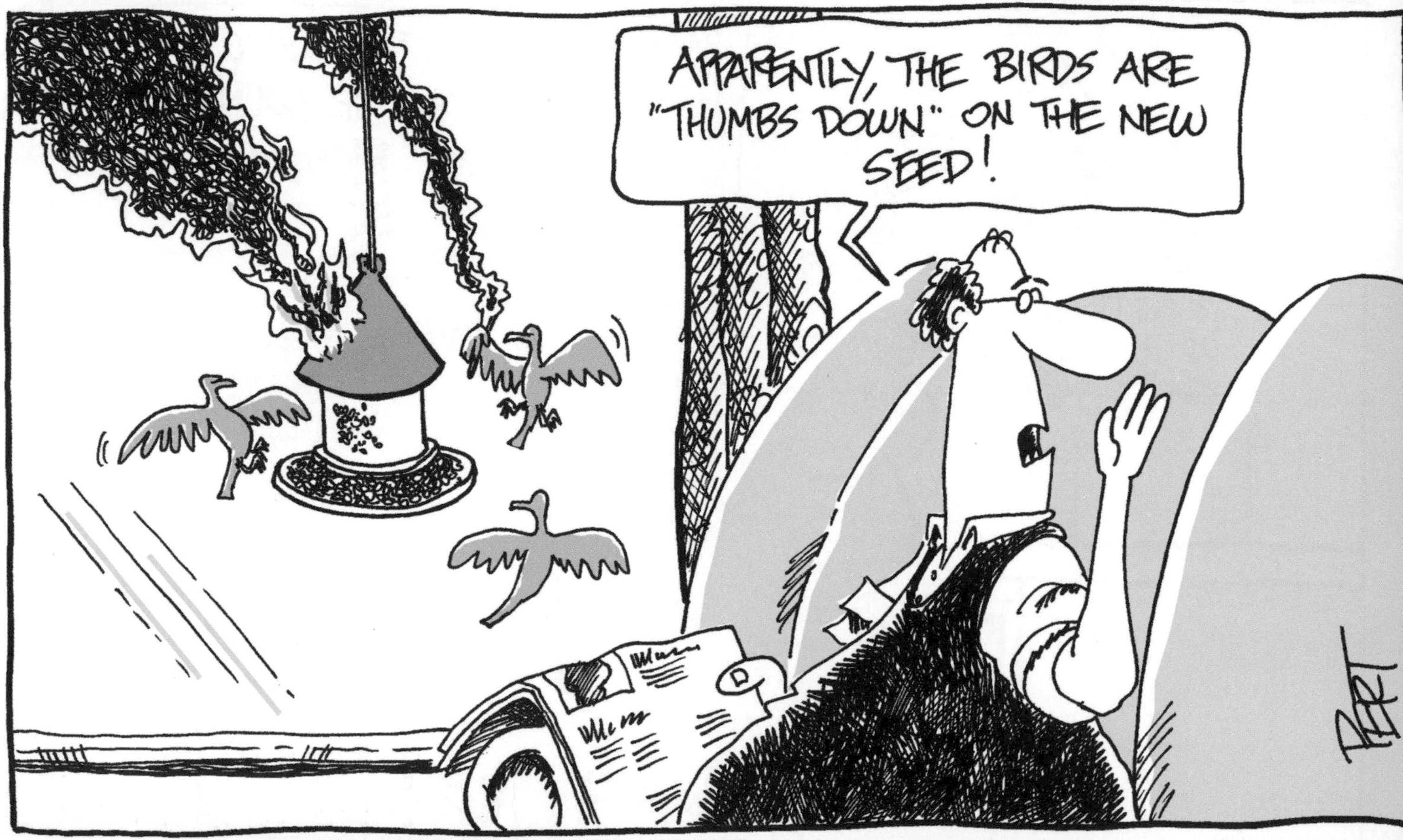
APPARENTLY, THE BIRDS ARE "THUMBS DOWN" ON THE NEW SEED!

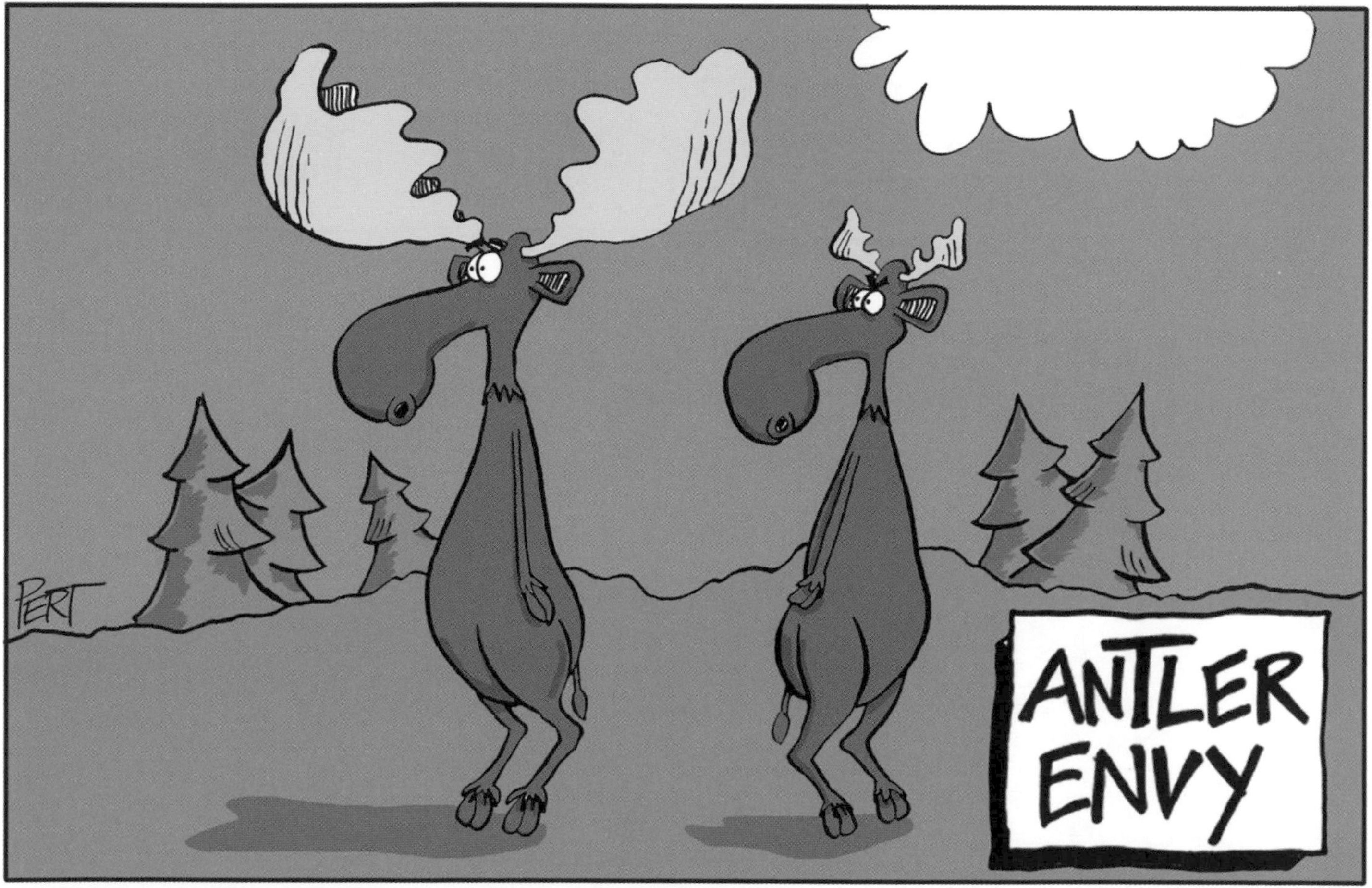
PERT
ANTLER ENVY

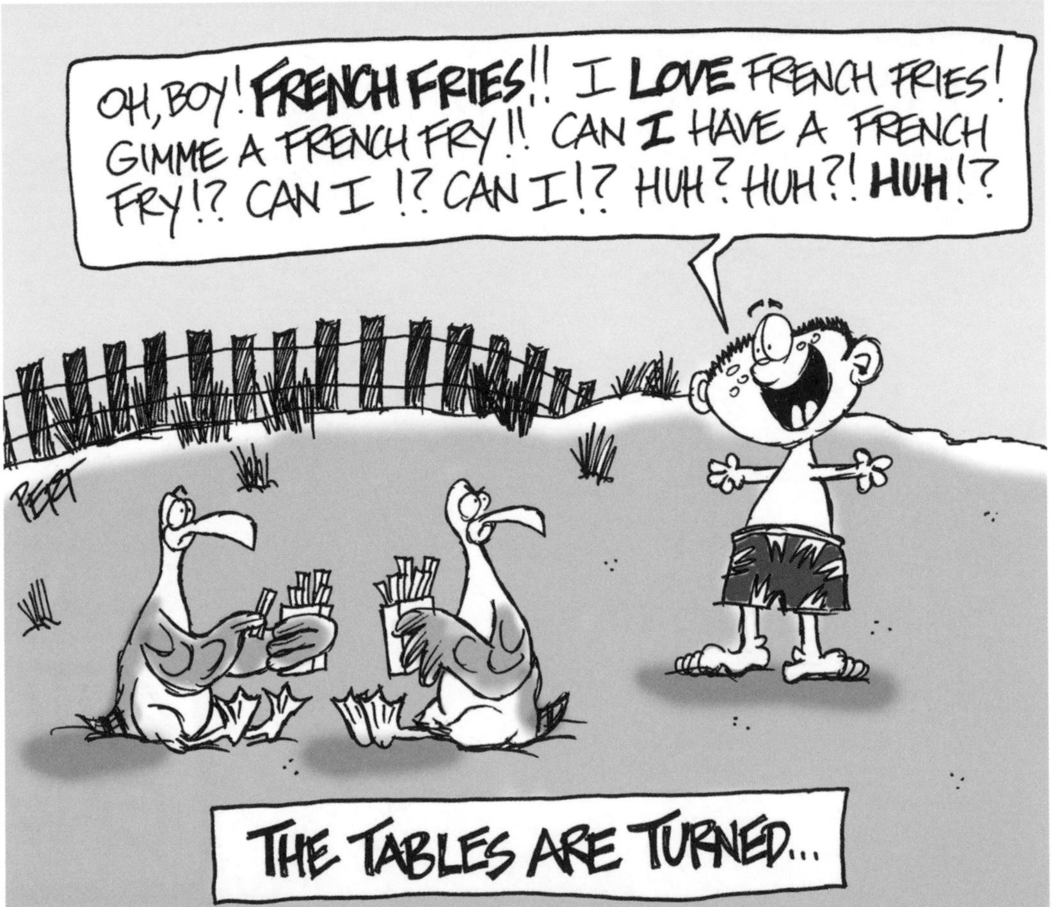
OH, BOY! FRENCH FRIES!! I LOVE FRENCH FRIES! GIMME A FRENCH FRY!! CAN I HAVE A FRENCH FRY!? CAN I!? CAN I!? HUH? HUH?! HUH!?
PETT
THE TABLES ARE TURNED...

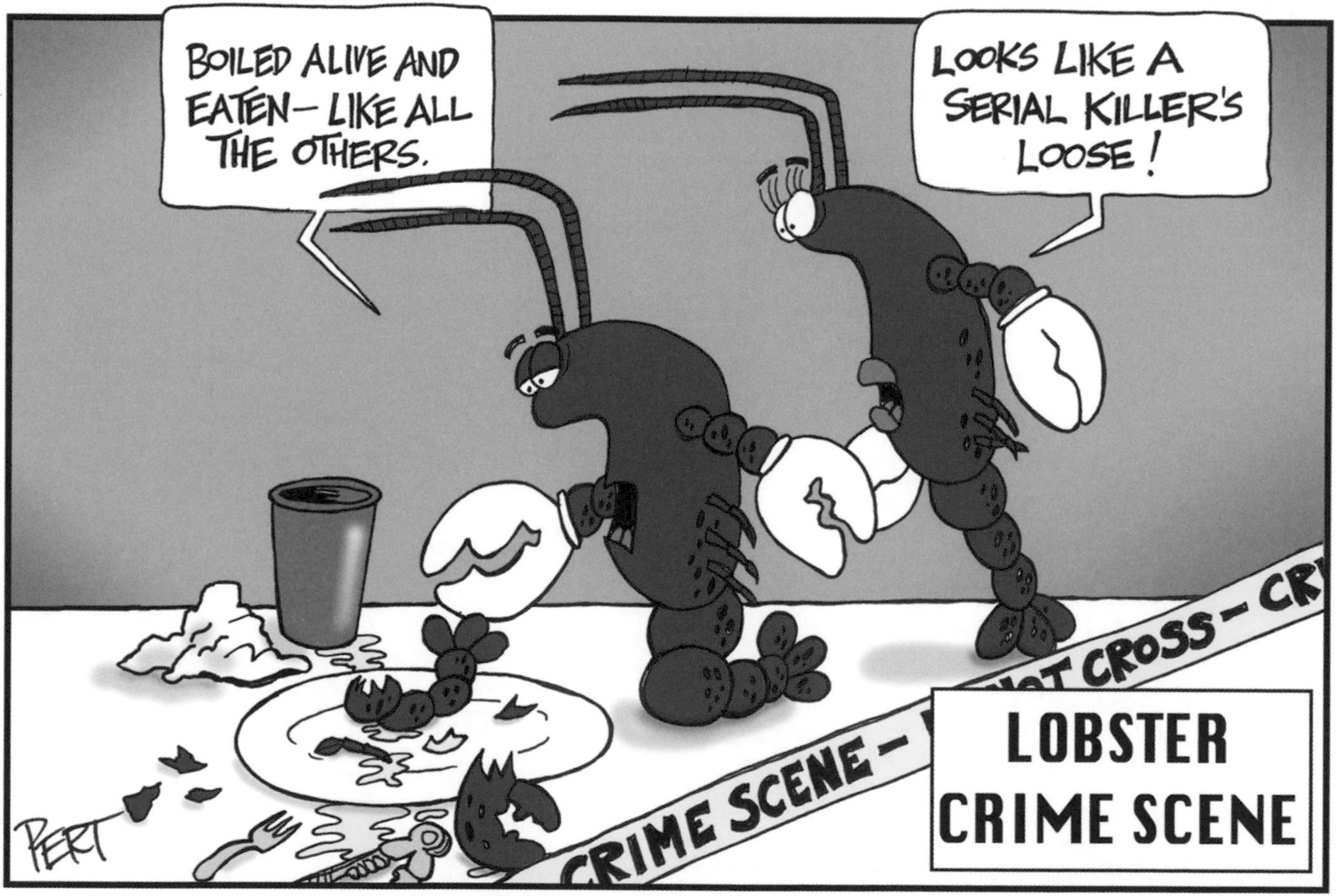
BOILED ALIVE AND EATEN– LIKE ALL THE OTHERS.
LOOKS LIKE A SERIAL KILLER'S LOOSE!
CRIME SCENE –
CROSS –
LOBSTER CRIME SCENE
PERT

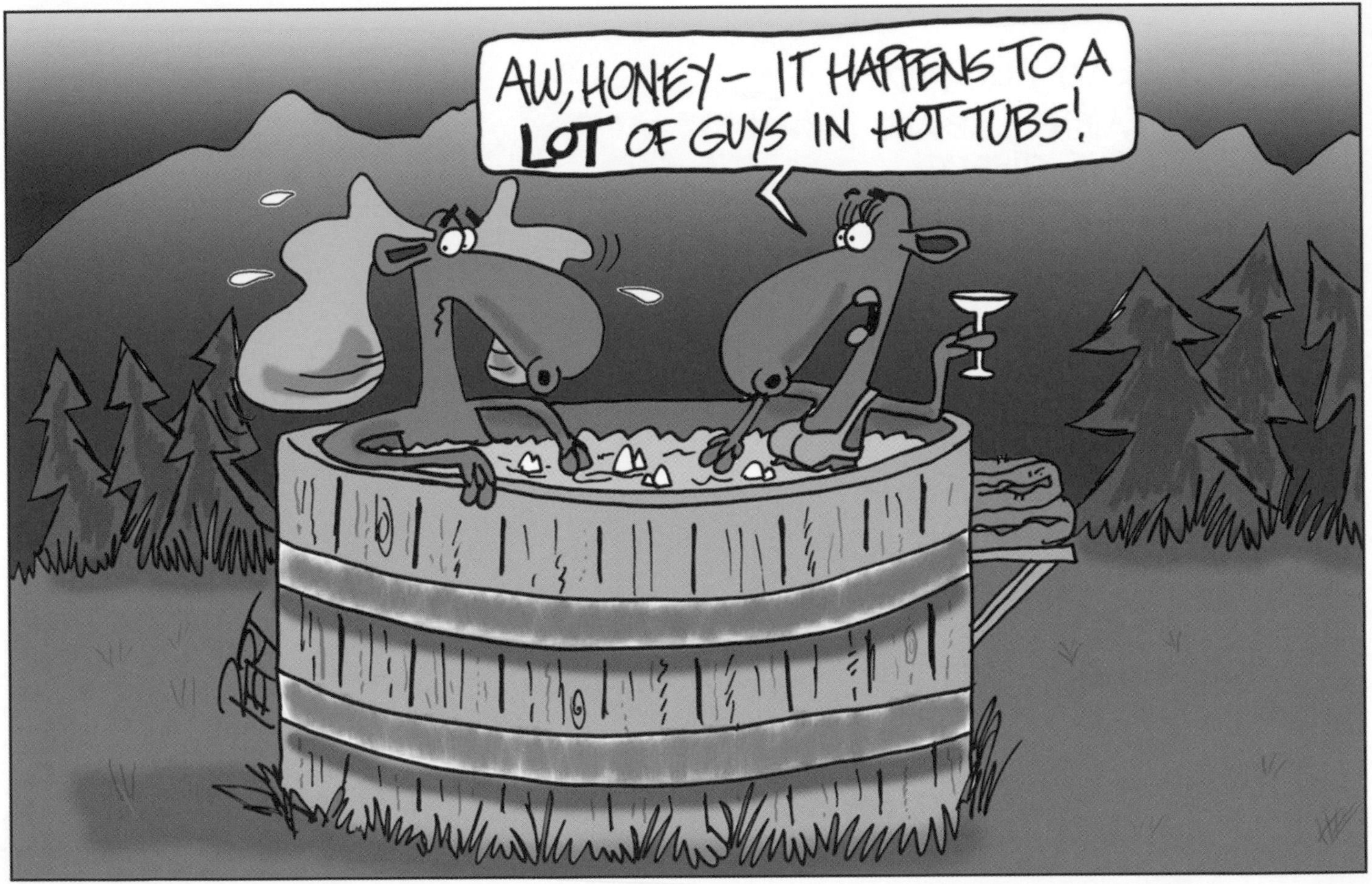
AW, HONEY– IT HAPPENS TO A LOT OF GUYS IN HOT TUBS!

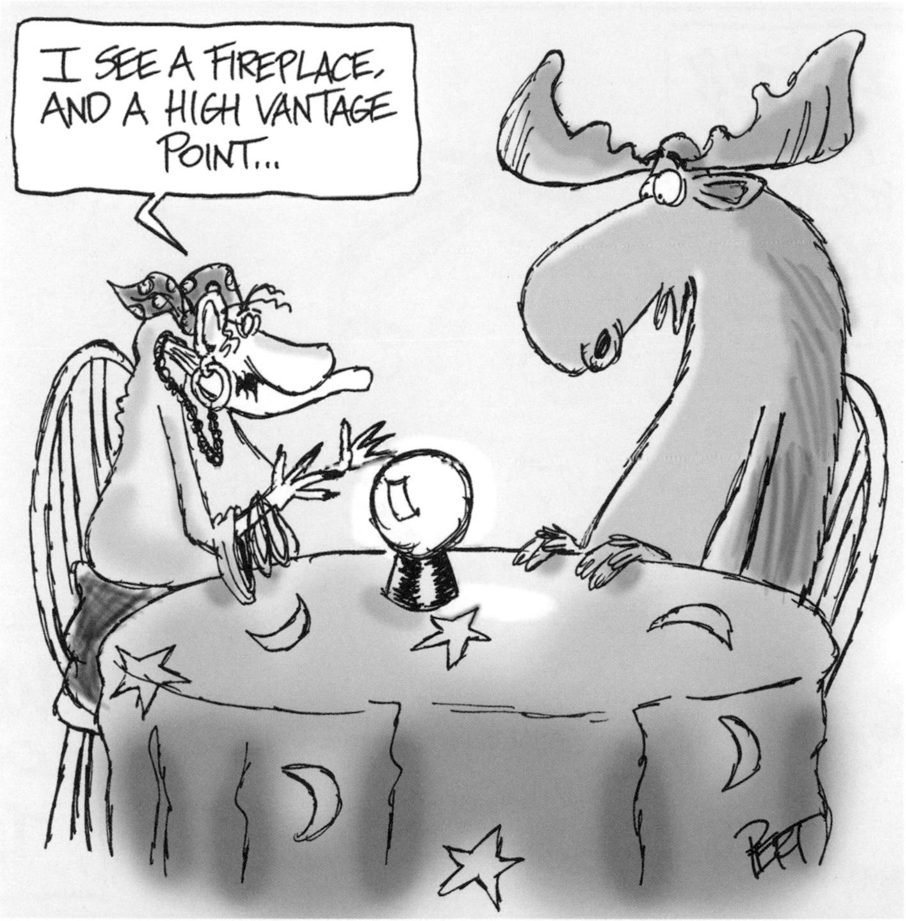
I SEE A FIREPLACE, AND A HIGH VANTAGE POINT...
BERT

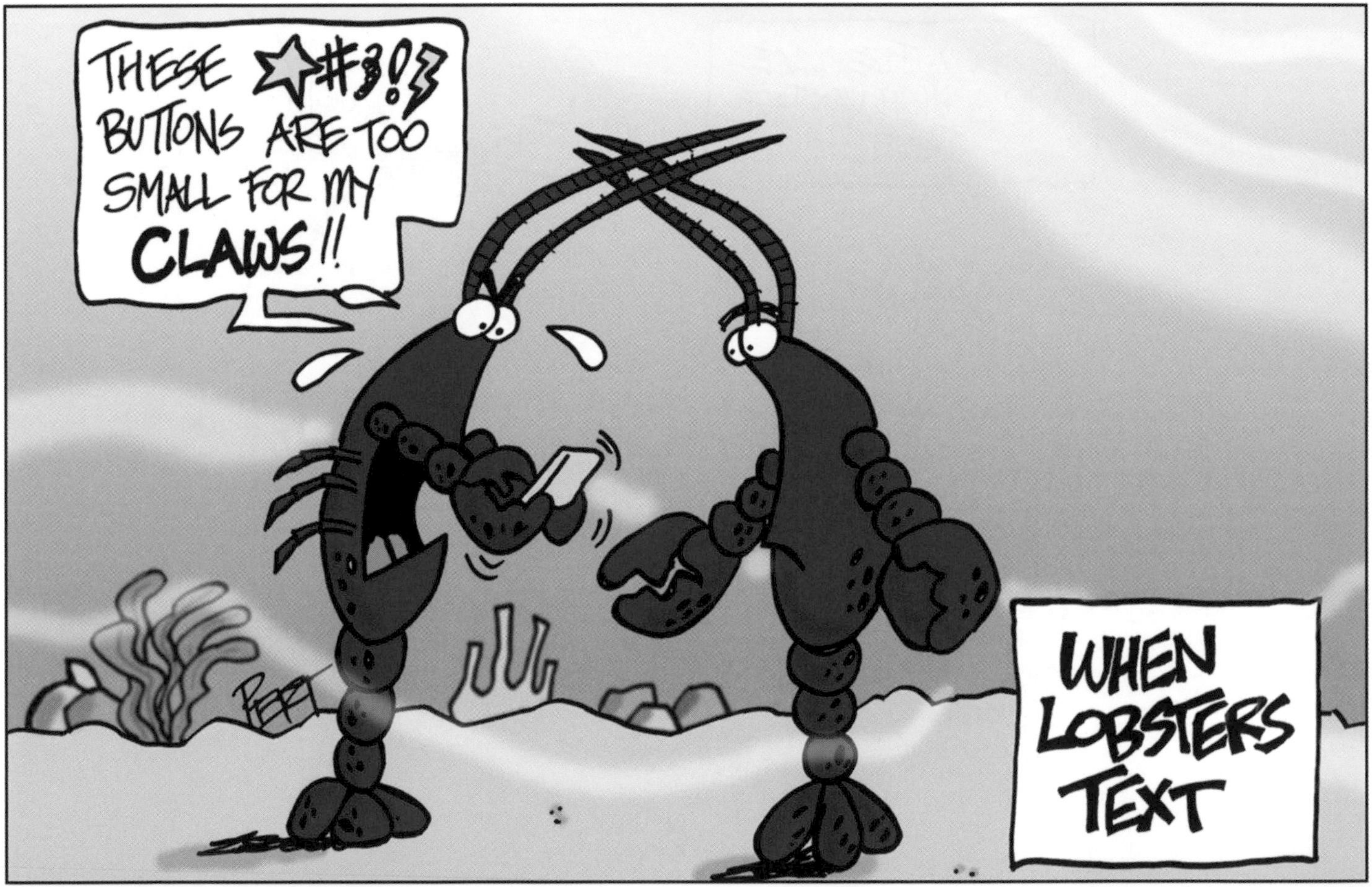
THESE BUTTONS ARE TOO SMALL FOR MY CLAWS!!
WHEN LOBSTERS TEXT

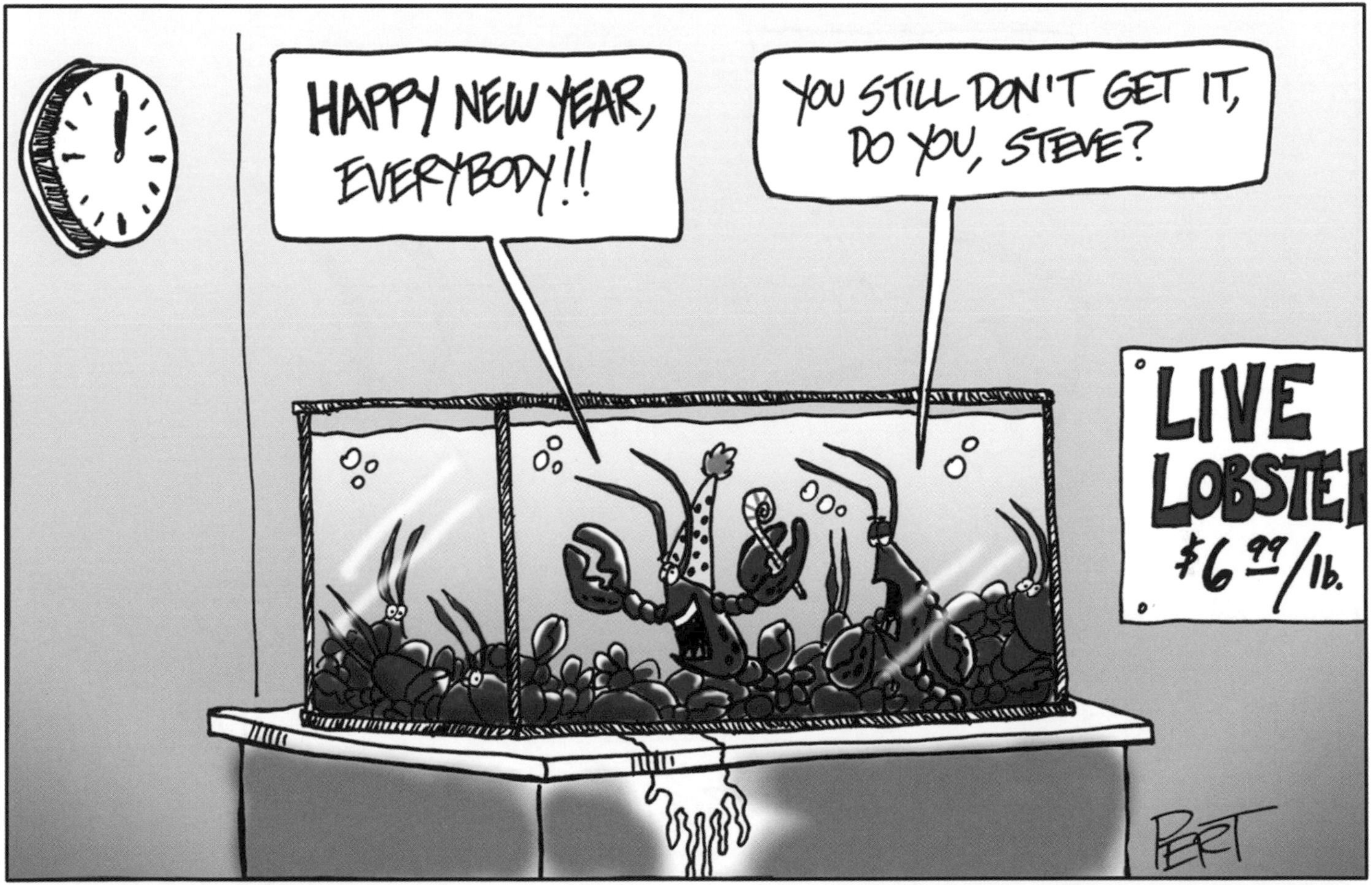
HAPPY NEW YEAR, EVERYBODY!!
YOU STILL DON'T GET IT, DO YOU, STEVE?
LIVE LOBSTE
$6 99/lb.
PEART

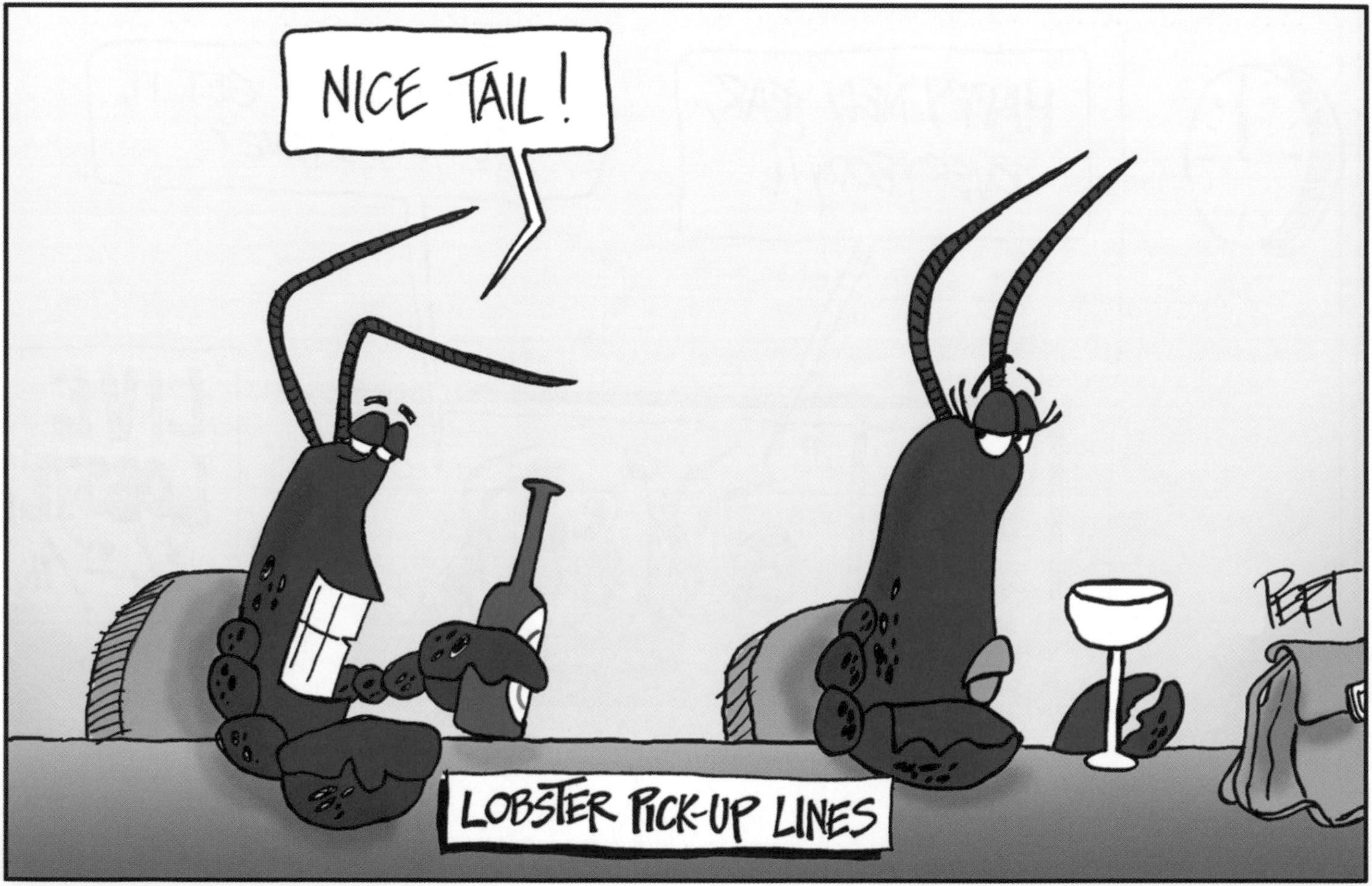
NICE TAIL!
PERT
LOBSTER PICK-UP LINES

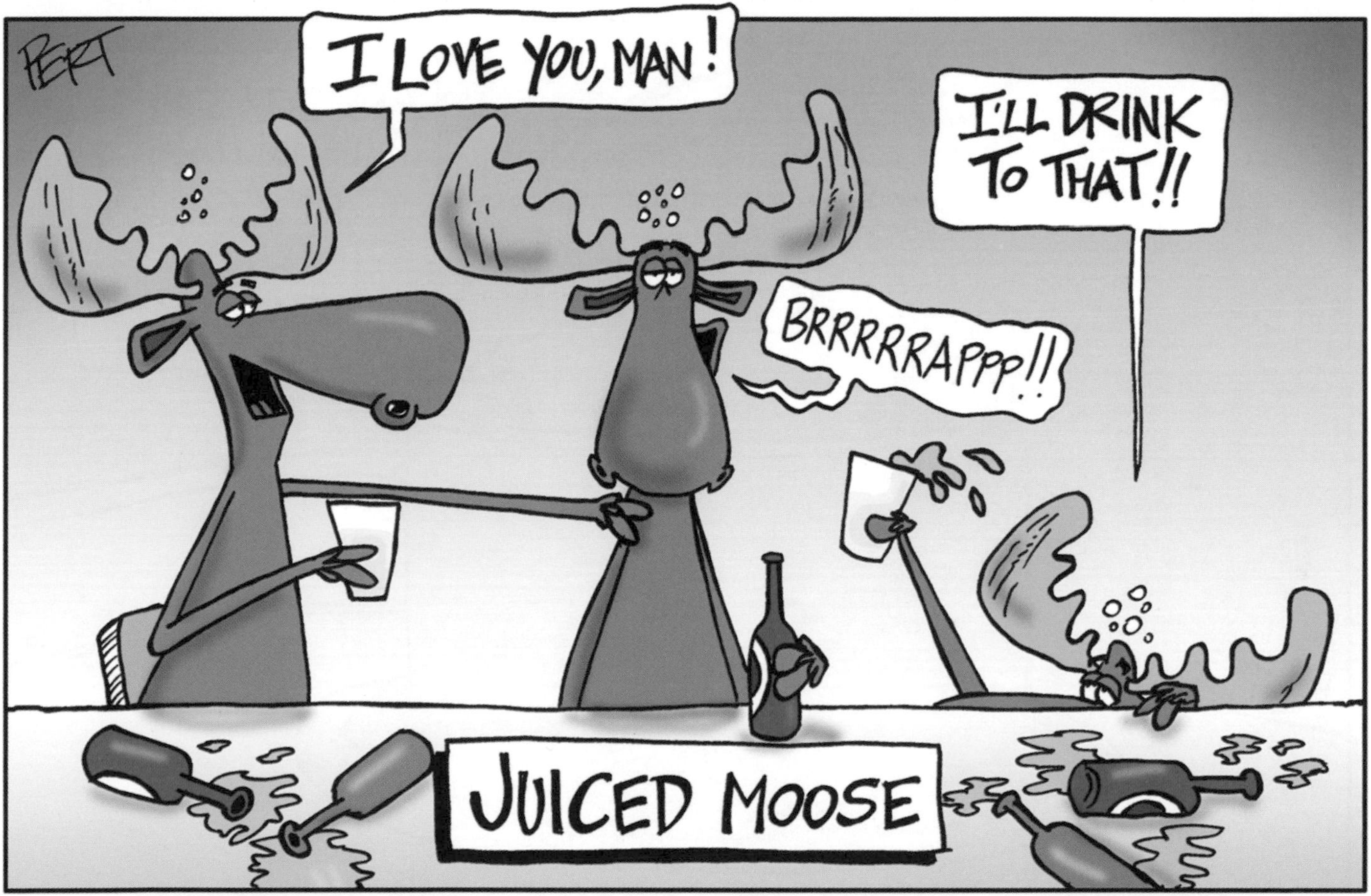
PERT
I LOVE YOU, MAN!
BRRRRRRAPPP!!
I'LL DRINK TO THAT!!
JUICED MOOSE

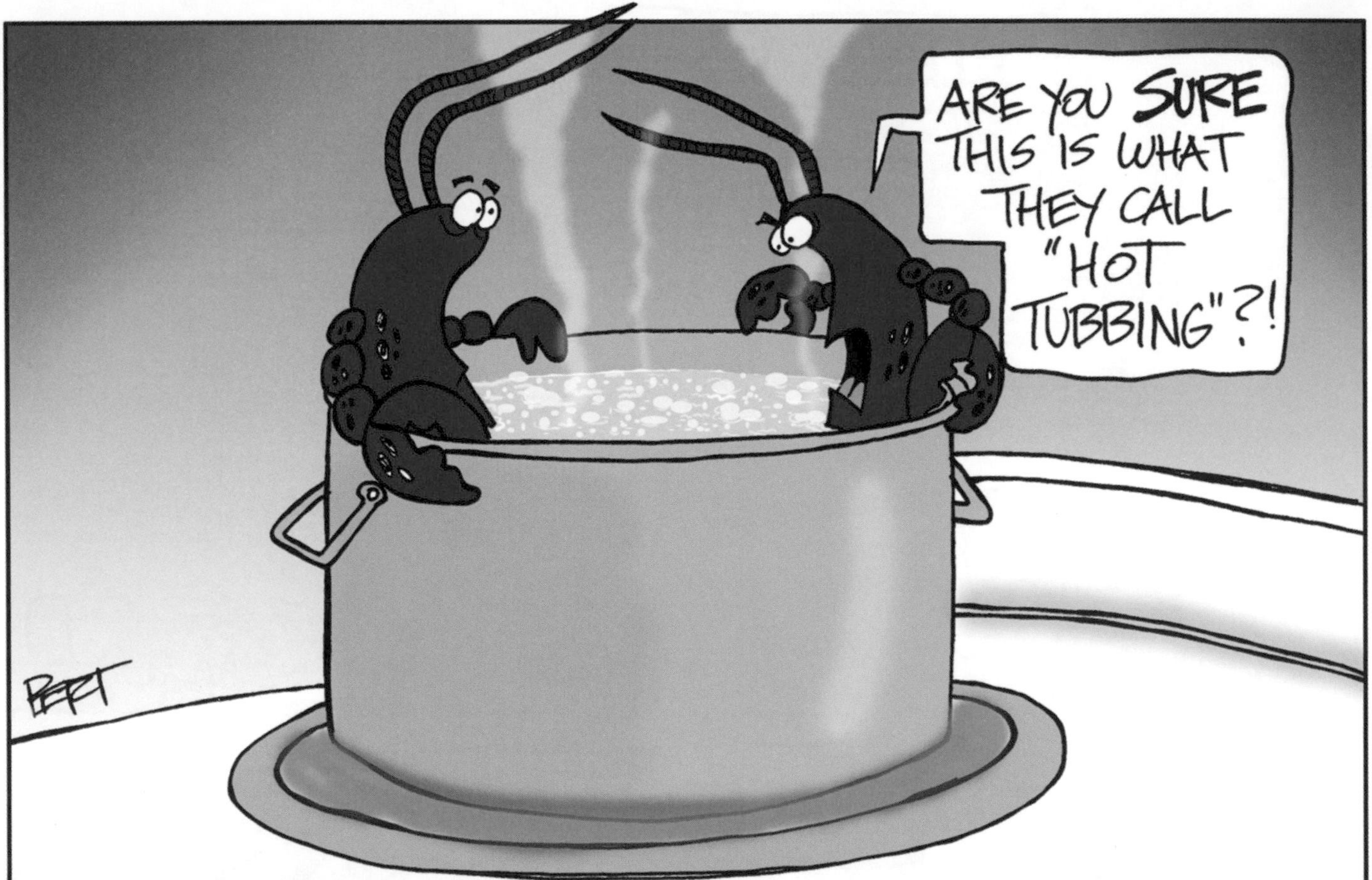
ARE YOU SURE THIS IS WHAT THEY CALL "HOT TUBBING"?!
BERT

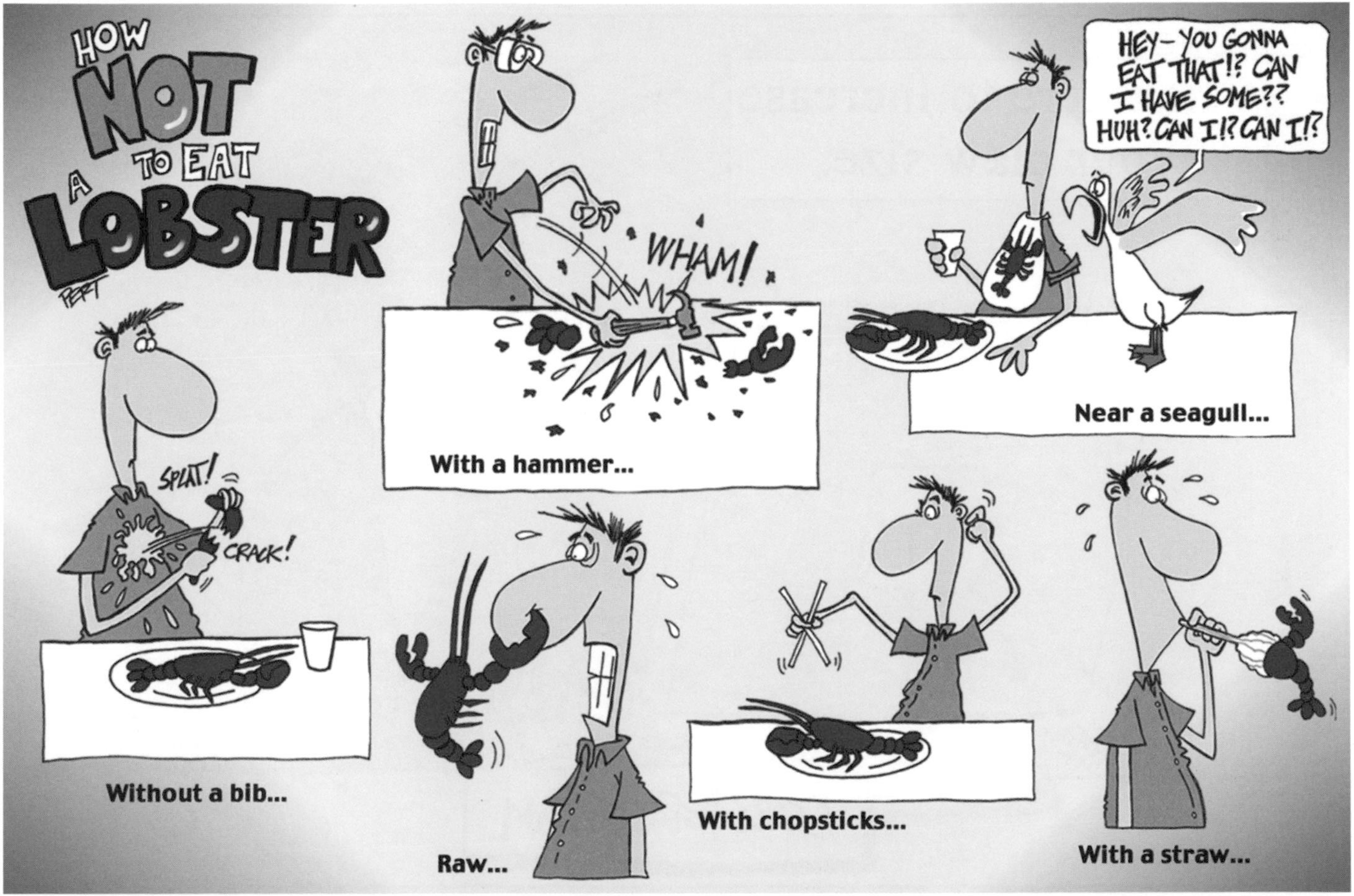
HOW NOT TO EAT A LOBSTER
PERT
WHAM!
With a hammer...
HEY–YOU GONNA EAT THAT!? CAN I HAVE SOME?? HUH? CAN I!? CAN I!?
Near a seagull...
SPLAT!
CRACK!
Without a bib...
Raw...
With chopsticks...
With a straw...

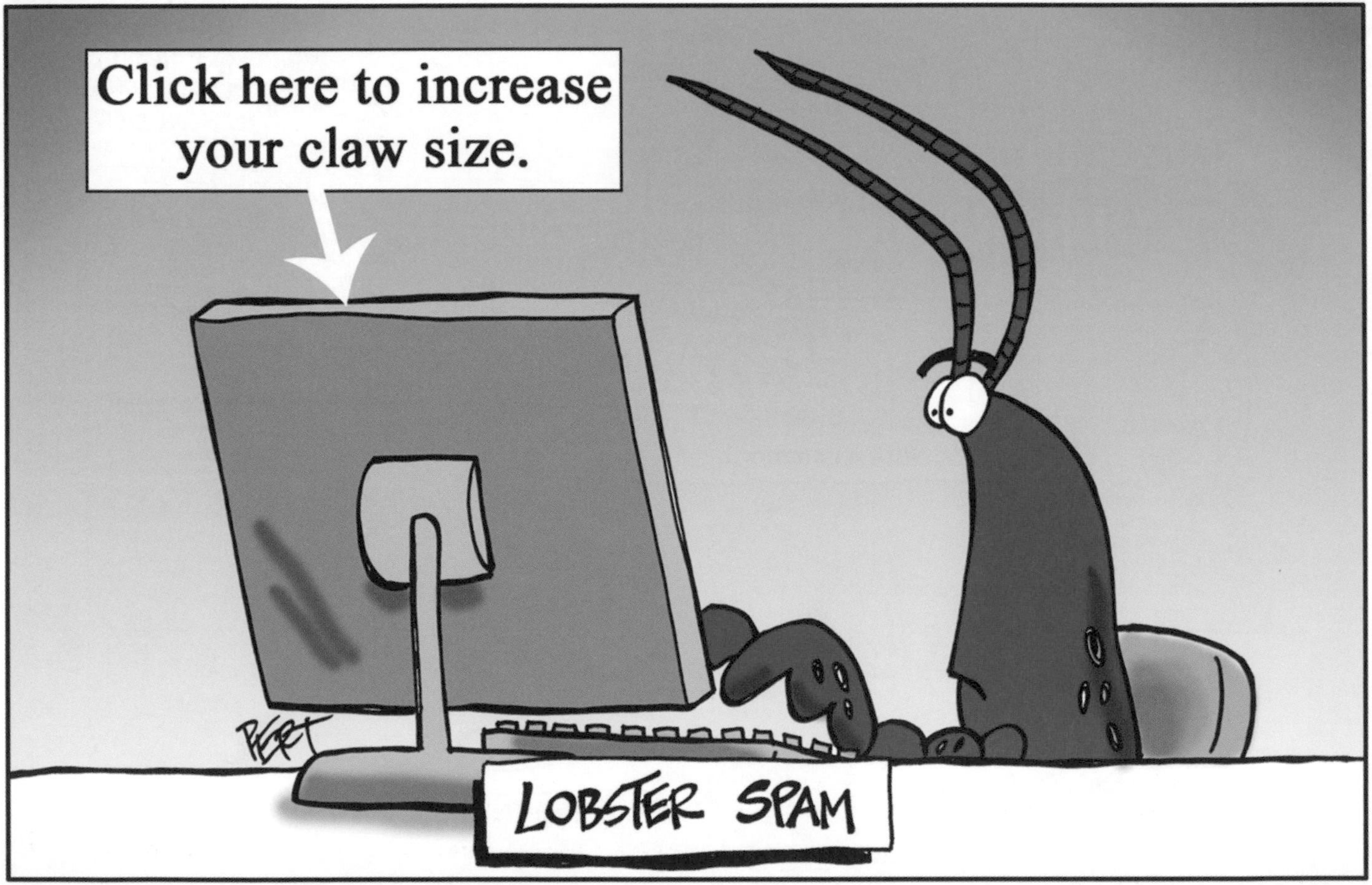
Click here to increase your claw size.
LOBSTER SPAM

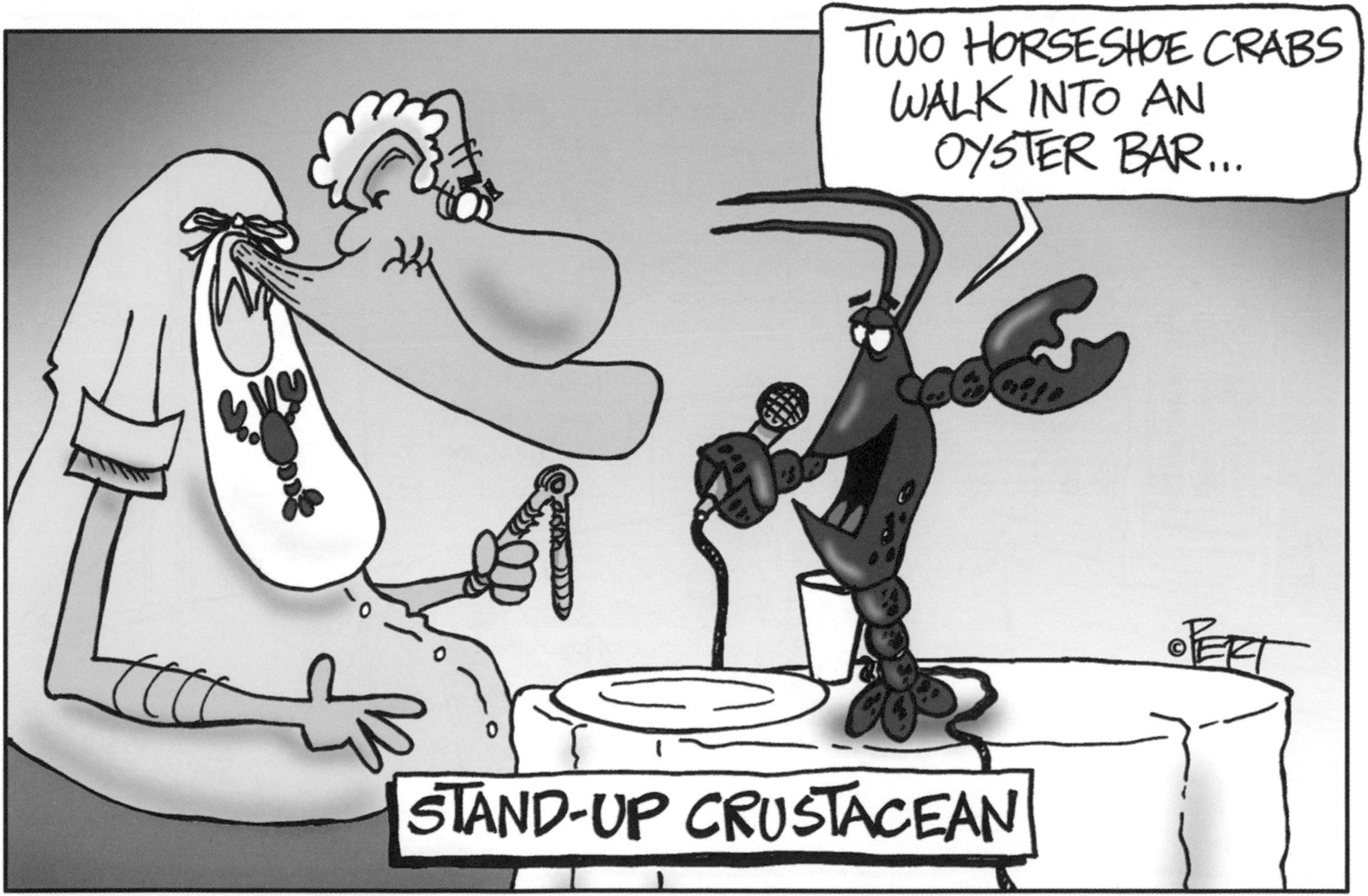
TWO HORSESHOE CRABS WALK INTO AN OYSTER BAR...
©PERT
STAND-UP CRUSTACEAN

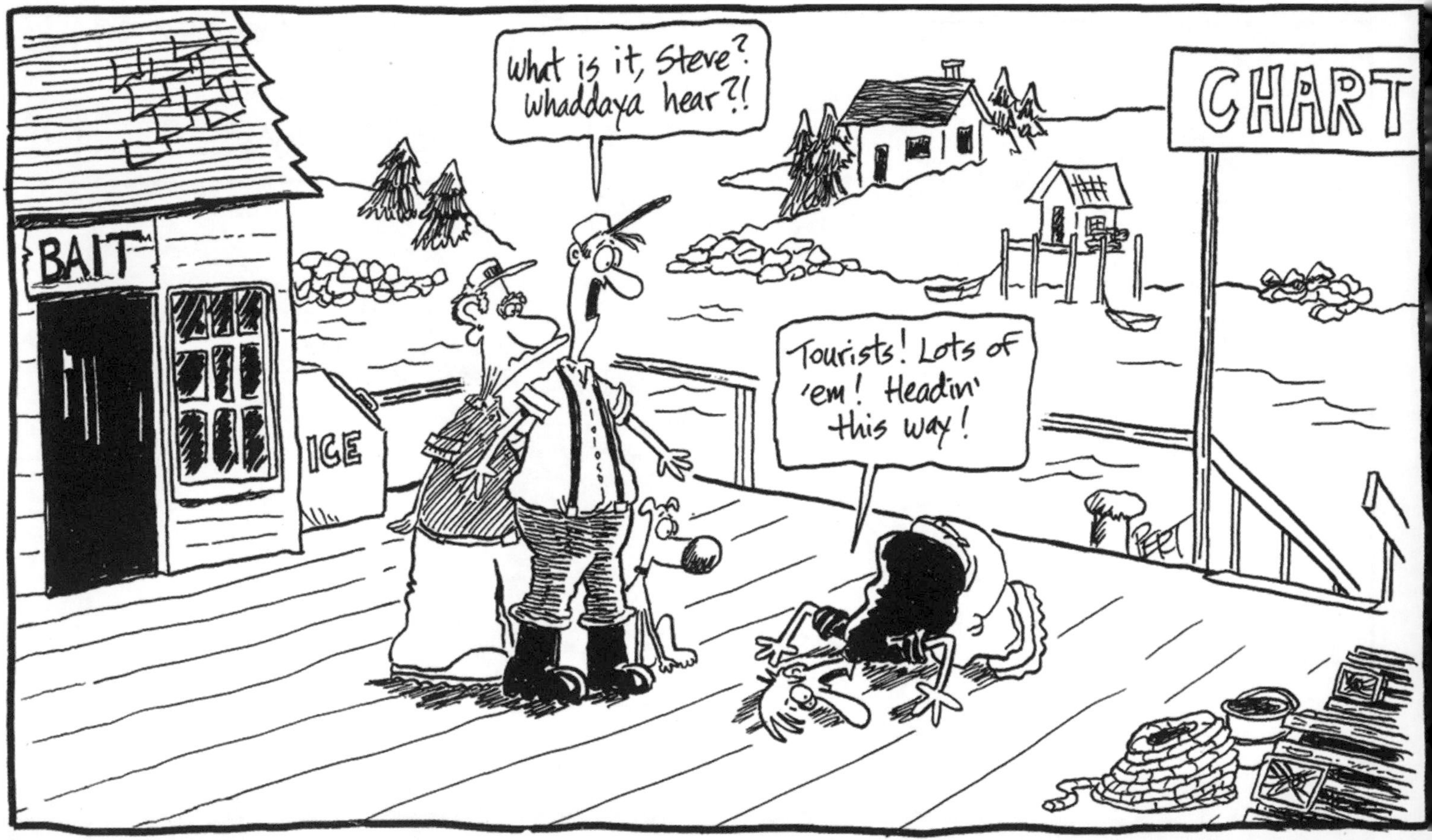
BAIT
ICE
CHART
What is it, Steve? Whaddaya hear?!
Tourists! Lots of 'em! Headin' this way!

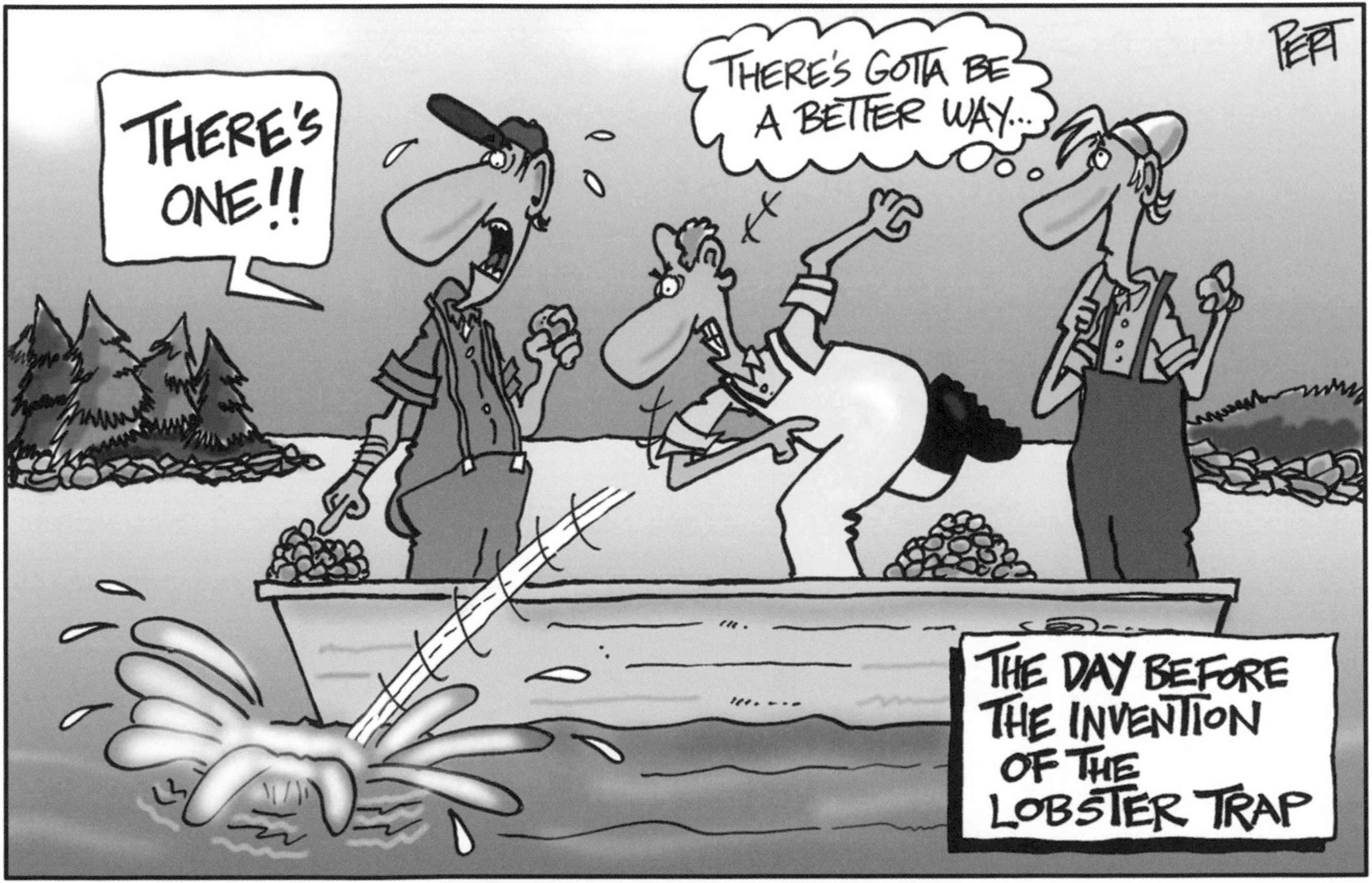
PERT
THERE'S ONE!!
THERE'S GOTTA BE A BETTER WAY...
THE DAY BEFORE THE INVENTION OF THE LOBSTER TRAP

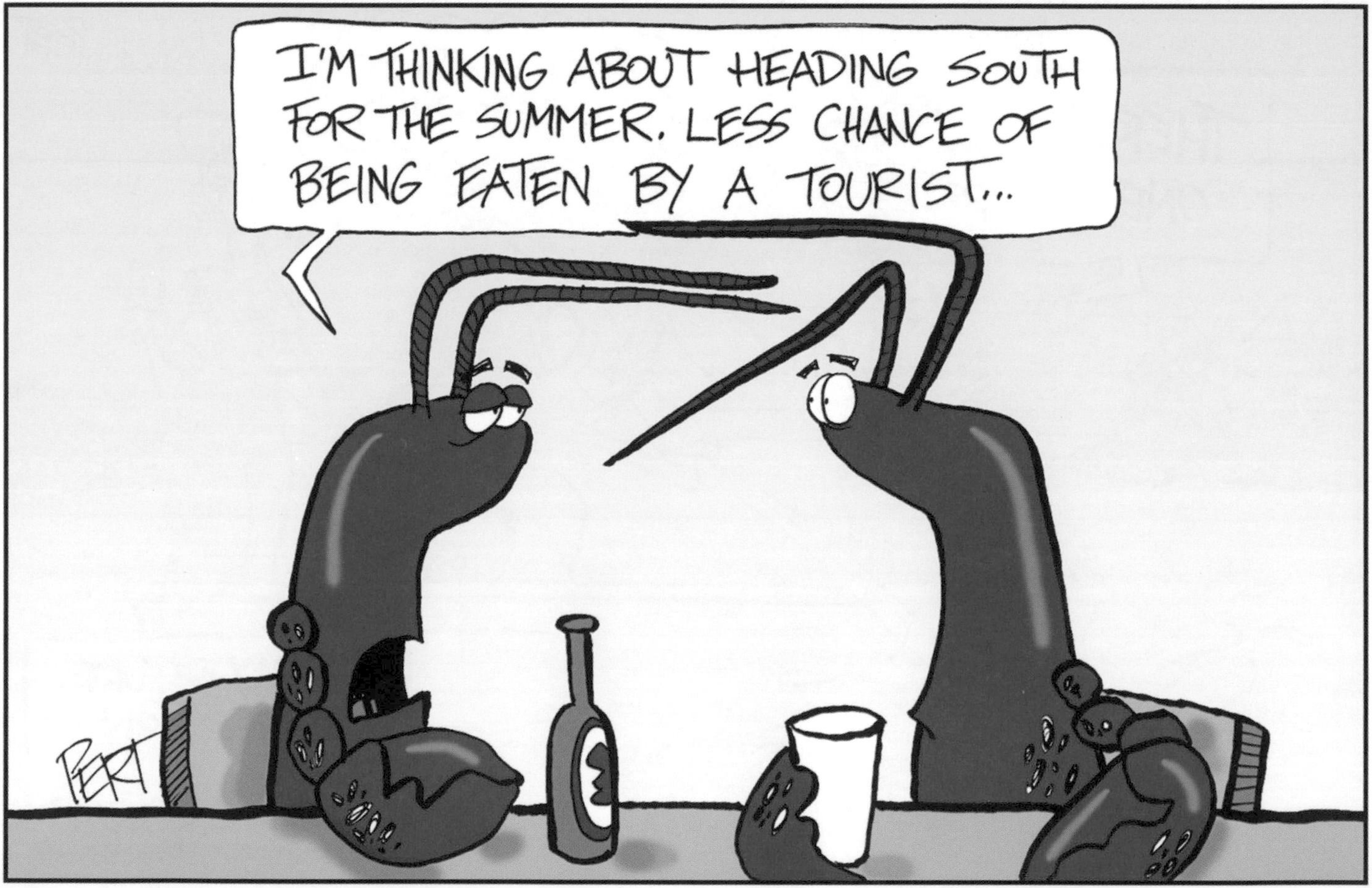
I'M THINKING ABOUT HEADING SOUTH FOR THE SUMMER. LESS CHANCE OF BEING EATEN BY A TOURIST...
PERT

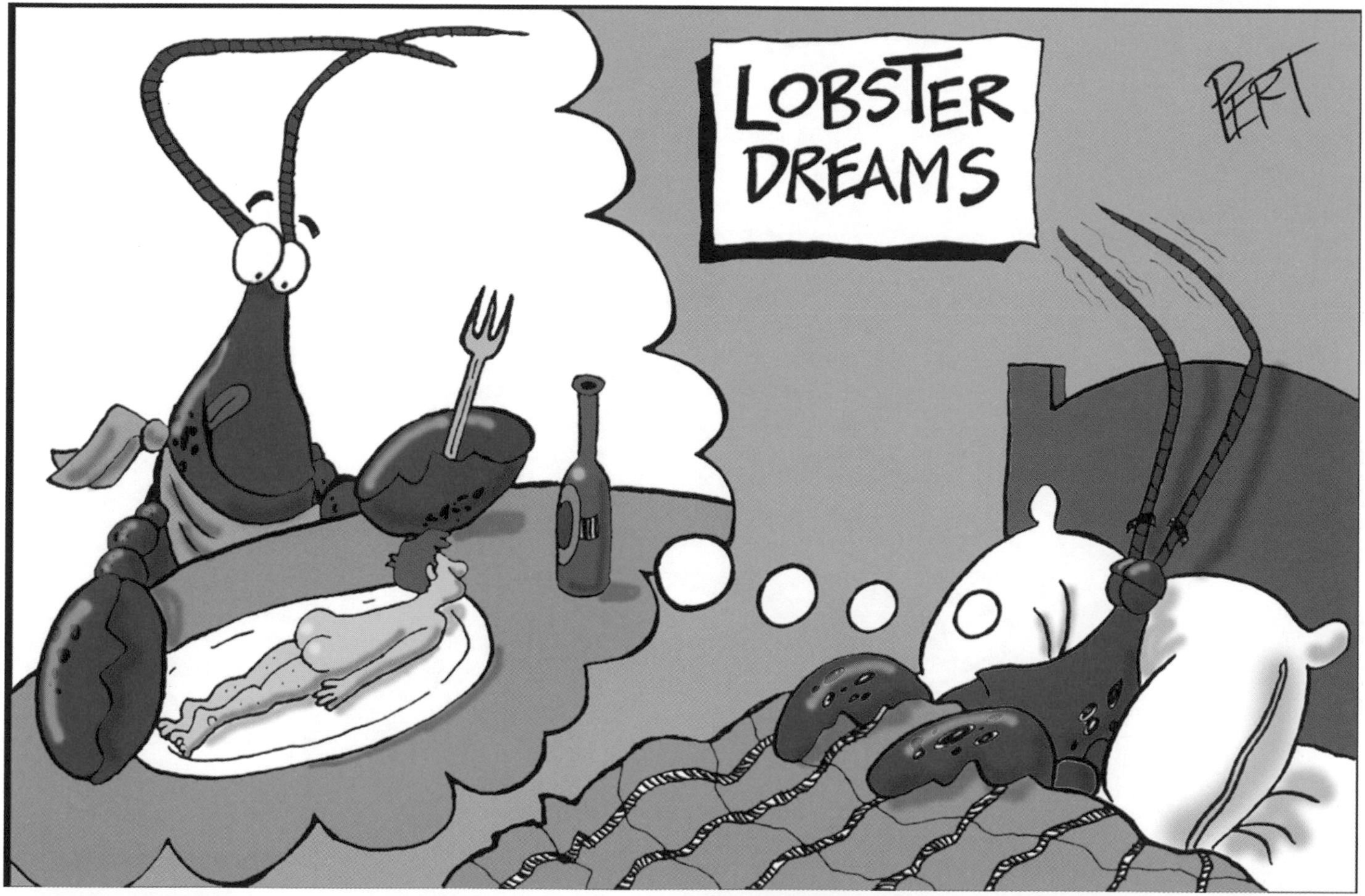
LOBSTER DREAMS
PEERT

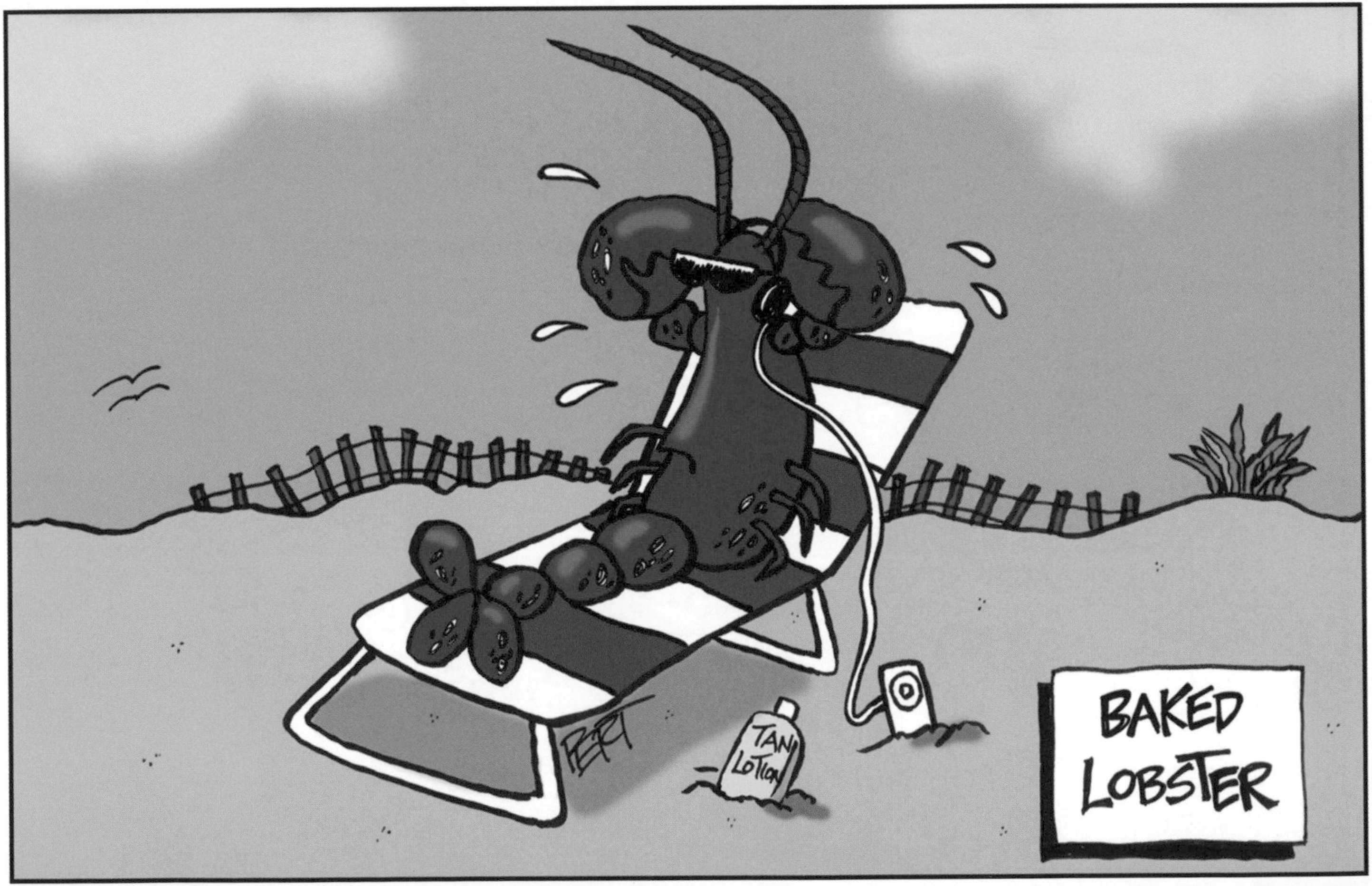
TAN LOTION
BAKED LOBSTER

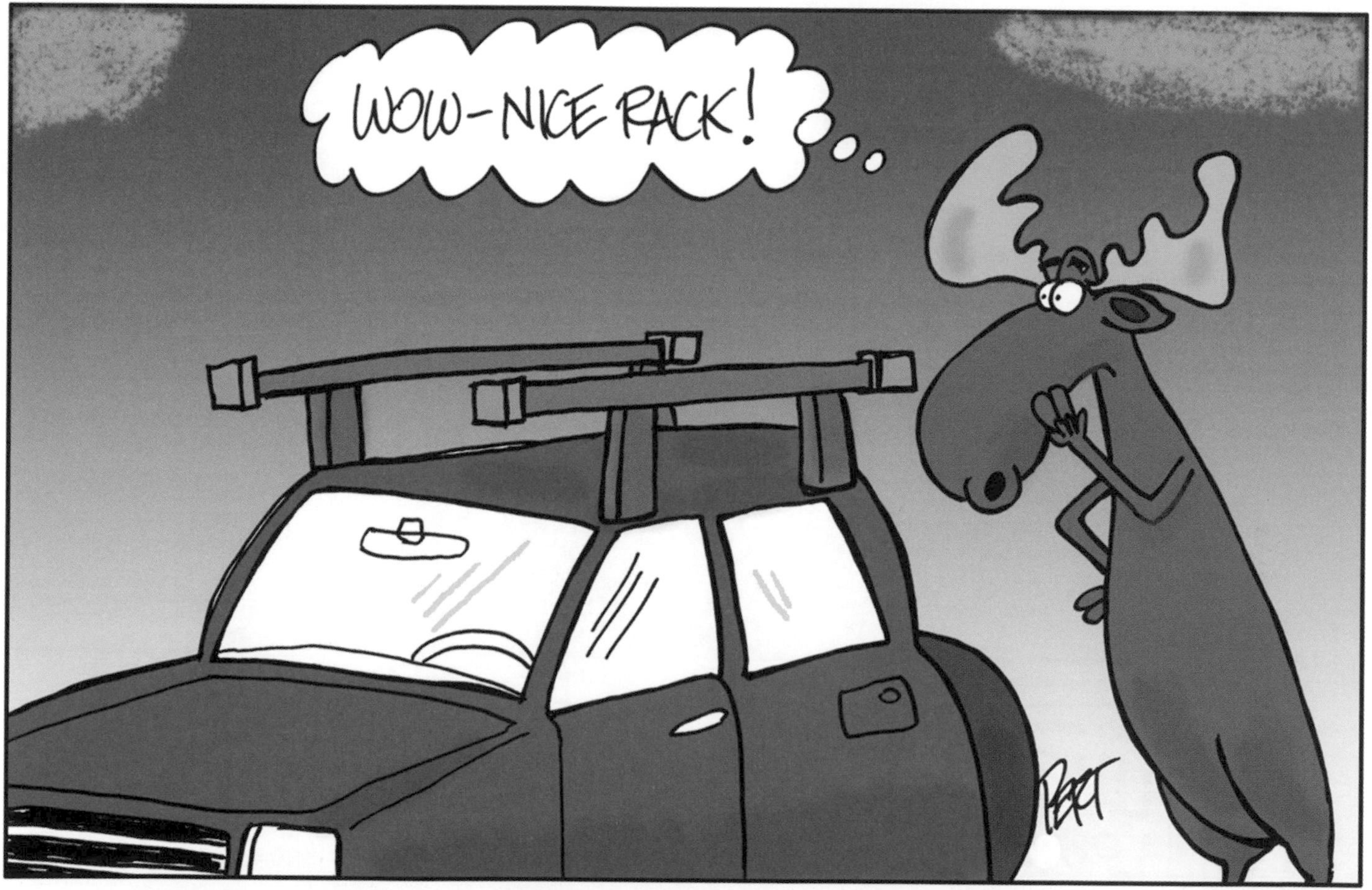
WOW-NICE RACK!
BERT

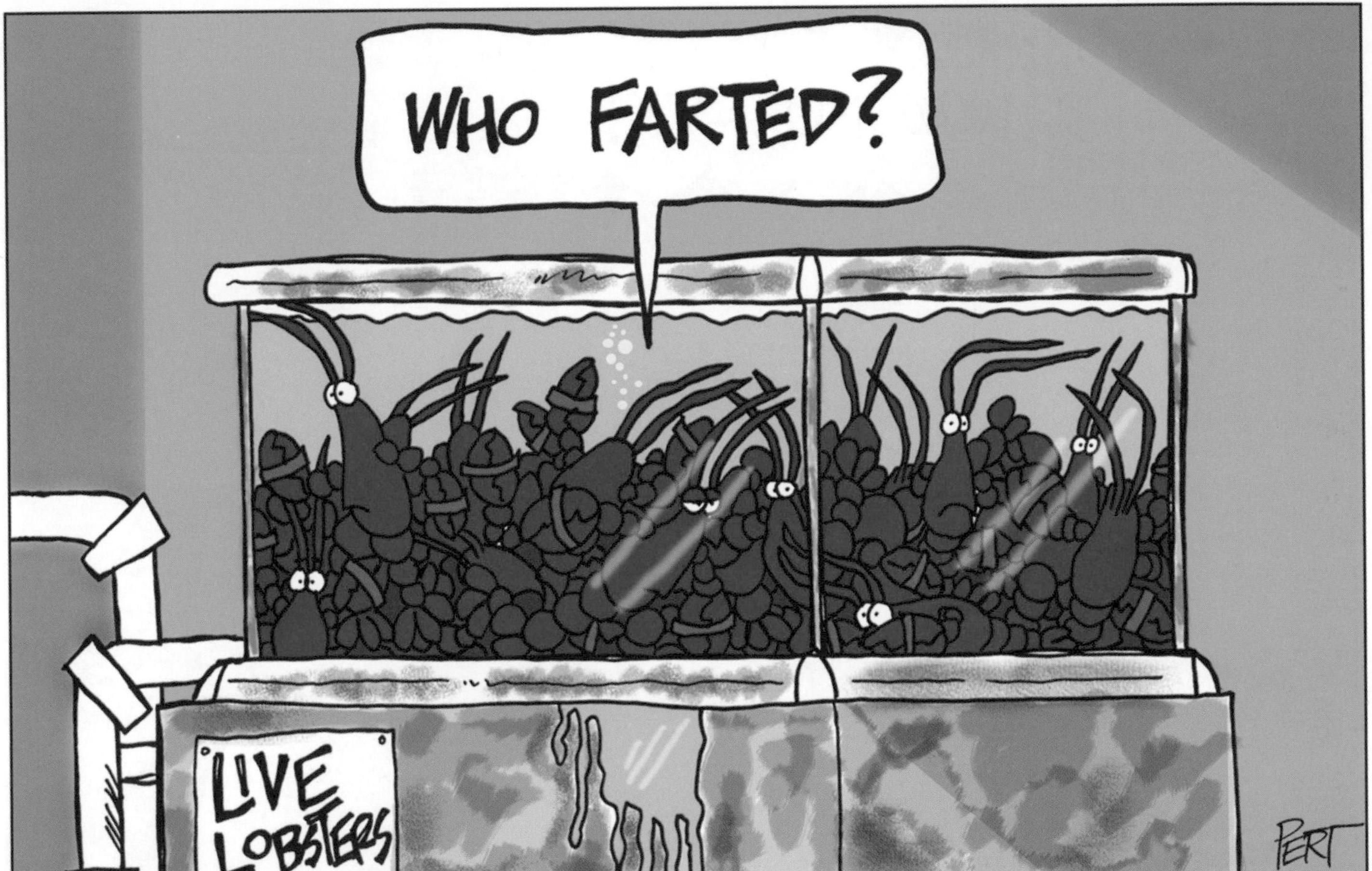
WHO FARTED?
LIVE LOBSTERS
PERT